The National War Labor Board

Supplementary Volumes to
The Papers of Woodrow Wilson
Arthur S. Link, Editor

THE EDITORIAL ADVISORY COMMITTEE

Katharine E. Brand August Heckscher
Henry Steele Commager, *Emeritus* Richard W. Leopold
John Milton Cooper, Jr. David C. Mearns, *Emeritus*
William H. Harbaugh Arthur M. Schlesinger, Jr.

A list of volumes in this series will be found
at the back of the book.

Valerie Jean Conner

The National War Labor Board

Stability, Social Justice, and the Voluntary State in World War I

The University of North Carolina Press   Chapel Hill

© 1983 The University of North Carolina Press

All rights reserved

Manufactured in the United States of America

Library of Congress Cataloging in Publication Data

Conner, Valerie Jean, 1945–
 The National War Labor Board.

 (Supplementary volumes to The papers of Woodrow Wilson)
 Bibliography: p.
 Includes index.
 1. United States. National War Labor Board
(1918–1919)—History. 2. Industrial mobilization—
United States—History—20th century. 3. Industrial
relations—United States—History—20th century.
4. World War, 1914–1918—Manpower—United States.
I. Title. II. Series.
UA18.U5C66 1983   355.2'0973   82-13362
ISBN 0-8978-1539-X

The author wishes to thank *Labor History*
for permission to reprint a version of an
article that appeared in that journal.

Contents

	Preface	vii
Chapter 1.	Business, Labor, and Government in the Prewar Years: Prelude to Wartime Voluntarism	3
Chapter 2.	A New Deal for American Labor	18
Chapter 3.	Attack on Industrial Autocracy	35
Chapter 4.	Toward a Living Wage	50
Chapter 5.	A Moderate Advance	68
Chapter 6.	Meeting the Government's Necessity	89
Chapter 7.	Democratizing Industry	108
Chapter 8.	The War Labor Board in Autumn	126
Chapter 9.	The Mothers of the Race	142
Chapter 10.	From War to Peace	158
Chapter 11.	Whither Industrial Cooperation?	173
	Notes	187
	Selected Bibliography	215
	Index	223

Preface

When President Woodrow Wilson reorganized war mobilization machinery following a "winter crisis" in 1917–18, he created the National War Labor Board. What follows is a study of how this "Supreme Court of Labor Relations" worked both to centralize federal war-labor policies and to secure voluntary acceptance of its rulings. The new agency, established in April 1918 specifically to stop labor unrest in war-related industries, had a formidable task. Yet if widespread cooperation between business and labor was possible during the war, the NWLB seemed well suited to encourage it. Half of its members had been chosen by the National Industrial Conference Board, an amalgam of employer associations; the others, by the American Federation of Labor. Former President William Howard Taft and Frank P. Walsh, the controversial chairman of the United States Commission on Industrial Relations from 1913 to 1915, served as joint chairmen. The potential for cooperation seemed even more likely because the members of the NWLB had themselves written the principles to guide the NWLB's settlements of labor disputes. The creation of the NWLB, nonetheless, marked an ambitious gamble in business-government-labor relations. War production demanded industrial peace. Presumably the spokesmen for competing private interests on the board had agreed on the meaning of what they had written, but could their words alone prevent strikes and lockouts?

The meaning of words became the first problem. The NWLB's principles defied easy interpretation because they reflected the contradictory organizational goals of the men who wrote them. The principles affirmed the rights of employees to join trade unions and to bargain collectively with their employers. They acknowledged the rights of workers to a living wage and of women to equal pay for equal work. They lent support to the concept of an eight-hour day. But those concessions to organized labor were undercut by other principles that warned against using the war emergency to pursue prewar objectives, upheld the "open shop" where it existed, and ordered the NWLB to consider local customs and existing conditions in all its rulings. In short, the principles pledged the NWLB to both undermine and uphold the status quo. The board's members, moreover, meant to define them to set precedents to outlast the war. In these circumstances, the viability of "voluntary cooperation" as an instrument of mobilization became immediately suspect.

Enormous problems generated by the war economy further militated against an easy industrial peace. First, American workers were understandably restless. With the advent of war, the cost of living had soared. By the end of 1917, food costs were 85 percent above the 1913 average; clothing costs, 106 percent; and medicines, 130 percent. Inflation and the increased demand for industrial labor after the United States entered the war encouraged workers to join labor unions and to strike 3,500 recorded times between April 1917 and early 1918 for higher wages, shorter hours, collective bargaining, and union recognition.[1] A new problem emerged as large numbers of women assumed jobs traditionally held by men, and women's low wages threatened the standard of living. Second, employers fought to retain control of their shops. Despite the wartime cost-plus contracts that protected the profit levels of those who did business with the federal government, businessmen generally wanted protection from labor agitation and without federally attached strings. Third, both organized business and organized labor read the NWLB's principles with an eye to the future. Like the members of the board, they were inclined to support only those policies that lent strength to their visions of postwar industrial relations.

Regardless of predictable problems, necessity mandated the voluntary aura that enveloped most of the administration's war bureaucracies. Neither the president nor the private interests to be directly affected by mobilization policies accepted in the abstract the theory of federal coercion, even in time of war—especially in a war being fought in the name of democracy. The image of general cooperation in federal policies was therefore essential for ideological reasons. Practical considerations also necessitated "voluntary" action. The longstanding antipathy of the American people to a powerful central state had produced a federal bureaucracy ill-equipped to mobilize the economy in a national emergency. Bureaucracies in the private sector, in contrast, were more experienced and sophisticated. Business organizations had long worked to rationalize the economy in their own best interests. Even in matters of social welfare, corporate liberals had a deeper tradition of leadership than did the federal government. Businessmen had played a commanding role in shaping the outcome of minimum wage and workmen's compensation legislation in the states, while the federal government's role in such matters had generally been to encourage uniform actions by private interests and within the states.[2] Matters of similar import would now become the national purview of the NWLB. In essence, then, the structure of the NWLB, and of most other war bureaucracies, grew directly from existing tradition.

None of the dollar-a-year men who poured into Washington to fill the war bureaucracies found it easy to rationalize the economy on a voluntary basis. The legendary War Industries Board, for example, foundered badly in its first year. The president revitalized the WIB under the leadership of Bernard Baruch at just about the same time that he created the NWLB. Because of the president's commitment to voluntarism and reluctance to increase the power of businessmen in government, as Robert D. Cuff has shown, Baruch's new powers remained far short of those of an economic dictator. Instead, he emerged as a power broker who successfully manipulated elements of the business world into following his lead.[3] Baruch, however, did not have to contend in the WIB with two equal groups of men who represented organizations that had entered the war in fundamental disagreement over what results the war should yield at home. Taft and Walsh did.

In the NWLB, the advantage went mostly to labor. Never before had the federal government authorized pervasive policies to govern working conditions in American industries. Never before had representatives of organized labor shared equally with businessmen in determining federal labor policy. Both of those conditions had developed because the war brought the leadership of the AFL and the Wilson administration to a realization of mutual usefulness. By the time that the NWLB was created to keep workers on the job, Samuel Gompers had spent more than a year advertising the AFL's loyalty to the government. He had squelched radicalism in the AFL and in return expected the kind of recognition for his organization that business interests had traditionally enjoyed from the government. The problem was to make voluntarism the instrument of social justice as well as of stability. Normally, voluntarism allowed the strong to govern the weak; and despite its official equality in the new bureaucracy, labor was disadvantaged by recent history. With history as the enemy, Taft and Walsh therefore had to stimulate—or simulate—a consensus on the very issues that had caused strikes and lockouts for fifty years.

The creation, composition, principles, and powers of the NWLB marked it as the hybrid child of progressivism. For almost twenty years, prominent national business and labor organizations had groped toward uniform labor policies devised by private interests and implemented voluntarily. Two federal commissions had supported labor's right to organize and had advocated collective bargaining.

Reformers and political theorists had urged a larger role for the government in industrial affairs. Many such thinkers had embraced the welfare state implicit in the New Nationalism, which called for a strengthened federal executive and discriminatory action on behalf of the labor movement. Many others, wary of class legislation and federal coercion, took comfort in the more traditional rhetoric of the New Freedom. The business and labor organizations, the commissions, the reformers, and the theorists had all called for national solutions to industrial problems. Then the war made national policies imperative; and when the NWLB was established to impose them, it echoed the recurring themes of two decades. A structural monument to the New Nationalism, the NWLB owed much to New Freedom ideology. A creature of the federal executive that recognized labor's voice as equal to management's, it was nevertheless wholly devoid of real power—unless the president should decide to supply it.

That last was important. The president had, or could get from Congress, powers to compel compliance with an NWLB decision as long as the war was on. By the spring of 1918, Wilson had told workers that unruly horses would have to be corralled, and whether or not they knew it, employers were subject to the same strong hand. The president, in other words, could impose "voluntary" rulings on occasional recalcitrants. But if the NWLB could reach no decisions, or if indecision began to characterize its work, the administration would need another avenue to maintain uninterrupted production.

Because they deal with policy and the difficulties that accompanied its development, these pages focus on a handful of industrial disputes that came before the NWLB for adjustment. Each case has been selected because its settlement forced the definition of one of the NWLB's principles or because it illustrated the measure of wartime conflict between business and labor. This study also admits a secondary focus on the partnership of Taft and Walsh as joint chairmen because these men led the NWLB in fact as well as in name. Because of their efforts, the board laid the foundations for the major labor legislation of the New Deal and the Kennedy years. The Wagner Act, the Fair Labor Standards Act, and the Equal Pay Amendment to that act all germinated as federal policy in the program that the joint chairmen prodded the NWLB to adopt.

In the sixteen months before the NWLB self-dissolved in August 1919, the board moved in a world of public relations, press releases, and precedents. It considered roughly 1,250 cases, many of which it referred to other agencies, and made awards or findings in almost 500 of them. Much of the credit for the implementation of those findings belongs to the NWLB's staff, which at its peak numbered 250 newspapermen, lawyers, college professors, feminists, statisticians, stenographers, and students. For many of them, working for democracy at home was more important than fighting in foreign trenches. Others, unable to serve abroad, believed that serving with the War Labor Board was the next best thing to being there. Their story remains largely untold here, but they deserve recognition. They kept the NWLB functioning on a daily basis, and without them the NWLB could never have begun what Frank P. Walsh called "a new deal for American labor."

As I end this project, I cannot help thinking of all the persons who have contributed so much, personally and professionally, to its completion. Most of them know who they are. A few of them I must single out for special thanks for support when I needed it: to my friends, students, and colleagues at The Florida State University, especially to Jean G. Hales, who gave unstinting service as sounding board and critic over many, many months; to Winifred J. Newcomb, the late Harry J. Dell, and S. J. Makielski, Jr., who always listened and asked the right questions; to Arthur S. Link, for his generous professional courtesy and incisive critical reading of an earlier draft of this manuscript; to John Milton Cooper, Jr., Jordan A. Schwarz, and Robert D. Cuff for their helpful suggestions concerning a later draft; to William H. Harbaugh, for his consistent help and encouragement at every stage of this work; and finally, to my mother, Valerie W. Conner, who characteristically refused to lose faith.

The National War Labor Board

Business, Labor, and Government in the Prewar Years: Prelude to Wartime Voluntarism

> So far as employers in distant places do come into competition with each other, their interests . . . may often be promoted by the coalescence of the local unions of their men: It tends to the establishment of uniform conditions throughout the industry, and thus moderates the severity of competition between employers. This effect is most marked when widespreading organizations of employers are also found . . . and when they settle wages, hours, and other conditions by direct agreement with the unions.
>
> —United States Industrial Commission, 1902

Wartime voluntarism was a natural, if not inevitable, development. Since the 1890s, national business and labor organizations had turned to the federal government for help in achieving their organizational goals. Yet, even as they worked to scuttle laissez faire, those organizations reflected the fear of federal coercion that had characterized American society since the eighteenth century. They clung fiercely to their own independence and to the traditional belief that democracy thrives best under limited government. At the turn of the century, there emerged within both groups a "vital center," committed to stabilization and standardization in industrial affairs. Many of these moderates also wrestled with a separate problem, which was how to achieve industrial democracy without destroying economic freedom. The means that they chose to resolve both matters was the means through which they believed political democracy had flourished, voluntary cooperation. The federal government could act as watchdog, establish certain guidelines for industrial behavior, and provide occasional forums for debate. But the real work of harmonizing the relations among businessmen and between employers and employees was best left to private interests. Such ideas, so prevalent in 1918, were embryonic in 1898 when the United States Industrial Commission investigated the conditions of labor and capital.

The fear of federal coercion permeated the Industrial Commission's final report. After four years of investigation, it recommended a program to promote industrial justice and efficiency with a minimum of federal interference. Government, nonetheless, had a vital role to play in industrial affairs. Its primary function, so the report implied, was to bolster the drive toward nationally uniform conditions already begun by the private organizations of the 1890s. Unwilling to see the powers of Congress revolutionized to that end, the commission looked more to the states. Congress should, of course, strengthen existing labor regulations for industries engaged in interstate commerce and for federal employees. But to increase dramatically the scope of federal action, the commission believed, was unacceptable. Clearly, cooperation in the passage of uniform state laws was the more democratic alternative.[1]

Ideally, however, the commission envisioned a society in which labor legislation would be all but superfluous. Repeatedly throughout its final report, it suggested that the enactment of needed reform by law, even nationally uniform law, was less desirable than securing the same ends without governmental intervention. Differences in state constitutions limited the potential of uniformity through state action. Confusions over the extent of the police powers of the states not only weakened the prospect of uniformity but also negated the possibility of legislation on vital questions in industrial relations. Finally, even uniform laws sustained by the courts were sure to be evaded unless laboring men could force compliance with them. If labor was that strong, the commission reasoned, the laws themselves would become unnecessary.[2]

The best way to achieve a just and efficient industrial society was through what the commission called "industrial democracy." Introduced in 1897 by Beatrice and Sidney Webb, British Fabian reformers, the phrase was interpreted loosely to include a variety of means through which laborers could acquire some measure of control over the terms of their employment.[3] Although the commission took notice of such plans as stock purchasing and cooperative production, it dismissed both as ineffective tools for the democratic reorganization of industry. "By the organization of labor, and by no other means," the report concluded, "it is possible to introduce an element of democracy into the government of industry." Only through organization could workers "effectively take part in determining the conditions under which they work." This became "true in the fullest and best sense only when employers frankly meet the representatives of the workmen, and deal with them as parties equally interested in the conduct of affairs."[4] Simply put, the Industrial Commission equated "industrial democracy" with "collective bargaining," another term that it noted was only just coming into use.[5]

The organization of labor was thus the cornerstone on which the Industrial Commission built its comprehensive program for national industrial reform. The national trade unions worked for the standardization of production costs and working conditions in major industries. When persuaded to cooperate for that purpose, business associations and powerful labor unions could eliminate the fragmented conditions that had caused industrial unrest. Such cooperation could not only prevent disruptive strikes but also end abuse of employees by employers and ease the competition among employers for competent workmen. Even local industries would profit from the national organization of craft unions, for their efforts to set national standards would increase the mobility of the work force. Finally, standardized conditions would erase the competitive disadvantage of states with advanced labor legislation. For all these reasons, the commission believed, "legislation is needed only where organization fails."[6]

Significantly, the report endorsed union goals in language that anticipated both the practical and the humanitarian tendencies in the Progressive ethos. The right to organize was essential to counterbalance the "growth of great aggregations of capital under the control of single groups of men."[7] In general, since wage earners were the weakest economic component in America, successful union efforts to strengthen their relative economic position strengthened the nation as a whole. More specifically, evidence indicated that shorter hours made for more on-the-job efficiency. Higher wages boosted the economy by increasing consumer buying power. More leisure time and a better standard of living encouraged workingmen to better their skills and to develop the qualities essential for constructive citizenship. Equal pay for women and limitations on the employment of children not only aided the unions but also furthered the welfare of the women and children themselves, and hence of the community at large.[8]

Most important, the growth of organized labor symbolized for the commission the best insurance for the future of capitalism and the American system of government. The national trade unions, already a brake against socialism, further protected the existing economic and political systems because the leaders of large organizations tended necessarily to be responsible and conservative men. Even persons out of sympathy with the labor movement had testified to the high "general character and ability" of the national union chiefs. This was especially true when the organizations themselves reflected democratic principles, such as the AFL's affiliates did.[9]

In sum, the commission report mirrored an America awakening to new socioeconomic realities but committed to old political values. It preached national uniformity and endorsed the essence of virtually every proposal for the reform of labor relations that would receive serious consideration in the next twenty years. Clearly, the commission envisioned collective solutions to national problems, even as it clung to Jeffersonian concepts of individualism and limited government. "Industrial democracy," in these circumstances, became the logical means to achieve both ends.

Theoretically, the commission's logic betrayed no flaw: Voluntary associations such as the trade-union affiliates and business organizations of the 1890s themselves eschewed coercion and preserved the image of individual freedom for the workers and employers who joined them. Voluntary cooperation between the representatives of both groups would extend the methods of political democracy into the national industrial arena. As cooperation succeeded, the need for governmental intervention would decrease. In reality, however, the harmony of the commission's scheme with popularly held Jeffersonian ideals was strained. The scheme did preserve the ideal of limited government, but the fundamental thrust of the report was that industrial democracy—a necessary correlative to political democracy in the modern state—demanded the sacrifice of economic individualism to the actions of formal, organized interest groups of equal strength.

On the practical level, therefore, the commission's emphasis on voluntarism and collective agreement appealed to important groups of elites, be they associations of business, labor, or reform. Such a program was ideally suited to "enlightened" businessmen, who thought in terms of a national economy and were both willing and able to make concessions to the work force in return for future harmony. Likewise, the program suited conservative labor leaders who accepted capitalism and were willing to work piecemeal toward increased political and economic power for their constituents. Finally, it offered hope to those middle-class reformers whose conception of the ideal society included little more than the capitalist state stripped of obvious inequities. For all those groups, voluntary collective action, supplemented by appropriate legislative guidelines, suggested the potential for change without the threat of revolution. In fact if not in theory, "industrial democracy" provided for the sharing of power among already powerful organizations.

For others, however, the thrust of the commission's report was noxious. Socialists took little comfort in proposals designed to strengthen an economic system that they abhorred. Local-minded businessmen, meanwhile, saw potential ruin in the triumph of voluntarism, collectivism, and legislated uniformity. For socialists, the commission's recommendations fell short of meaningful reform; for small businessmen, they moved the locus of power too far from home. This dissent from the left and from the right threatened the very heart of the commission's moderate program, for it belied the consensus upon which the commission predicated reform.

In actual fact, consensus had broken down even within the commission itself. Several members refused to sign the report. Fearing equally their large competitors and governmental intervention, these spokesmen for small business interests had retreated behind a wall of individualism in defense of their economic future. Two vice-presidents of the recently organized National Association of Manufacturers protested against both the ideal of standardized working conditions and the congeniality that their colleagues encouraged between large labor and large capital.[10] Climatic conditions, as well as differing kinds and status of industry, they insisted, made uniformity impracticable. They argued, moreover, against "any iron-clad rule adopted or suggested from a central power" and supported "the inalienable right of private contract" in order to fulfill America's destiny as the "leading manufacturing nation of the world." The report, one dissenting commissioner noted, catered to "unrestricted and uncontrolled organization of special classes of labor," which in cooperation with large-scale employers could demand and exact tributes from less powerful segments of the economy.[11]

Within months after the Industrial Commission's report was issued, voluntarism broke down in Pennsylvania. The long and bitter struggle in the anthracite coalfields ended only after President Theodore Roosevelt appointed a commission, which then settled the dispute and mandated voluntary cooperation for the life of the award. Although the United Mine Workers failed to win recognition per se, Roosevelt did appoint a labor leader to the commission, and the mine workers were represented equally with the operators on the board of conciliation created to implement the settlement.[12] The settlement lent important support to the ideas advanced by the Industrial Commission. It also set a precedent for presidential action in times of national crisis, even as it provided organized labor with its first measure of real power under the auspices of the federal government.

But the coal strike graphically demonstrated the imperfections of voluntarism as a tool for reform. Historically, the concept of voluntary cooperation had been devised to perpetuate democracy in a relatively small and homogeneous society. It assumed a fundamental commonality of interests and a basic equality of power among citizens.[13] In the United States, such a society had reached its apogee in colonial New England. In the twentieth century, voluntarism merely perpetuated the existing power structure. What voluntarism obviously could not do was equalize the power of business and labor. The coal strike had required the intervention of the federal government because the operators had seen no common interests with their employees. In 1902, the miners got a Square Deal only because the operators were forced to share power with them.

The coal strike and its aftermath also helped to clarify the divisions within the business community which had appeared within the Industrial Commission and which hindered the orderly progress of labor relations throughout the Progressive era. On the one hand, the business-dominated National Civic Federation, organized in 1900, recognized the organization of labor as a permanent fact of industrial life and endorsed the concept of collective bargaining. During the strike, the NCF had worked unsuccessfully to bring the miners and the operators together.[14] The National Association of Manufacturers, however, found a "great danger" in the NCF's conciliatory approach to trade unionism and resented the government's method of restoring peace to the anthracite fields.[15] Like the NCF, the NAM believed that private interests could best solve industrial problems and that businessmen should organize to that purpose. Yet, while the NCF accepted the implications of the emerging collectivist society, the NAM steadfastly refused to see the irony of its attempts to organize American employers for the preservation of individualism.[16]

The program of the National Civic Federation between 1900 and 1904 harmonized perfectly with the Industrial Commission's majority report. A blue-ribbon coalition of America's most prominent public and private figures, the NCF promoted industrial justice as a by-product of industrial peace. It provided a national forum through which representatives of special-interest organizations might come together and discuss common problems. John Mitchell, president of the United Mine Workers, had been among its first members. Through its Industrial Department, the NCF also offered mediation and conciliation services to strife-torn industries, and it pioneered the tripartite commission—composed of representatives of labor, capital, and the public—which the government later adopted.[17] Under the formal leadership of Mark Hanna, the Ohio businessman-politician, and Samuel Gompers, president of the American Federation of Labor, the NCF was mutually useful to businessmen and labor leaders in search of industrial order.

The National Association of Manufacturers—as its members on the Industrial Commission had so well demonstrated—reflected the views of less prominent and less secure businessmen. Rather than tame labor by inviting it to dinner, the NAM decided to fight back. While the NCF preached its message of conciliatory collectivism, the NAM opened fire on the AFL and on federal meddling in industrial problems. In 1902, the president of the NAM, Theodore Search, warned against union efforts to broaden the eight-hour law for governmental employees and to secure protection from injunctions under the Sherman law. By the following year, the NAM had reacted even more strongly against what it considered increasing inroads into economic freedom. At their annual convention in 1903, the manufacturers heard President David Parry criticize the government's interference with the "natural wage law" in the anthracite settlement. Labor's success in that strike, he warned, had "fired the minds of labor leaders everywhere with an exalted idea of the power they possessed." To Parry, organized labor was nothing but a socialistic "mob power." Recent support for labor's demands by the press, the public, and certain members of Congress revealed "the deep-seated powers of an organization which . . . [is] dominating to a dangerous degree the whole social, political, and governmental system of the nation."[18]

In the wake of Parry's remarks, the delegates adopted what became the basis of the NAM's labor policy for years to come. Not until after World War I did the NAM acknowledge any real difference between Gompers's objectives and those of the labor radicals whom he opposed. The "Declaration of Principles" of 1903 defended the "personal liberty" of employer and employee. It claimed no hostility to the organization of labor, per se, but condemned the purposes for which labor organized. In particular, it opposed meaningful collective bargaining, which the NCF supported in principle, and denounced union recognition, which the AFL considered the prerequisite for successful collectivism. In general, the NAM rallied behind the open shop and demanded freedom for management in setting the conditions and rewards of labor.[19]

The vehemence of the NAM's antiunion position foreshadowed

things to come. The optimism of the Industrial Commission's recommendations and the NCF's program gave way to widening rifts within and between business and labor associations. When the organizational drive launched by the AFL stalled in mid-decade, the NCF broadened its program to accommodate the new status quo. Never entirely comfortable with labor, many NCF businessmen—especially those who refused to deal with unions in their own shops—now embraced welfare capitalism as a means to contain union growth.[20] The NAM continued to reject both the strained democracy and the obvious paternalism inherent in the NCF approach. By 1905, the conservative hierarchy of the AFL was beset by socialists' demands to dissociate the AFL from the NCF and by escalating NAM-sponsored open-shop campaigns. For the moment, Gompers and Mitchell had little trouble defeating the socialists in the AFL, but the manufacturers' attacks were more difficult to counter. In an effort to meet them, the AFL leadership chose to reinvigorate traditional union demands for labor's political and economic independence.[21]

In 1906, the American Federation of Labor entered national politics directly. Its "Bill of Grievances" stressed to Congress the basic program that it had sponsored since the 1890s. Among other things, the AFL continued to demand extension of the federal eight-hour law to include all workers on governmental contract, an antiinjunction law, and exemption from the antitrust act. That year organized labor elected six members to Congress, among them William B. Wilson of Pennsylvania, one of the founders of the United Mine Workers and its secretary-treasurer since 1900. Wilson believed strongly in the need for a separate Department of Labor and worked toward that end for the next six years. The AFL turned partisan in 1908. Rebuffed by the Republicans, it supported William Jennings Bryan for the presidency and many Democratic congressional candidates.[22] The Supreme Court that year had given labor special reason to be active. The Court had struck down prohibitions against "yellow-dog" contracts* in the Erdman Act of 1898; termed secondary boycotts† conspiracies in restraint of trade; applied the Sherman Act, for the first time, to labor organizations; and confirmed the use of the labor injunction.[23] In

---

*A "yellow-dog" contract, which is now illegal, was an employment contract that required an employee to sign a pledge that he would not be a member of a labor union while employed by the company that issued it.
†A secondary boycott, which is prohibited by both the Taft-Hartley Act (1947) and the Landrum-Griffin Act (1959), is a boycott in which employees who oppose policies of their own employer also refuse to patronize another employer, a third party, in an effort to strengthen their relative position.

1910, labor sent fifteen men to Congress, including Representative Wilson, who became chairman of the House Committee on Labor in 1912, and, in that year, the AFL helped Woodrow Wilson to win the presidency.[24]

The AFL's foray into politics unnerved the businessmen of the NCF. It raised the specter of class politics, which they had all along sought to prevent. It suggested that labor was willing and perhaps able to win for itself what the NCF had been trying to secure for it and thereby become an independent force with no further need to cooperate with business. Furthermore, the AFL's antagonism toward the Supreme Court suggested a possible full-scale attack on the judiciary, which the NCF businessmen defended as the mainstay of private property. To protect its business-labor coalition, therefore, the NCF sponsored the Hepburn bill in 1908 to give both business and labor protection from the Sherman Antitrust Act. The bill, which failed to satisfy labor completely, went down to defeat, and the NCF coalition was close to falling apart. The following year, the Civic Federation found a means to reinvigorate its relationship with the AFL when it persuaded Samuel Gompers that workmen's compensation legislation would go a long way toward satisfying labor's social needs. Even then, the relationship remained strained, for it had become clear that the NCF businessmen did not agree with the AFL's fundamental political and economic goals.[25]

Within the AFL, continued support for the NCF began to take its toll as socialistic elements persisted in their distrust of the businessmen. Socialists within and without the labor federation had been pleased at the AFL's entry into politics, for they had hoped that a new labor party would emerge to supersede the NCF connection. When it did not, John Mitchell, an NCF loyalist, was forced from the presidency of the UMW in 1907. By 1911, the miners had made membership in the NCF cause for automatic expulsion from the union, and Mitchell, head of the NCF's Trade Agreement Department since 1908, reluctantly left the coalition that he had served for almost a dozen years. That same year, James O'Connell, first vice-president of the AFL and member of the NCF executive committee, was replaced as president of the International Association of Machinists by a socialist, William H. Johnston.[26]

Meanwhile, the AFL's political activity and persistent relationship with the NCF greatly disturbed the NAM. The manufacturers, of course, had stimulated labor politics. Their efforts, and those of other employer associations which sprang up to defend the open shop, had stymied organized labor's growth and decreased its normal influence in Congress. After 1906, the NAM redoubled its efforts to keep labor's influence minimal. In 1908, the NAM's *American Industries* told its readers to "Go into Politics," and the association rallied behind William Howard Taft. That year the manufacturers and their allies fought the Hepburn bill and financed the court cases whose outcome so enraged the AFL. The NAM's antiunion sentiments, although genuine enough, were fed by inordinate fear of federal power and traditional hostility toward larger competitors. It fought labor legislation, in part, to restrain the scope of federal action. And, while the NAM denounced the Hepburn bill as a labor giveaway, association members resented the bill as much because of the obvious advantage that it offered to big business.[27]

In 1910, the cold war turned hot when members of the Bridge and Structural Iron Workers Union dynamited the Los Angeles *Times* building. The bombing, which shocked the nation, inadvertently took the lives of twenty workers. For several years, the BSIW had battled the tough-minded open-shop policies of the National Erectors Association. Simultaneously, in Los Angeles, Harrison Gray Otis, owner-editor of the *Times*, had led a local manufacturers' association in a successful campaign to make the city the open-shop stronghold of the West Coast. The BSIW men had hoped to discredit Otis, the NEA, and other antiunion forces by making the explosion appear accidental—the result of leaking gas—evidence of unconcern for employee safety among autocratic employers. Instead, they went a long way toward discrediting the labor movement. The incident also profoundly disturbed a group of social reformers, most of whom had connections with *The Survey*, a leading organ of social justice, and had long been interested in industrial democracy. At their urging President Taft requested, and Congress approved in 1912, plans for a new commission to investigate the causes of industrial unrest.[28]

The United States Commission on Industrial Relations, which President Wilson appointed in 1913, followed the model of the NCF: business, labor, and the public had equal representation. Moreover, eight of its nine members also belonged to the NCF. The three labor representatives, who included James O'Connell, were all conservatives. Nevertheless, the NAM and its fellow open-shop organizations were suspicious of the CIR. The NAM had good reason, for as James Weinstein points out, it, basically, was what the commission would investigate. With neither labor radicals nor "anarchic" businessmen within its ranks, the CIR was designed to promote the kind of reform that had been the hallmark of the NCF's program since 1900.[29]

Among the most prominent of the commissioners was John R.

Commons, economist at the University of Wisconsin. Commons, one of three members who represented the public, had superb credentials. He had been on the staff of the Industrial Commission, written for *The Survey*, and worked as a conciliator for the NCF. Commons and his fellow Wisconsinite Charles McCarthy, director of the CIR's Research Division, worked hard to generate the same broad consensus among society's "responsible" elements which the NCF had always sought. McCarthy, who had earned the Ph.D. under Frederick Jackson Turner, had helped to inaugurate the so-called "Wisconsin Idea" that gave experts an unprecedented role in the government of the state. Under his leadership, Wisconsin had pioneered a legislative reference service, which employed scholars to draft proposed statutes. Although critics scoffed at McCarthy's "bill factory," it nevertheless embodied the elitist concept of democracy at work. It provided the means through which intelligent and scientific social planning could supersede laws passed for mere partisan or parochial purpose. Commons and McCarthy hoped to put the Wisconsin idea to work in the CIR.[30]

When the commission's funds were cut short in 1915, its chairman, Frank P. Walsh, reordered CIR priorities and dismissed McCarthy. Walsh was forced to choose between financing extensive research or continuing the public hearings through which he had broadcast the plight of the working man and woman. He curtailed the research. During the preceding year, the hearings had effectively dispelled whatever remained of the myth of class harmony in America. For Walsh that was among their important accomplishments. The colorful chairman had little patience with mild-mannered men in search of consensus. What he wanted the commission's investigation to reveal was the irresponsibility of American employers. When it did, he would propose measures to give labor its fair share.[31]

Always flamboyant and often belligerent, the Irish lawyer from Kansas City, Missouri, was an unreconstructed muckraker who thrived on controversy. He courted publicity for the commission's hearings; he dug deeply into the Colorado coal strike and depicted John D. Rockefeller, Jr., as a cunning liar; he saw his work as a crusade against poverty. "The poorly nourished," he argued, "are weak comrades in a war on rotten industrial conditions, adulterated food, vice, and wholesale murder, or any other of those countless evils that have an economic basis."[32] Walsh took testimony from powerful industrialists and from their common laborers, gave both sources equal weight, and never missed a chance to tell the press what he had discovered. "There seems to be an idea that the . . . Commission . . .

was appointed to keep things quiet," he said in the face of mounting criticism. "This is not my idea."[33] When the Chicago *Evening News* attacked him as "unjudicial," he claimed to be an investigator and not a judge. "I have no judicial poise," Walsh agreed. "I don't care to have judicial poise. Judicial poise is a bar to human progress."[34]

But more than method and temperament separated Walsh from Commons and McCarthy. The Missouri lawyer, like the Wisconsin scholars, was committed to reform. Walsh, however, shared neither their enthusiasm for social planning nor their reverence for scientific legislation. He did not belong to the NCF, nor did he share its preoccupation with industrial harmony. Furthermore, he abhorred the elitist implications of the Wisconsin Idea. His concept of democracy was somewhat more egalitarian and considerably less "efficient." Walsh wanted to help labor escape its dependence on well-meaning benefactors. He therefore encouraged the kind of class politics that the NCF found so distasteful. John R. Commons understood the difference. The issue, he believed, was "whether the labor movement should be directed toward politics or toward collective bargaining. . . . I wanted them to avoid politics and to direct their energies toward . . . building up strong organizations of self-governing unions." Walsh wanted them to avoid neither.[35]

When it was all over, the Commission on Industrial Relations was torn apart by its own findings. Walsh and the three labor members issued a report that the other five members rejected as prounion propaganda.[36] Commons and Mrs. J. Borden Harriman, who also represented the public, strove for balance in a report of their own, and the employer group issued separate conclusions that pointed to abuses perpetuated by organized labor. *American Industries* described and dismissed them all in a burst of familiar rhetoric: "The one signed by the Chairman and the labor union officials and that produced by Professor Commons and Mrs. Harriman are socialistic in tone throughout. The report which bears the name of the employers is individualistic as might have been expected. . . . We are not disappointed with the product of the Commission's labors; nothing constructive was expected of it and nothing constructive has been produced."[37] Actually, the Walsh report was more incendiary than socialistic, and Commons's was neither; but the NAM's journal correctly perceived the fundamental antagonism of both to the employers' more conservative stance.

Among other things, the three reports disagreed on the meaning of "industrial democracy." Even the employers agreed that labor was "thoroughly justified in organizing and in spreading organization in order better to protect itself against exploitation and oppression."[38] They also believed that the democratic ideal could be realized through scientific management, which would increase productivity and eliminate waste. The AFL, however, had gone on record against scientific management, and the Walsh report upheld labor's position when it reinforced the conclusion of the CIR's turn-of-the-century predecessor —namely that industrial democracy meant "collective bargaining." A joint agreement between an employer association and a national trade union, the Walsh report explained, is superior to legislation because "it is more comprehensive, is more elastic, and more nearly achieves the ideal of fundamental democracy that government should to the greatest possible extent consist of agreements . . . voluntarily made."[39] For Commons, too, collective agreement on working conditions was essential; but the Wisconsin professor also wanted to establish permanent impartial governmental authorities to help business and labor to reach accord on proposed new legislation as well.[40]

Both Walsh and Commons carved out a much larger role for the federal government than had the Industrial Commission at the turn of the century. Walsh wanted the government to set rules conducive to human welfare and advantageous to an independent labor movement and then to step aside while labor battled with management for its own destiny. Hence he proposed land and tax laws to redistribute the wealth and prohibitions against judicial interference with state and federal laws. His report also called for laws to establish the eight-hour day and the six-day work week, to abolish child labor, and to provide equal pay for women. Finally, it condemned the open shop as an antiunion tactic and called for federal protection of the rights to organize and to bargain collectively. Commons, on the other hand, saw the government as an adviser, but not a dictator, to both sides. Yet he believed that government had a duty to encourage equality of power between employers and employees. His collectivist solution to industrial unrest included the creation of a national advisory council consisting of the secretaries of labor and of commerce and representatives of employer and labor associations, along with similar state industrial commissions.[41] Commons, in other words, wedded the NCF's traditional ideology to the Wisconsin Idea, while Frank Walsh wanted government to help labor to achieve the goals that it had sought since the 1890s. Taken together, most scholars agree, the two reports anticipated both the mobilization machinery of World War I and the labor legislation of the New Deal.

The CIR, of course, solved no industrial problems, but it gave the labor movement a new hero and the NAM a new nemesis. "Who can say the money had not been well spent," chided *American Industries*, "especially when one considers that Chairman Walsh has permanently disqualified himself for any other official position."[42] Praise for Walsh, however, poured into the White House from trade union locals and even a few socialist groups.[43] Before the CIR hearings had got under way, the IWW leader, Bill Haywood, had dismissed the commission as a "tragic joke, perpetrated by legislative jugglers."[44] When they ended, Eugene Debs wrote to Walsh that the commission's work had "measureless value to the working class and to the cause of humanity."[45] For Samuel Gompers, too, Walsh had won the "confidence of the people" by exposing the "burdens that have been heaped upon the wage earners of this country."[46]

All of this increased the confidence of radicals and of the labor movement in the Wilson administration. To the general public, the Walsh report *was* the commission's report. In 1968, James Weinstein correctly observed that a major effect of the commission's work was to stem the tide of socialism, for Walsh spoke for the government as he castigated the nation's industrial evils. That was the key. His exposé helped to soften criticism of the system, for it demonstrated that the system could flay itself.[47]

The New Republic understood that fact in 1915. Walsh, it proclaimed, had determined from the beginning not to write the typical governmental document or to sponsor "dull and unmanageable inquiries, of use only to a few professors who want to write books." Furthermore, he "realized that the question of industrial relations was not so much a matter of quantitatively ascertaining truth as it was a matter of what workingmen and employers thought and felt about the facts." He had, therefore, paid little attention to the experts, and, instead, had "set out to dramatize for the newspapers the psychology of industrial relations." He had been an agitator, determined that "the poor and the oppressed . . . should find in a governmental official . . . some one who could voice with official sanction their indictment of America." Because of that, Walsh had become "the leader around whom American radicalism had tried to rally." At the same time, the commission had respected organized labor more than any previous governmental body. For that reason, *The New Republic* concluded, "Mr. Walsh has in all probability done a great deal to reestablish the confidence of labor in the promise of political action. He has also done much to stiffen the labor movement and conserve it against . . . despair."[48]

Other political developments in Wilson's first term justified the AFL's confidence in political action. The president's New Freedom and Gompers's voluntarism were cut from the same cloth. From the beginning, Gompers enjoyed Wilson's attention, and in 1916 the hierarchy of the AFL and the Wilson cabinet scheduled unprecedented joint luncheon meetings. By then, the president had signed the Clayton Antitrust Act and the Seamen's Act, both important victories for organized labor, and when the railroad brotherhoods threatened a nationwide strike that year, Wilson forced through Congress the Adamson Act, which mandated an eight-hour day on interstate rails. The Clayton Act, the Seamen's Act, and the Adamson Act became the labor legislative landmarks of the Wilson years.[49] None of them, however, fell outside the scope of federal power envisioned so long ago by the Industrial Commission.

Even more important than the headline-grabbing legislation was the new Department of Labor, the creation of which Taft had reluctantly authorized on his last day in office. Wilson's appointment of William B. Wilson, the AFL's choice, as the first secretary of labor, provided the labor movement with a powerful, independent voice in the federal executive. Secretary Wilson, not surprisingly, shared the president's and Gompers's commitment to voluntary action. In 1913, the department's Division of Conciliation gradually began to assume the conciliatory functions that the NCF had pioneered. Except for controversies in interstate commerce, which were provided for separately in the Newlands Act of that year, the division could enter any industrial dispute on the request of employers or employees. Although poorly funded and infrequently used in its early years, the division's record of success was good. By 1916, it had made the idea of federal mediation viable.[50]

The Labor Department came at a perfect time to further industrial harmony through voluntary cooperation. Both business and labor associations had been generated and then fragmented by twentieth-century problems. The Commission on Industrial Relations had demonstrated, once and for all, that purely private interests could not forge industrial consensus. While the AFL had emerged from the fracas seemingly vindicated, industrial tensions had bankrupted the NCF. In 1916, organized business began to speak through the National Industrial Conference Board, an organization of manufacturing associations that was neither so progressive as the NCF nor so obviously reactionary as the NAM.[51] The federal government's new role in industrial conciliation—along with the recent legislation, the Walsh exposé, and Samuel Gompers's persistent conservatism—created the conditions that made possible the "partnership" of the AFL and the NICB under governmental supervision during World War I.

# 2

A New Deal for American Labor

> The Presidential Doctrine of Labor is to give labor an equal voice in the affairs of the nation with capital; an equal right with every individual in the country to enjoy the privilege and credit of winning the war.
>
> —Frank P. Walsh, *The Forum*, August 1918

The prewar experience had demonstrated the limits of voluntarism in the absence of a countervailing force to equalize the volunteers. Both business and labor organizations, however, retained their historic antipathy toward coercion as America mobilized for war. Dominant interests within both groups also saw an unprecedented opportunity to cooperate with the government. They hoped thereby to further their own ends and to effect national solutions, however temporary, to the continuing problems of industrial relations. Once the war had put inevitable strains on the economy, the Wilson administration sought effective machinery to satisfy governmental needs and insure the cooperation of private interests. The Labor Department's Division of Conciliation was insufficient for such a responsibility; and the National War Labor Board, created a full year after the United States went to war, was the administration's ultimate answer. The NWLB formalized voluntarism under governmental auspices and gave labor the equal voice it had long demanded.

"Nobody is surprised at anything in Washington these days. . . . Sworn enemies are friends, working side by side to win the war." So wrote a Washington correspondent in the late spring of 1918. In the corridors of the new labor building, William Howard Taft soothed everyone with his infectious good humor, and Frank P. Walsh chuckled right along with him. "Some might interpret this," the reporter warned, "to mean that capital, in the person of Mr. Taft, is in superior position, and that labor must fight doggedly on in order to wrest a modicum of its rights from its ancient enemy." Such, he concluded, was not the case. The National War Labor Board was too well balanced to give advantage to either side, and people who appealed to it for justice came away believing in a decent world.[1] Impressed by the NWLB's public image in its early days, the reporter had written his story to reflect what everyone in Washington hoped was true.

Evidence that Taft and Walsh had learned to respect each other that spring and were working well together was indeed newsworthy. They had differed vehemently in the past, particularly over the conduct and conclusions of the Commission on Industrial Relations. Taft, after all, had sought and secured congressional approval for the commission in 1912, only to have his own appointees rejected. Frank Walsh, the headline-grabbing social reformer and labor lawyer who turned the commission's operations into a vehicle for personal expression, had not even been Wilson's first choice to be chairman. To Taft by 1915, Walsh had destroyed whatever promise the commission had once held. (Walsh, for his part, had decided that Taft's attitudes toward industrial problems were among the things that the commission needed to probe.) Ironically, both Taft and Wilson had appointed the same conservative leaders to represent labor. Now Frank Walsh was leading them away from the cooperation with capital for which Taft had yearned and toward radical dissent.

All of this fed Taft's temperamental and ideological disaffection from the commission's investigations, and, no doubt, encouraged his refusal to participate in its work. The summons came in 1915, when the commission turned its attention to "Labor and the Law" and invited Taft to testify. While serving as federal judge for the Sixth Circuit in the 1890s, Taft had sentenced Frank M. Phelan to six months in prison for encouraging a boycott in contempt of court. Phelan, an organizer for the American Railway Union during the Pullman strike, had persuaded Cincinnati railway workers to walk out in protest against the dismissal of three switchmen who declined to route Pullman cars on the Cincinnati, Hamilton, and Dayton Railroad. The stoppage of work on those grounds, Judge Taft held, was illegal under the Interstate Commerce Act. Men could refuse to work in protest against their own working conditions, the judge reasoned, but they could not halt traffic in sympathy with the dissatisfaction of other workers.[2] Many supporters of organized labor believed that Taft's decision had cut the heart out of labor's right to strike. Two decades later, Walsh wanted to ask him about it, but Taft wrote Basil M. Manly, coordinator of the commission's hearings, that he had no time to appear.[3]

If Taft was too busy to cooperate with the commission, he found the time to join its host of critics, and—in the process—to infuriate Frank Walsh. Disgusted by the tumult that accompanied its end, Taft dismissed the commission's multiple findings before he saw them. By forsaking "judicial poise" in the investigations, Walsh had not sought the truth, Taft told the St. Louis Businessmen's League in the summer of 1915: "The result is that no one will pay any attention to the report of the Commission."[4] Characteristically, Walsh returned the fire: "Without desiring to appear caustic or critical toward the distinguished gentleman," he said,

> might I suggest that he should have, at least, waited until . . . he could have considered the . . . recommendations of the staff . . . which includes the greatest educators and experts of the nation, before his denunciation of the report as a whole. Thus, perhaps, the personality of the chairman . . . might not have beclouded the "judicially minded" seekers of the truth.
>
> This advice, might I also hazard, applies particularly to my exalted critic himself, who, it will be recalled, after the delivery of an address upon labor conditions at Cooper Union . . . a few years ago, was asked . . . what the thousands of unemployed workmen were to do for food the coming winter, and who unjudicially as well as unscientifically, threw up both hands and exclaimed "God knows."[5]

In succeeding years, the two men had continued old habits. Frank Walsh, who had by now alienated the NCF hierarchy of which Taft was a part, also drew predictable fire from the NAM. *American Industries*, for example, ridiculed the Committee on Industrial Relations, a private group that Walsh organized to lobby before Congress. Nor did his work behind the scenes in support of the Adamson Act please any of the business interests that he had antagonized.[6] After he returned to private practice in Kansas City, Walsh continued to rail against American industrialists, publicly sympathized with the IWW, and flirted temporarily with a new career as owner and publisher of the Kansas City *Post*. Taft, meanwhile, continued his duties at Yale University, where he had taught constitutional law since leaving the presidency. After 1915, when he assumed the presidency of the League to Enforce Peace, he also worked for a new world order governed by an international set of rules. Although Walsh inclined toward pacifism and Taft hoped to see America remain neutral, both men accepted the decision for war when it came. Seemingly, they agreed on little else in the spring of 1917.

Long before America abandoned neutrality, business and labor organizations clamored for power while mobilization machinery slowly emerged to coordinate production with military needs. In 1916, both sides received initial recognition in the Council of National Defense and its Advisory Commission. Cabinet members made up the CND, while the seven-member National Defense Advisory Commission

(NDAC) represented groups in the private sector: transportation, labor, general industry, finance, mining, merchandising, and medical science. In creating the two agencies, Robert D. Cuff concludes, the Wilson administration accepted a major premise of its early mobilization effort, which was that private interests should fill the gaps in governmental ability to guide the war economy.[7] By the following year, business interests had clearly provided the lion's share of guidance.

Business advocates of efficiency and industrial self-regulation had spearheaded the drive for the CND and NDAC in an effort to generate a workable partnership between business and government. Rising professionals, including engineers, proponents of scientific management, and leaders of the Chamber of Commerce were in the forefront. The "dollar-a-year" men who subsequently settled into many of the war bureaucracies echoed the need for voluntary, uniform solutions to industrial problems, much as the Industrial Commission and the National Civic Federation had done years earlier. Although the cooperation that they envisioned was largely among themselves, these "business synthesizers" promoted the partnership with full cognizance of its national implications. Theoretically, at least, their sentiments helped to unite enlightened business elements that had arrived at similar conclusions since the turn of the century. Less enlightened elements, from the outset, therefore seemed vanquished.[8]

Preparedness and mobilization had no such unifying effect on organized labor. On the contrary, those issues further divided the conservatives and radicals who already vied for control of the labor movement. As the nation moved toward war, socialists and other radicals remained convinced that the European conflict threatened the interests of the working class. They stood by organized labor's traditional beliefs that preparedness for war generated war and that militarism transformed laborers into cannon fodder for the ruling class. Conservative unionists, however, gradually adjusted their antipathy toward militarism to accommodate preparedness. The key figure in their transition, logically, was Samuel Gompers.[9]

Under constant pressure from Ralph Easley, who had organized the NCF and remained its chief spokesman, Gompers became persuaded of the immorality of peace at any price. Germany, he believed by 1915, threatened the democratic ideal to which he was devoted, and pacifist societies at home unwittingly aided the German cause.[10] Accordingly, Gompers adopted the tactics and some of the rhetoric of his business counterparts in 1916. In the process of doing so, he redefined preparedness to include the AFL's longstanding goals.

Preparedness differed from militarism, the AFL chief wrote in

March 1916, for preparedness furthered "freedom," while militarism spelled "repression." Indeed, the militarist preoccupation with rearmament perverted the fundamental meaning of preparedness, which included a "comprehensive policy . . . to meet all of the problems of life." Because preparedness required "the coordination and utilization of national forces and resources," it demanded national concern for human welfare. Preparedness also required that mobilization machinery be structured to further democratic ideals.[11] By so broadening the definition of preparedness, Gompers held out the promise of the AFL's cooperation in what he considered the inevitable participation of the United States in the anti-German coalition. He also devised the rationale for his consistent demand that labor be represented on all mobilization boards.

As labor's representative on the National Defense Advisory Commission and chairman of the NDAC's Committee on Labor in 1917, Gompers worked hard to increase labor's relative power in the emerging war bureaucracy. Even before the declaration of war, he called a special labor conference in Washington to underscore labor's loyalty and to clarify labor's position. At the conference, representatives of seventy-nine affiliated unions, five affiliated departments, and five unaffiliated unions signed a statement drafted by the executive council of the AFL which offered "our services to our country in every field of activity to defend, safeguard, and preserve the Republic of the United States of America against its enemies, whomsoever they may be." While pledging labor's loyalty the statement also reflected Gompers's definition of preparedness. It denounced militarism and reinforced Gompers's demand that labor be represented in all agencies established to formulate national defense policies. Most important, the statement argued that organized labor had "earned" the right to speak for the wage earners of the country. Therefore, the leaders who signed it urged the government to cooperate with them and to establish union standards in both public and private establishments essential to war production.[12]

Then, apparently, Gompers gambled. In April 1917, his NDAC committee recommended that the Council of National Defense support existing standards in industrial employment. Changes, said the committee, should be made only after approval of the CND itself. When the statement inevitably jarred organized labor, Gompers explained that the committee meant only to keep standards high. Regardless of that, significant elements of the labor movement as well as the NAM, which called a special meeting to endorse the recommendation, read the statement as an acquiescence in the open shop.[13]

Perhaps they read it right. Gompers, it seems, counted on his special relationship with the Wilson administration to achieve the closed shop informally. If the government dealt with the unions, employers, in order to prove their patriotism, might also accept union standards.[14]

Initially, the first phase of Gompers's strategy seemed to be working and without the cooperation of more radical labor leaders. In June, the AFL chief officially relaxed union demands for the closed shop. In turn, Secretary of War Newton D. Baker agreed that the War Department, as employer, would observe union standards in building sixteen army cantonments.[15] This Baker-Gompers agreement seemed a reasonable trade-off. It was an important psychological victory for organized labor because it seemed to open the way for similar agreements with other governmental agencies. The Cantonment Adjustment Commission, established to fulfill the Baker-Gompers agreement, became the first labor board of the war. Its three members represented the constituency recognized long ago by the NCF in its conciliation work: business, labor, and the public. Subsequent labor boards generally followed the CAC structure. Some, like the National Adjustment Commission, which mediated differences between the International Longshoremen's Association and shipping operators, specifically guaranteed union rates and hours. The NAC, therefore, upheld the Baker-Gompers agreement.[16]

On balance, however, the new adjustment machinery reflected the government's need for efficient production rather than a commitment to union goals. Governmental pledges to adjust wages and hours were necessary to keep workingmen on the job in a time of spiraling inflation, increased production needs, and acknowledged labor shortages. None of the new governmental commissions intended to further the closed union shop in a hostile environment. To do so would spell disaster, for none of the commissions had the power to compel employers to accept their rulings. Consequently, the adjustment machinery dissatisfied many labor leaders who wanted to use the war emergency as a catalyst for sweeping reform. For them, the Baker-Gompers agreement was a hollow victory. In the building trades and among longshoremen, union standards already prevailed.[17] Acceptance of those standards by the government marked only the acceptance of the status quo.

Men who remained skeptical about the Gompers strategy, such as William L. Hutcheson of the United Brotherhood of Carpenters and Joiners, were vindicated in August 1917. The disparity between governmental needs and union goals became clear that month, when Gompers tried to move the government beyond an acceptance of the status quo. Gompers and the Labor Department's troubleshooter, Louis B. Wehle, reached an impasse when the two men sat down to draft plans for the Shipbuilding Labor Adjustment Board. Because this board would handle disputes in the construction and repair of shipbuilding plants, Gompers suggested that its awards follow current union standards in the districts in which the plants operated. For Gompers, the suggestion merely extended the Baker-Gompers agreement, but Wehle termed the idea a "radical departure" from it. He objected to Gompers's idea because "it would have automatically transformed many open shops into union shops." Wehle then disregarded Gompers and prevailed on the affected unions within the AFL to accept adjustments according to standards existing within individual plants. Only Hutcheson rejected the plan.[18]

By autumn, the critical weaknesses of the war-labor adjustment machinery were all too obvious. The government had encouraged neither significant change nor standardized working conditions. As a result, the Shipbuilding Labor Adjustment Board was forced to adjust its basic principles. Soon after the creation of the SLAB, sixty thousand shipyard workers on the Pacific Coast walked out, demanding, among other things, better pay. The settlement granted uniform wage scales all along the coastline. Shortly afterward, the board's charter was amended to provide for district-wide settlements as a matter of course. Not surprisingly, the revised charter also seemed conducive to existing union standards. The board, said the revised charter, would henceforth base its wage adjustments on prevailing rates that had been established "through agreements between employer and employees and are admitted to be equitable."[19]

The early problems of the SLAB fed a growing awareness that autumn that piecemeal federal labor policies were inadequate. Just as it was impractical to adjust separately the conditions in each shipyard, so it was impossible for a myriad of governmental adjustment boards to forge a coordinated program. Furthermore, some of the munitions and supplies industries had no adjustment boards at all. Throughout the war industries, moreover, employers under governmental contract competed for laborers who changed jobs whenever profitable. Less mobile employees went out on strike. Both the rapid turnover and frequent walkouts slowed vital production. When the number of strikes in the first six months of the war (2,314) exceeded those in the same months of 1916 (2,296),[20] President Wilson became concerned. Business and labor organizations, similarly displeased, began to formulate ideas for a centralized labor board.

The president was particularly distressed about increasing unrest in the West. Frequent strikes and rapid turnover in the Arizona copper mines, the California oil fields, and the Pacific Northwest forests seriously curtailed production in industries essential to the war effort. In Arizona, labor problems had already led to strong-arm tactics. In July, the sheriff of Cochise County, with a force of 2,000 "deputies" and the support of mining company officials, had forcibly deported almost 1,200 miners—some of them IWW members—from Bisbee, Arizona, into New Mexico.[21] In Washington that summer, Gompers urged presidential action to ease the growing tensions. In August, the president sent J. Harry Covington, chief justice of the Supreme Court of the District of Columbia, on a tour of the West as his personal representative. That September, Wilson dispatched a team of personal emissaries, among them Secretary Wilson and Felix Frankfurter, a professor at the Harvard Law School who was then advising the secretary of war on labor policies, to conduct a full inquiry throughout the region. Once there, this President's Mediation Commission was to seek out political leaders, employers, and employees in an effort to formulate guidelines to prevent further production losses.[22]

When the President's Mediation Commission began its western investigation, the National Industrial Conference Board had already completed recommendations to the same end for the Council of National Defense. The NICB called for the establishment of a tripartite federal board with general jurisdiction in war-related industries. The NICB's scheme boasted the endorsement of the seventeen national manufacturing associations that it represented—including the NAM —along with the approval of twenty-one state and local employer groups. The report pledged the cooperation of businessmen in "an equitable system of adjustment, *for the period of the war.*" The underlying policy of the new board that the NICB envisioned, however, reflected a conservative interpretation of the Gompers recommendations to the Council of National Defense, which the CND had subsequently adopted. Essentially the board would work to maintain existing conditions.[23]

The NICB's report reflected the fears of American employers, as much as anything else. The men who signed it were satisfied with things as they were. Existing wages and hours pleased them; union goals threatened their power and their pockets. What they wanted now was an "unambiguous interpretation"[24] of the government's commitment to the status quo. As guidelines for settling disputes, the NICB therefore asked that the proposed new board consider revisions in prewar hours and safety regulations *only* when specifically requested by the government. Wages, the NICB suggested, should be measured by prewar local standards and modified only to meet demonstrated increases in the cost of living. Above all, the manufacturers wanted a cease-fire with organized labor. Although they portrayed "the institutions of a free people" threatened by men who sought to unionize open shops, they were nonetheless willing to call off their war against the unions as long as the unions sought no further power. If labor gave up the right to strike, the manufacturers would deal with employees' grievances through governmental adjustment machinery. Finally, to remove all doubt of its commitment to prewar conditions, the NICB reached back to 1902 to find a statement suitable for the Council of National Defense to adopt as its "guiding principle." The report of the Anthracite Coal Commission, once so reprehensible to some members of the NICB, now served to defend the open shop: "That no person shall be refused employment or in any way discriminated against on account of membership or nonmembership in any labor organization; that there shall be no discrimination against, or interference with, any employee who is not a member of any labor organization by members of such organization."[25]

The American Federation of Labor had different ideas, and its forum to present them was the AFL's thirty-seventh annual convention in Buffalo, New York, in November. At the convention, the federation repeatedly underscored labor's loyalty, reinforced its ties with the administration, and answered the National Industrial Conference Board. The gathering was distinguished from its predecessors by its spirit of cooperation, its commitment to the war effort, and its principal speaker, who was the president of the United States. Gone were antiemployer invectives; muted were the cries for the closed union shop. The theme of this convention, John Fitch wrote in *The Survey*, was "loyalty to the government," and the keynote address set the tone.[26]

On a week's notice, President Wilson took an all-night train ride to open the two-week meeting. Before an enthusiastic crowd on Monday morning, 12 November, he praised Samuel Gompers as a man who knew how to "pull in harness." He himself had left the capital, Wilson said, because there were so many people there "who know things that are not so," and he wanted to talk with men who were "up against the real thing."[27] Then he thrust ahead with his message: America could win the war only if industrial production was maximized.

The fundamental lesson of the war, the president explained, was that both sides must yield to common counsel. He voiced hopes for a national body through which both capital and labor could meet face to face and reminded his audience that settlements were always possible when both sides wanted to "do the square and right thing." Wilson then reached for audience support. "While we are fighting for freedom," he said, "we must see among other things that labor is free." The administration, he told the cheering crowd, would maintain "the instrumentalities by which the conditions of labor are improved." Yet the president knew how to be firm with his friends in Buffalo. There would be no sympathy for the uncooperative or the impatient: "The horses that kick over the traces will have to be put in the corral."[28]

Inspired by Wilson and led by Gompers, the convention seized the opportunity to please the friendly administration in Washington. The president had told the delegates that labor was "reasonable" more often than capital, and Gompers believed that the best way to get what he wanted from the government was to demonstrate just how reasonable labor could be. In a resounding roll-call vote, the delegates routed the pacifists within their ranks and endorsed the American Alliance for Labor and Democracy—a Gompers-devised propaganda organization studded with prowar socialists and founded to oppose the antiwar Peoples Council of America.[29]

Its patriotism thus recorded, the convention then answered the National Industrial Conference Board. The tone of the AFL's recommendations for a tripartite board was in keeping with Gompers's definition of preparedness. The convention insisted that wages be considered "as to equity" before they were adjusted to the increased cost of living. It described the right to bargain collectively through representatives selected by the workers as "fundamental," and it declared that any adjustment board should consider prevention of the right to organize a violation of the board's principles. Efficient production, the AFL said, required mutual goodwill; only if employers recognized the essential rights of their employees could that efficiency be sustained. Significantly, however, the recommendations avoided comment on the open shop and hedged on surrendering the right to strike. The AFL said only that production should not cease "except as a last resort."[30]

In January 1918, the Department of Labor moved to avert labor's need for a "last resort." The President's Mediation Commission had already concluded that employers were responsible for much of the western turbulence. Their refusal to deal collectively with employees and their hostility toward wage and hour changes had encouraged the strikes. To increase production, the commission concluded, the government needed to provide some means to achieve collective agreements as well as to create efficient national mediation machinery.[31] That month, at the suggestion of the Council of National Defense, Secretary Wilson appointed a tripartite advisory council to consider ways to bring about better correlation of the War, Navy, and Labor departments' labor policies. On 28 January, Wilson followed the advisory council's advice and took the final step. He asked the NICB and the AFL each to nominate five men to the War Labor Conference Board, which would centralize governmental policies and design procedures for a supreme national adjustment agency.[32]

The five labor leaders represented unions absolutely vital to war work. Before the declaration of war, their unions had resisted Gompers's headlong rush to preparedness, and even now they spoke for divergent factions within the AFL. All of the labor leaders, however, now supported the war effort. Redheaded Frank J. Hayes, a native of What Cheer, Iowa, was president of the UMW. As chief of the largest labor organization in the world, he commanded special attention. At the AFL's November convention, Hayes, a young militant, had led a successful minirevolution to drive John B. Lennon, veteran of the Commission on Industrial Relations and AFL treasurer for almost thirty years, from the executive council. Forty-four-year-old William L. Hutcheson of the carpenters was the labor representative most often in the news. Leader of the AFL's second largest affiliate, Hutcheson still battled for the union shop and standardized wages for his 320,000 men. While he sat in Washington writing a document to curtail production losses, members of his union crippled the East Coast shipbuilding industry in a massive mid-February strike. Thomas A. Rickert, president of the United Garment Workers since 1904, was less rebellious than Hayes and Hutcheson. A long-time supporter of arbitration and mediation, Rickert was an obvious choice for the WLCB. Thomas J. Savage, a member of the executive council of the International Association of Machinists, represented a union with strong leftist tendencies. Its socialistic president, for whom Savage spoke, William H. Johnston, had come to power in 1911, in part by opposing the influence of the NCF on the labor movement. (After the war, Johnston and Hutcheson would cooperate in an abortive attempt to replace Gompers as head of the AFL with the mineworkers' John L. Lewis.) Like Hayes, Johnston in 1918 was nevertheless ready to gamble that wartime cooperation would ultimately aid the unions. Labor's fifth representative, Victor Olander, had important regional ties and national credentials. Secretary-treasurer of the Illinois State Federation of Labor, Olander had also been second vice-president of the International Seamen's Union since 1902.[33]

The industrialists on the WLCB represented a similar cross section of the business community. All of them stood firmly behind the open shop. Two of them, Loyall A. Osborne and William H. VanDervoort, had helped to draft the NICB's report in September to the Council of National Defense. As chairman of both the executive committee and the advisory committee of the NICB, Osborne was well steeped in what he called "considerations of industrial policy." A resident of Stockbridge, Massachusetts, and vice-president of the Westinghouse Electric and Manufacturing Company, he was the group's natural leader. VanDervoort, also a member of the NICB's advisory committee, was president of an engineering company, an automobile company, and an ordnance firm, all in East Moline, Illinois. Leonor F. Loree, president of the Delaware & Hudson Railroad and numerous coal and iron companies, was a protégé of Edward H. Harriman. At sixty, he was an acknowledged transportation expert. B. L. Worden of Newark, New Jersey, presided over the Lackawanna Bridge Company and the Submarine Boat Corporation and also held significant governmental contracts. C. Edwin Michael completed the list of employer representatives. A one-time vice-president of the NAM, Michael was president of the Virginia Bridge and Iron Company in Roanoke.[34] Before the National War Labor Board had ended its work, Michael's own employees would appeal to it to grant them the right to bargain collectively with management.

The business and labor representatives chose Taft and Walsh as joint chairmen; then the twelve men struggled to produce a body of acceptable policies. The compromise report that they submitted to Secretary Wilson at the end of March 1918, condemned strikes and lockouts for the duration of the war and promised to eradicate the usual sources of industrial unrest. The WLCB men proposed the National War Labor Board, drawn from the same constituency and in the same manner as themselves. The principles that they drafted as guidelines for the NWLB borrowed much from existing agency boards, the NICB's report, the AFL convention's resolutions, and the conclusions of the President's Mediation Commission.[35] Even as the WLCB men reached accord, however, their report betrayed conflicting organizational goals. Consequently, the real strength of the principles lay in their ambiguity.

Certainly the most controversial principles concerned labor's wartime rights. The WLCB sanctioned existing open shops and union shops, but it also upheld labor's right to organize. The WLCB, for example, forbade employers to discharge men for union membership or for "legitimate" trade-union activities. The report denied workers the use of "coercive" means to bolster union power but nevertheless guaranteed their right to bargain "through chosen representatives" without interference from employers "in any manner whatsoever." The WLCB therefore went beyond both the report of the Anthracite Coal Commission and the recommendations of the NICB in an obvious effort to pacify workingmen. Even as it defended the open shop, it specifically invited labor unions to strengthen their ranks. To underscore that idea, the WLCB's report included the following statement: "This declaration . . . is not intended . . . to deny the right or discourage the practice of the formation of labor unions or the joining of the same by the workers . . . nor to prevent the War Labor Board from granting . . . improvement of their situation in the matter of wages, hours of labor, or other conditions."[36]

Other WLCB principles reflected the same curious determination both to protect the status quo and to undermine it. The proposed NWLB was to "regard" prevailing local conditions when it settled controversies, but it was not to be bound by the work standards of any particular area. The board would impose the eight-hour day when required by law and could otherwise adjust hours according to "governmental necessities" and the needs of the workers. In adjusting wages, it could do more than make increases to meet the rising cost of living. Indeed, it was pledged to establish a "living wage" and to "insure the subsistence of the worker and his family in health and reasonable comfort," which implied acceptance of the AFL's demand for equitable wages. The WLCB also called for equal pay for women for equal work. Theoretically, that principle was not even controversial by 1918. The U.S. Industrial Commission had urged equal pay two decades earlier, and both business and labor organizations had traditionally paid lip service to the idea. All of those groups, however, had defined the equal pay ideal narrowly, and, so, too, did the men of the WLCB. By limiting the wartime principle only to women who did work "ordinarily performed by men," they limited the kinds of jobs to which it applied; and, by warning against the employment of women on "tasks disproportionate to their strength," they discouraged the influx of women into certain jobs normally held by men.[37]

The supreme board devised by the WLCB offered hope to both sides but posed little threat to either. However one read the principles, the fact remained that the new board would have no real power. As originally envisioned, then later refined, its role was as follows: The NWLB could attempt to mediate any controversy in an industry vital to war production if no other agency had jurisdiction in the matter or when another agency had violated an NWLB principle. The board could arbitrate a dispute only if both parties agreed and if board members could approve the settlement unanimously. When the NWLB's members could not reach unanimity in an arbitration, the board would turn the matter over to an umpire—one of ten disinterested and distinguished citizens to be selected by President Wilson. The umpire himself would then serve as arbiter, and his award would be as binding—and as devoid of compulsion—as a decision of the NWLB. If either the employer or the employees in a dispute denied the board's jurisdiction, no formal award was even possible. In that event, the NWLB could only recommend a settlement and that by majority vote. Even when the board or an umpire had the initial cooperation of both parties, either party could refuse to accept an award. The NWLB's only power, therefore, was the force of moral suasion,[38] and this because the prospect of federal coercion was equally loathsome to businessmen and labor leaders alike.

Experienced observers cautiously praised the WLCB's work and approved the president's appointment of the members of the WLCB to serve on the National War Labor Board. Yet, all the while, they wondered if institutionalized voluntarism could stabilize industrial conditions. John Fitch of *The Survey* staff pondered publicly. "No one can read the Washington recommendations without being impressed by the spirit of tolerance and good will that made them possible," he wrote in the 6 April issue. Fitch, however, worried about the enforcement of those principles. Congress could legalize them, he suggested, or international unions and employers associations could formally endorse them, but in the end, Fitch, like the president and the WLCB members, came down on the side of continued voluntarism. Congressional enforcement, he decided, "would be a step of doubtful constitutionality and still more doubtful wisdom." No law, after all, authorized the creation of such a board with arbitrary power.[39]

James A. Emery of the NICB thought primarily about the new board's potential for efficient performance. Emery looked to statistics of production rather than to industrial reform. If the National War Labor Board could not halt strikes, he wrote in the *New York Times*, then the country was "likely" to demand an authoritative solution by the government. Great Britain, he reminded his readers, had worked an open-shop agreement with her highly organized trade unions as early as 1915 in return for the government's promise to curb employers' profits during the war. He ominously noted official German statistics that showed that the United States had lost more workdays from strikes in a single month than Germany had lost in an entire year. His thoughts were obvious. If labor did not cooperate with the new machinery, compulsion and an uncompromised open shop should supplant that machinery. Even so, Emery encouraged Americans first to try voluntarism and mutual concessions to achieve what other nations had accomplished through stronger measures.[40]

In Washington during May, the NWLB enjoyed continued support from the outside as it put together a staff and hammered out operational difficulties. In mid-month, the board approved a plan of procedure. Two members, one representing each side, would be assigned to adjust each jointly submitted case over which the NWLB had jurisdiction. To aid the two-man sections, impartial examiners sent from Washington by the NWLB's secretary would investigate every controversy under consideration. The secretary could also send two partisan field representatives to probe into a dispute. Only if a section could not agree on a proper disposition of a jointly submitted case, would the full board sit as arbiter. Only if the full board failed, would an umpire take over. In addition, NWLB sections would mediate cases submitted by only one party.[41]

To manage the docket, supervise the reports, and administer the board's work, the members selected W. Jett Lauck as secretary. Partisan passions, never far beneath the surface at any time the board met, had made the selection process difficult. Both sides, Taft wrote privately, wanted to claim the secretary for their ally, and no one under consideration for the job seemed to occupy "an indifferent position."[42] Lauck, a liberal economist, was considered labor's friend. A statistician for the Shipbuilding Labor Adjustment Board, he had once worked for the Commission on Industrial Relations.

The one question that the NWLB members faced with a solid front that month concerned the board's relative position in the war-labor bureaucracy. Taft and Walsh, as well as the business and labor representatives, felt threatened by the appointment of Felix Frankfurter to head the War Labor Policies Board, which would coordinate the wages and hours set by other governmental adjustment boards. The need for coordination was real enough, for even governmental departments competed for workmen, and certainly no uniform employment standards existed even within the government. But Frankfurter himself had designed the policies board and had subsequently announced that his board would consist of representatives of the Departments of War, Navy, and Agriculture, as well as the Emergency Fleet Corporation, the Railroad Administration, the War Industries Board, and the National War Labor Board. To Taft and Walsh, the plan smacked of personal ambition. When Secretary Wilson appointed the joint chairmen to sit with the Frankfurter board, they objected. Taft, personally antagonistic to the former War Department adviser, called Frankfurter "the hot dog of war, no longer of War." Both he and Walsh spoke to the NWLB membership candidly. The policies board, they charged, was nothing less than the vehicle that Frankfurter had chosen to supersede their own board. Like "a good Chancellor," Taft added, "he wants to amplify his jurisdiction and he is very anxious to say that this Board is under him." No one on the NWLB wanted that.[43]

Aside from their distrust of Frankfurter, Taft and Walsh also recognized the imprudence of their membership on both boards. The NWLB, the joint chairmen believed, was a judicial body; the War Labor Policies Board, an administrative agency. If the policies board took a stand contrary to NWLB principles, there could be appeals to the latter from the rulings of the former. "We believe, therefore," said the joint chairmen to Secretary Wilson, "that it would be unwise for us to embarrass the National War Labor Board . . . by participating in the proceedings of the Policies Board in matters which may reach the War Labor Board for disposition."[44] The NWLB membership agreed; and when Secretary Wilson concurred, the NWLB had won the battle for autonomy.

Even while the board was triumphing over Frankfurter, there were signs—from within the NWLB and from without—that far graver problems lay ahead. Both the AFL and the NAM had officially endorsed the board's policies, but clearly much of the applause from opposite sides had come because opposing forces read the principles oppositely. Some observers worried that organized labor had become too complacent and that the conservatism of Gompers had stifled more liberal voices. One such analyst found the AFL president's self-congratulatory attitude about the new board as "unfortunate" as it was "human and natural."[45] Others felt that labor had profited most by the NWLB's creation, and a board member publicly warned the unions that they had not been granted "unlimited privileges."[46] Nor were Joint Chairmen Taft and Walsh of one mind. Taft, hesitant to speculate about the board's future work, was candid with his brother Horace; he did not know whether the NWLB would "be useful in really solving the questions [of industrial unrest] and maintaining a *status quo*, without strikes."[47] Walsh, characteristically, threw caution to the winds. The NWLB policies meant "a new deal for American labor," he told a New York reporter, "not merely a square deal under the old rules."[48] For Taft, the NWLB was intended as nothing more than a temporary judicial peacekeeping force; for Walsh, its larger purpose was in effect to legislate new standards that would outlast the war and permanently reshape industrial conditions. All of this pointed to what everyone on the NWLB must have known already: The principles would be much harder to put into effect than they had been to draft.

Nevertheless, the NWLB was the Wilson administration's ultimate response to the consistent demands of organized labor. The new board also fulfilled the need to create what the President's Mediation Commission had called a "single-headed" administration.[49] By the end of May, the board had the machinery to act efficiently, a secretary to maintain the machinery, and, after freeing itself from the War Labor Policies Board, the authority to proceed alone. In these circumstances, the AFL was optimistic. Symbolically, the board's very creation had been a major victory for Gompers, if only because it confirmed labor's vital role in the determination of industrial policy. The *American Federationist* saluted the board for recognizing this fact and called upon workers to organize so that they could participate intelligently. On that very question, the right to organize, the NWLB's powers would be challenged in the first major controversy referred to it.[50]

3
Attack on Industrial Autocracy

> If, after having taken the course that Carlton has, he does come over, he does submit himself to this tribunal, if you choose to call it such, it is a great step forward for us, because there is not any corporation that is as stiff-necked as he.
>
> —William Howard Taft, NWLB meeting, 10 May 1918

In the spring of 1918, the Commercial Telegraphers Union of America wanted the NWLB to define and enforce its most controversial principle. Even before the board began to function, the CTUA, an AFL affiliate, prepared to move against long-standing employment practices of the Western Union Company and the Postal Telegraph Company. Governmental war-labor policies had already lent significant verbal support to the right to organize. Now was the time, the CTUA believed, to defy these virulent antiunion firms. Between April and July, the ensuing disputes put both governmental policies and the NWLB machinery to a critical test. In the process, the conflict at Western Union, in particular, exposed deep-seated hostilities within the NWLB and threatened to destroy the board's usefulness at the very outset of its work. The difficulties in resolving questions about the right to organize and the preservation of the open shop laid bare the limits of voluntarism as a method of industrial adjustment. Finally, the Western Union crisis helped to clarify the government's commitment to labor's goals.

Newcomb Carlton, iron-willed president of Western Union, had an "understanding" with the forty thousand men and women in his employ. For over a decade, the company had prohibited its employees from joining an organization that believed in the right to strike. That policy, in effect since an abortive CTUA strike in 1907, eliminated labor unions from the organizations which company employees might join. Whether or not the arrangement constituted a legal contract had made little difference over the years. The policy, Western Union explained in 1918, was "so well known that it was understood that those who accepted employment were considered to have agreed thereto."[1]

If Carlton's antiunion employment agreements did constitute contracts, however, the Supreme Court had made them seemingly inviolable. In December 1917, the court had sanctioned such a policy when enforced through signed individual agreements. The majority of the court sustained the Hitchman Coal and Coke Company's "yellow-dog" contracts—individual contracts that the company had initiated following its own troubles in a 1907 strike—which required the West Virginia miners in its employ to abstain from union membership. The court also upheld an injunction issued some years before that prohibited the United Mine Workers from activity at Hitchman after the introduction of the new contracts.[2]

Frank Walsh, who anticipated circumstances such as those at Western Union even while the WLCB drafted its principles, had urged specific condemnation of the individual contract despite the Hitchman ruling. Half of the board, of course, would never have agreed to such a direct assault on employer prerogatives. Nor would the bulk of American employers have accepted it. Joint Chairman Taft, too, had opposed Walsh's proposal. The clauses in the principles that guaranteed the right to organize and to bargain collectively were broad enough to discredit that kind of contract, Taft believed, but subtle enough to spare the board a clash with the court.[3] While the principles neither invited men to break existing contracts nor condemned individual contracts made before the war, they nonetheless asked employers to abandon policies that restricted legitimate union activities. The board also specifically announced that "employers should not discharge workers for membership in trade unions." Theoretically, it could easily interpret the principles to circumvent antiunion tactics such as the individual contract.

Before the board could act, however, publicists for both employer associations and trade unions interpreted the NWLB's policy to serve their own purposes. C. Edwin Michael, NWLB member and NAM spokesman, assured employers that the board could not successfully defend men who organized in violation of contracts. The right to organize, he wrote in *American Industries*, was secondary to "existing legal arrangements."[4] The American Federation of Labor, on the other hand, congratulated the board for reversing Hitchman. It also applauded the NWLB's departure from the "old time 'legal' view" that considered unions "conspiracies calculated to do nothing but mischief to society."[5]

As speculation about the import of the NWLB's principles continued, S. J. Konenkamp, CTUA president, plotted a course to determine who was right. Sunday, 28 April, would be organization day for the CTUA, and the target companies were Western Union and the Postal Telegraph. Working conditions had improved at Western Union since 1914, when management admitted to Frank Walsh that employees were underpaid, but in 1918, so the CTUA charged, workers for both firms were still undervalued because the companies insisted that "nothing short of force" could persuade them to hire union labor. The Postal Telegraph maintained control over its work force through a compulsory employees' association, and Western Union management dealt with its employees singly. The force of numbers was what the union counted on now to change those policies.[6]

By the end of April, the union had predicted in mid-March, thousands of telegraphers would unite from coast to coast, ready to see "what the companies are going to do about it."[7] Initially, the challenge seemed foolhardy. Then, from the West, and from Washington, Baltimore, New York, and Boston, organizing committees began to report more support than in 1907. In Savannah, the Organizing Committee of Five urged telegraphers to see the district leader: "Pack the FOUR DOLLARS initiation & dues on your hip and GET RIGHT WITH GOD."[8] In the end, however, the union's campaign came to little: Newcomb Carlton summarily dismissed eight hundred Western Union employees who had joined the CTUA. Then, as Konenkamp dramatically threatened to strike, the NWLB entered the controversy at the union's request.[9]

Carlton's obvious violation of the intent of war-labor policy and Konenkamp's threat to violate it further put the board in a difficult position. To maintain credibility, the NWLB would have to stand firm against the Western Union dismissals and then assess the union's right to organize in light of the company's policies. To make peace between the intransigent employer and the determined union leader, the board had to grapple with complicated legal and procedural problems. The critical legal questions were whether or not contracts existed at Western Union and whether or not their existence bound the board to predetermined action. Procedurally, the NWLB faced both internal and external difficulties. Could its business and labor representatives reach accord on the disposition of the case, and, if so, could they persuade Carlton and Konenkamp to agree voluntarily to accept the award? Failure to settle the case could fatally weaken the board; and Carlton's refusal to accept the board's good offices or the rejection of its decision by either Carlton or Konenkamp could reduce an NWLB ruling to an academic pronouncement.

The board assigned the case to Taft and Walsh, whose dissimilar mindsets colored the negotiations at the outset. On Friday afternoon, 10 May, Walsh proposed the obvious solution to his colleagues: Western Union should be directed to reinstate the discharged employees and to cease discrimination against the union during the war. But Taft spoke against the motion in logical and practical terms; the case, he explained, was not a joint submission. (Newcomb Carlton had already denied the board's jurisdiction.) It was "too bad," he continued, that either side could ignore the NWLB as they chose, but that was the "inevitable result of an absence of legal power and the character of the Board."[10] As long as Carlton maintained his uncooperative attitude, the board could make no award. Certainly it could not issue "decrees" such as Walsh had proposed. To adopt the Walsh motion in these circumstances, Taft argued, would cut off discussion with the company and end all hope of negotiating a workable agreement. Instead, he proposed that the board first negotiate with Carlton.

Taft suggested that Loyall Osborne call upon Carlton, a close friend of the Westinghouse executive, in an effort to persuade the Western Union chief to grant the joint chairmen an interview. Carlton's testimony was necessary because the board disagreed on the legal status of Western Union's employment policy, but Taft also wanted to meet with Carlton for another reason. If Carlton could be persuaded to cooperate with the board, he would set an important example for other employers. Furthermore, having participated in its mediation, he would have difficulty maintaining his denial of jurisdiction when the board proposed a settlement.

Walsh and the labor members at first dismissed the former president's suggestion. They either failed to see or rejected the political repercussions inherent in his counterproposal. Accordingly, Walsh insisted that the board had the power to act immediately and that it had sufficient information upon which to base its action. The company had violated the NWLB's principles. That was all the labor members needed to know. Determined not to show Carlton what amounted to special privilege, the labor members also resented Osborne's potential interference in a controversy assigned to another section. Osborne, however, set their minds at ease by suggesting that he would simply get Carlton "into a frame of mind to come back here with a less-stiff-necked attitude." He would neither act as personal mediator nor "attempt to put into his mouth the maintenance of his position."[11]

When Osborne visited his friend on his way home to his Stockbridge estate the next morning, he made limited progress. Carlton agreed to meet Taft and Walsh and even to have them meet the company's board of directors. Yet the stubborn telegraph executive saw little purpose for either meeting. The conferences, Carlton believed, would only bring pressure from the NWLB to reinstate the employees and to permit the CTUA to organize the company, and he would do neither. Carlton, Osborne reported, had "professed to want to do everything to increase the prestige and influence of the National War Labor Board" except change his employment policies. The union, he said, would ruin the company and "destroy its usefulness as a war instrument." Of that, Osborne concluded, "I believe he is fully convinced."[12] In short, Newcomb Carlton's attitude remained unchanged. He feared neither the CTUA nor the NWLB.

Carlton's willingness to talk encouraged Taft's determination to make him listen and put the differences between the joint chairmen in their proper perspective. Whatever his private feelings may have been, Taft worried most about the probable consequences of open defiance of the NWLB, especially if met by a weak response. As he wrote to his son Charles in France, the case had become a "crisis" that the board might not surmount. His dilemma was evident: "We don't sympathize with an attempt to exclude the union," he explained, "though I generally think we would prefer to let the *status quo* remain during the war; but . . . we have declared in favor of the right to organize."[13] Actually, Taft agreed substantively with Walsh. His real opposition to the Walsh motion of 10 May had been procedural. Although he believed that formal employment contracts antedating the war were protected by the board's principles, he could not agree to extend that protection to informal customs of employment;[14] and, to his judicial mind, Carlton had yet to prove that he held formal contracts.

Taft offered Carlton a package drafted by Walsh when the two men met alone in Philadelphia on 15 May. It included not only the motion of 10 May but also a procedure to accomplish collective bargaining. The company was to reinstate its employees and on the following conditions: (1) Western Union would bargain with a committee of its employees for revised wages, hours, and working conditions, and if no settlement was reached, the company would submit the dispute to the NWLB; (2) the company had neither to recognize nor deal with the CTUA; (3) the union would abandon the strike, would not itself initiate proposals for change and, like the company, would take unresolved problems to the board; and (4) if any employee who belonged to the CTUA violated this agreement or the NWLB's rules, Western Union could discharge him with the board's support.[15]

Carlton rejected the proposal and within a week offered a substitute plan intended to bribe both the NWLB and his employees. To allow the union to organize and then to deal with organized employees, he still maintained, would render the company unable to fulfill its obligations to the public and to the government. Nor did he concede the need for Western Union employees to join an outside organization. The company already practiced nascent welfare capitalism: Employees worked a basic eight-hour day and enjoyed paid vacations, semiannual bonuses, pension and health benefits, and life insurance. Yet, he wired to Taft on 22 May, the company agreed that, in the right circumstances, the workers should have the benefit of collective bargaining, too. A company-wide referendum could decide the matter democratically. The employees could elect to join the CTUA, or they could vote to form an association of their own within the company.[16]

In essence, Carlton offered his employees either the right to organize or the right to bargain collectively but not both. If they chose the first alternative, the company would no longer dismiss workers solely for joining the union, but neither would it deal with CTUA officials—regardless of their status as company employees. If, on the other hand, the employees voted against affiliating with the CTUA, Western Union would sponsor their organization of an association whose officers would be elected from within their ranks. Thereafter management and employee representatives could bargain together and submit unresolved problems to the NWLB for arbitration.[17] Under the Carlton scheme, therefore, Western Union employees who wanted to deal collectively with management had to eschew the union and accept instead an employee association similar to that in operation at the Postal Telegraph Company.

Taft stood firm. Unable to persuade the Western Union chief to meet further, he scribbled out a heated six-page message on 27 May. The joint chairman wanted Carlton to know how he felt about the company's attitude and the case itself, even before he talked to Walsh and Osborne. In the first place, Taft explained, the NWLB's principles did not permit the "closed non-union shop in the status quo to be maintained." Second, Carlton's justification for discharging the eight hundred employees was weak: "A mere understanding that men will be discharged who join unions does not constitute . . . a contract on their part not to join unions." When those contracts did exist, furthermore, they failed to satisfy NWLB policy if they had been concluded after the establishment of the board. Patently, Carlton's proposal did not "square" with the NWLB's principles because it limited the right to organize during the war. The Walsh plan, Taft reasoned, posed no threat to company efficiency and made continued exclusion of union members from Western Union employ unnecessary. Urging Carlton to reconsider, he added in ill-concealed disgust, "You may show this to Mr. Osborne."[18]

That same week, letters from CTUA leaders throughout the country poured into the joint chairmen's offices. Since the dismissals had begun, four weeks had passed with no relief. Without a settlement, the letters warned, the men would strike despite war-labor policy. Inevitable questions put the board's prestige on the line. Who was more powerful, the government or Western Union? Did the NWLB have the power to enforce its own principles? "Have we the right to organize? Reinstatement and reimbursement for the time lost is all we ask." The union officials demanded no less than the concessions that Taft and Walsh had tried to secure and wrote off Carlton's proposed referendum as a ludicrous ploy: "If the workers have the right to organize, then that right is an individual right to be exercised by one, one hundred, a thousand, or ten thousand."[19]

From the other side, the NWLB business members worked hard to end Taft's opposition to the Carlton proposal. Their only hope for success lay in persuading the former president to qualify the right to organize. If they won here, they could probably preserve employer prerogatives for the duration of the war. If they lost, Taft would vote with the opposition, not only in this case, but no doubt in countless others. Clearly, more was at stake at Western Union than the fate of a few hundred telegraphers.

Under Osborne's leadership, the NWLB employers lectured Taft on considerations of "industrial policy" and majority rights. L. F. Loree urged appreciation for the needs of the nonunion employees who, he said, constituted 92 percent of the workers in war industries.[20] Osborne was patronizing and almost rude. Taft could not understand the employers' fear and distrust of labor unions because, he said, the former president had not been "fighting the battle for industrial independence." Organized labor, Osborne charged, meant "to evade the spirit of our principles by insisting on the letter of them." As for Walsh and the labor members, he continued, they wanted to interpret the NWLB's principles to benefit unions instead of individuals. Rejection of Carlton's proposal "on technical grounds" would brand the NWLB as the tool of organized labor. Osborne warned Taft that the employer members could never support "Mr. Walsh's impossible motion."[21]

Two days later, on Saturday, 1 June, the full board met in the Belmont Hotel in New York to hear the Taft-Walsh report. Afterwards, because Carlton steadfastly refused to accept the board's jurisdiction, the members could propose recommendations in the case by majority vote. Sitting at the end of a long session and frustrated by Carlton's continued immobility, the joint chairmen were eager to end the case without prolonged debate. Everyone in the room had made up his mind on the issues, and everyone knew it. Taft had been unswayed by last-minute appeals from the NWLB employers, even after he had attended a special caucus that they had called for that morning. The report was a documented history of the futile negotiations with the Western Union president and included Walsh's plan for settlement, Carlton's substitute scheme, and Taft's telegram of 27 May rejecting it. It concluded that the company "should" accept the Walsh plan and suggested, in view of Carlton's attitude, that efforts at mediation be ended. Taft and Walsh then moved the report's approval and publication. If they could not subdue Newcomb Carlton, they could publicly humiliate him. The country could judge him as it saw fit; and, in the joint chairmen's minds, there was little doubt what the judgment would be.[22]

The debate that followed revealed a hardening of the lines on both sides. At the meeting of 10 May, Osborne had disapproved of "yellow-dog" contracts during the war. Now he emphasized that employers who traditionally forbade their employees to join labor unions should be permitted to continue to do so. So strongly did he and the other employer members dissent from the Taft-Walsh report that they demanded the right to file a minority statement if a majority voted to publish the former. The labor representatives, on the other hand, agreed with the report to the extent that it upheld the right to organize regardless of the existence of legal contracts. They dissented, however, on the ground that mere humiliation of the company was meaningless. The controversy, they insisted, should be referred to President Wilson for further action.[23]

All of this indicated that none of the members cared very much about interpreting the NWLB's principles in strict accordance with the Supreme Court. Taft, the man most likely to agonize over such matters, had resolved the potential conflict between the principles and the Hitchman case by ignoring it. The employer members were eager to cite Hitchman but only if it bolstered their case. Since it apparently did not in this instance, they endorsed Carlton's plan as the only one offered in the spirit of compromise. Walsh and the labor members, of course, had never pretended to care. Machinist Tom Savage frankly believed that the public had a right to know if the NWLB meant what it said. It was time, he said, for the board to settle its differences over the meaning of the principles that its members had drafted. Victor Olander was more blunt: "It is remarkable," he said to the businessmen, "that you gentlemen never turn to the principles and read them. It is so plain that I can't understand why you don't agree to a mild statement of this kind."[24]

In the end, the joint chairmen deserted the business and labor constituencies that they had been selected to lead in order to preserve their report. Taft voted with Walsh and the labor members to defeat the employer members' demand for reconsideration of the Carlton plan; and Walsh voted against labor's proposal to send the problem on to the White House. Thereafter the joint chairmen and the labor members sustained the report, and the NWLB business members declined to wash their linen in public. Instead, they dissented from the report without giving reasons.[25]

Taft and Walsh had ended this phase of the Western Union controversy in complete accord. Mutual skepticism, if not more, had given way to mutual trust. Much of the credit for their cooperation, no doubt, belonged to Newcomb Carlton, who drove the emotional Walsh and the literal-minded former president into each others' arms by his refusal to treat seriously with the agency that they headed. In another sense, of course, Taft's adherence to the NWLB's principles was hardly surprising, and his commitment to labor's rights to organize and to bargain collectively within the confines of the open shop neatly reflected his long-time adherence to NCF ideology. Walsh, moreover, had demonstrated the ability to rise above partisanship and to compromise when necessary. The most important consequence of these events was the emergence of the joint chairmen as the real leaders of the board.

Although the joint chairmen had managed to salvage the board's image as a viable instrumentality, they had failed to deter Newcomb Carlton. As expected, he refused to comply with the majority's recommendations. This time, he offered reasons sure to appeal to other industrial leaders. Carlton accused Taft and Walsh of misreading the NWLB's principles in order to tie employers' hands. Since both existing union and nonunion shops were protected in the principles, he said, it was "equally clear that organizations non-union in character should also pursue that policy during the period of the war." If the Taft-Walsh ruling gained acceptance, he predicted, the NWLB would "furnish a cloak behind which a propaganda for the unionizing of labor in every industry may be carried on without . . . hindrance."[26]

By early June, then, the viability of voluntarism was seriously endangered. At one and the same time, the Western Union president had defied a governmental agency and fanned the flames of labor unrest. As *The Survey* observed, the company's actions would not "help much in winning the war, nor . . . go far toward convincing the workers of the country of the disinterested loyalty of those private employers for whom they work." A railroad telegrapher echoed those sentiments and more: "The Courts are jailing men who are not as dangerous as Mr. Carlton is to [the] military success of [the] United States." Meanwhile, after conferring in Washington with Gompers, Konenkamp returned home to Chicago and renewed threats of a strike—this time in four hundred cities—if the eight hundred telegraphers remained locked out. Back in Washington, Frank Walsh supported speculation that the federal government might nationalize the wires for the duration of the war.[27]

These events, which left war-labor policies and the rationale behind them in shambles, brought the inevitable response from President Wilson. Still hopeful that employers and employees could cooperate voluntarily in the national interest, the president appealed personally to both Carlton and Clarence McKay, president of the Postal Telegraph Company, to acquiesce in the board's decision. It was, he wrote on 11 June, their "patriotic duty to cooperate in this all-important matter with the government, by the use of the instrumentality which the government has set up."[28] Such action would also set a useful example for other employers. McKay agreed immediately. But Newcomb Carlton waited nearly a week to reply. In the interval, he consulted with the NWLB employer members and made final plans to establish the company union that the NWLB majority, and now the president, had deemed unacceptable.

Things got worse on 17 June when Carlton defied Wilson and then took his case before the public. He meant to persuade both the president and the nation that his intended company union could better serve the national interest than the plan of the NWLB's majority. To do so, he discredited the union campaign as an attempt to provide "the nucleus for the disorganization of our service" at war's end, denied any conflict between the company and its employees, and promised the president that a Konenkamp strike would be ineffectual. Under his proposal, he explained to Wilson, the Western Union family could work in an atmosphere free of hostile outside forces and "would be glad to have the advice and counsel of the National War Labor Board."[29] In a forty-page pamphlet released to the public about the same time, the company reiterated its arguments and revealed its plans: Western Union employees would have a constitutional convention in Chicago on 10 July. Democratically chosen delegates would then meet at company expense to hammer out negotiating procedures and the means to increase employee participation in the formulation of company policy. All told, the pamphlet predicted, this collectivization scheme would so encourage employee "loyalty and enthusiasm in cooperating with the management that an uninterrupted and competent service to the public may be assured."³⁰

The letter that Carlton sent to the White House on 17 June defended the company's refusal to comply with the NWLB on specious grounds and had been devised in collusion with the NWLB employer members. That same day those employers sent a telegram to Wilson which supported the company's behavior. Both communiques attempted to nullify the president's request through a novel interpretation of NWLB procedures. The employers' telegram, sent from Stockbridge, denied —four times—that the board had reached a decision in which to acquiesce. Indeed, the promulgation of the majority opinion, so the statement charged, was "calculated to mislead" people unaware that bona fide decisions required unanimity. The employer members had explained that procedural refinement to Carlton, whose own letter to the president reflected their help—and went ludicrously beyond it. Having failed to reach a decision, Carlton wrote to Wilson, the board should have appointed an umpire to arbitrate a settlement.³¹

The procedural defense brought swift reaction, especially from NWLB insiders. The Newark *Evening News*, too, saw through Carlton's attempt to envelope the issues in a smoke screen. The case, said the *Evening News*, had become a test of the workability of the board's machinery.³² In New Haven, William Howard Taft seethed. Angered that Carlton had kept the case from going to an umpire and then faulted the board for not appointing one, Taft excoriated Carlton's use of half-truths in a bid for public support. "After his not consenting to the action of the Board," he wrote to Walsh, "there was no chance for us to go on . . . to the arbitration. . . . He knows it or ought to know it, for he has lawyers." Privately, Taft blamed Osborne for Carlton's strategy.³³ He also dismissed as rubbish the Western Union president's claim that his employees had no complaints.³⁴ From Kansas City, Frank Walsh sent a wire to the president to protest against the procedural subterfuge and to underscore his complete agreement with Taft on the proper disposition of the case.³⁵ In Washington, Secretary Wilson asked the president to intervene further. Western Union apparently would accept the NWLB's jurisdiction on all issues except the right to organize, he surmised, but the board could perform its functions only if the company recognized its authority to deal with that issue. Therefore the secretary of labor urged Wilson to "insist upon" the company's submission to the NWLB and adherence to its decision without qualification.³⁶

In St. Paul, the American Federation of Labor was profoundly disturbed about the future of wartime industrial relations. For the labor leaders assembled there in annual convention, the Western Union debacle had exposed an effort by private employers to define governmental labor policy. The most important objective in the Carlton-NWLB employer plan was to squelch the growth of organized labor and to do so with the sanction of the Wilson administration. Gompers interrupted the proceedings to send President Wilson an ominous message. Western Union, he said, sought merely to continue its old policies under a new label. Its proposal was "out of harmony with [NWLB policies] and renders it very difficult, if not impossible, to prevent interruption of work essential to the successful conduct of the war."[37]

Most telling of all, *The New Republic* saw in the board's own principles an inherent weakness that encouraged men like Carlton to stand their ground. Carlton, it admitted, was in many respects an enlightened employer whose social vision surpassed that of many of his colleagues. His blind spot, of course, was organized labor. Labor unionists, it declared, should therefore be grateful to Carlton for presenting the real issues in such sharp relief. Even if no grievances existed at Western Union, the company had offered no more than the perpetuation of employer and employee as master and servant. As for the NWLB, it had compromised the central issue: "It permits unions to exist and to grow, but does not incorporate them into the organization of industry." If the board survived this crisis, the magazine predicted, ultimately it would have to choose sides.[38]

For almost a month, until the administration broke the stalemate in mid-July, tensions ran high. Konenkamp planned his strike for Monday, 8 July. To avert the disruption of the wire service, President Wilson asked Congress to authorize federal control of American communications systems. On hearing the news, Taft wrote to an old friend with obvious satisfaction: "It is quite evident . . . that the President is making Carlton's asinine performance an excuse for urging this legislation. How often the scriptural text comes to one: 'You may bray a fool in a mortar with a pestle, yet will his foolishness not depart from him.'"[39] On Sunday, 7 July, Konenkamp canceled the strike—but only on the personal assurance of Secretary of Labor Wilson that "exact justice" would result from congressional action.[40] Nine days later, the president signed a joint resolution empowering the government to nationalize telegraph and telephone facilities for the duration of the war. Konenkamp's objective was fulfilled; what the CTUA president had been unable to do with his 2,500 member union, the government had done for him, or so it seemed.

In any case, that was how most Americans read the facts that summer. The NWLB and, more importantly, organized labor had triumphed through the intercession of President Wilson. Western Union had fallen. As the nationalization of the wires became imminent, the *New York Tribune* lamented the fate of the American employer. The NWLB, said a *Tribune* editorial, had knocked down "the only bar which employers could set up against the unionization of their shops."[41] Indeed, some analysts believed that the federal takeover would accomplish the first step in labor's plans for postwar industrial relations. Among them, Hiram Moderwell of the NWLB staff, wrote a frank salute to labor's tactics.

Moderwell's long article, published in the *Tribune* on 7 July, illumed a strategy at work. The right to organize, he explained, was the most important concession that organized labor had wrung from governmental policy makers. Without that license to build strength during the war, the labor movement could never have pledged its loyalty to the war effort or agreed to accept the continuance of the open shop. Moreover, labor leaders such as Gompers, a man "intimately interested" in the formulation of the NWLB's principles, had understood the need to establish a working definition of the right to organize from the outset. "The union leaders," Moderwell reported, had therefore "set to work in the most confident manner immediately after the formation of the Board. If they had had definite knowledge of the intentions of the White House, they would have acted exactly as they did." Given the special nature of the relationship between Gompers and the president, perhaps they had. Throughout the crisis, the CTUA had played by all the rules that the government had set up, while Western Union had not. When President Wilson intervened, labor's strategic gamble had paid off. He had forced a nonunion company to unionize and thereby identified further opposition to unions with opposition to the government. In short, Moderwell suggested that organized labor, knowingly and confidently, had set Western Union up.[42]

To the extent that it went, Moderwell's article made good sense. What it failed to consider, however, was the company's position. Indications, in fact, are that everyone intimately involved in the dispute wanted the wires nationalized. Frank Walsh had supported the idea as early as 1 June.[43] Two days later, the New York press had reported that "official circles" within Washington understood that both the company and its employees favored federal control.[44] By mid-June, the AFL had openly asked the president to take over Western Union.[45]

What, then, had the company and its employees hoped to gain

from Washington? The telegraphers said they wanted higher wages. Newcomb Carlton, it was reported, believed that federal administration of the wires would protect his profits from rising labor costs.[46] More likely, he guessed correctly that Postmaster General Albert Sidney Burleson would assume control of the wires. Burleson, the likely official for such a post, was so sure to be a brake against unionism that Carlton could surrender his company without surrendering principle. As late as 1917, the postmaster general had urged repeal of a law that, since 1912, had permitted government workers to organize as long as they declined the right to strike. So nearly did his ideas parallel Carlton's own, in fact, that the company's pamphlet had cited the postmaster general as an ally against the ideas of the NWLB's majority.[47] In view of Burleson's subsequent appointment, it seems, the NWLB's principles had been interpreted to effect the compromise they were designed to achieve. In that sense, the victory belonged to both Carlton and Konenkamp.

The mutual victory qualified, but hardly diminished, the substantial boost that the president's action gave to both the labor movement and the NWLB. What both needed and got was a precedent for future action, and that was important in the summer of 1918. The president, after all, had sustained labor's legitimacy—a fundamental goal of organized labor since the turn of the century. His action helped to make the NWLB viable. In fact, Wilson's intervention made voluntarism virtually involuntary; without it, the NWLB would have foundered and left the administration with no workable centralized labor administration. As it was, the majority had neatly sidestepped the narrow rulings of the Supreme Court. When Wilson enforced their ruling, he encouraged labor's confidence in the NWLB and greatly strengthened the board's image.

Image notwithstanding, the NWLB had emerged from the Western Union crisis with more power on paper than in reality. The board had reached no fundamental conclusions. It had been unable to make voluntarism work in part because of the inability of its own members to cooperate. Had Carlton submitted to its jurisdiction, the case would have gone to an umpire. Had that happened in so sensitive a case, the board itself would have been branded as ineffectual. Without both Carlton's defiance and the president's aid, therefore, the majority could have accomplished nothing. Beneath the headlines, the men most responsible for the board's reinvigorated image were Joint Chairmen Taft and Walsh. Had they not voted against the narrow interests of the men responsible for their appointments, there could have been no majority ruling for the president to enforce. All of this suggests that the board's definition of other principles would not be easy. In order for it to function in the future, Taft and Walsh would need to retain their ability to work together and to perfect a means to manipulate their colleagues into harmony.

# 4 Toward a Living Wage

MR. MICHAEL: If you want to know what I think the living wage is, I think the living wage is the average wage paid to a given craft in a given industry in a given community. Or I will go further and say the average maximum wage.
MR. WALSH: Unfortunately for your contention, we have defined the living wage as something else.

—Exchange at NWLB meeting, 10 July 1918

The NWLB's most idealistic principle pledged the board to set minimum wages so as to provide the American family with a "living wage" despite wartime inflation. Fundamental differences between the business and labor members, however, plunged the board into serious conflict over wage policy. Walsh and the labor members read the principles as a clarion call to reform. They wanted the NWLB to lead other adjustment agencies and the public at large toward permanent higher standards. The employers, again seeing the board as an instrument established to maintain the status quo, wanted to harmonize the board's work with that of existing agencies and to follow the "law" of supply and demand. These differences within the board became apparent when it entered a case in May at Waynesboro, Pennsylvania. From there a general discussion on the meaning of a "living wage" evolved almost naturally. As with all of the board's work, its ultimate actions in these matters fell somewhat short of idealism; but those actions nevertheless undermined existing conditions.

No single expression better served the Progressive generation's preoccupations with justice and efficiency than did the "living wage." By 1918, the phrase was commonplace. First called the workingman's "just payment" in 1891 by Pope Leo XIII, the concept of the living wage received widespread publicity in the writings of Father John Ryan. The Federal Council of Churches of Christ of America endorsed it in 1910. Throughout the Progressive Era, economists, social workers, and politicians called for legislated minimum pay rates to provide "living wages" and thus also encourage industrial efficiency and law and order. Theodore Roosevelt called for a living wage and endorsed a national minimum wage for women in 1912; and twelve states passed legislation to grant women and minors in certain occupations a minimum income before World War I. In 1915, the Walsh report of the Commission on Industrial Relations called the living wage a prerequisite for the welfare of the nation: Unless every worker was paid enough to support comfortably his wife and three children and to provide for ill health and old age, America could not develop a "strong," "contented," and "efficient" citizenship.[1] Walter Lippmann, an editor of *The New Republic*, was more succinct that year; a business that did not pay a living wage, he said, was "humanly insolvent."[2] President Wilson, himself, in accepting the Democratic nomination in 1916, had met the issue squarely: Americans "must hasten and quicken the spirit and efficiency of labour" by, among other things, "paying a living wage."[3]

When the NWLB promised American workers a living wage, the concept still lacked specificity. Good reformers by then called for a living wage almost automatically. There existed, however, no consensus on what it was or how it was to be achieved. A minimum wage was not necessarily a living wage—in many cases far from it. Indeed, legislated minimums in the minds of many tended, in practical terms, to become substandard maximums. The Supreme Court, furthermore, had yet to determine definitively whether legislated minimums were even constitutional. In 1917, the Court had sidestepped the wage issue in two cases that provided for time-and-a-half pay after limited hours of service.[4] When confronted with an Oregon minimum-wage law for women in a third case that same year, the Court sustained the law, but only by a vote of four to four.[5] In such a parlous state, establishment of a living wage by the NWLB was potentially the most practical solution to nationwide uncertainties.

Frank Walsh had little difficulty determining the broad outlines of what a living wage should be. It was what Leo XIII had called it in his encyclical *Rerum Novarum*, what Walsh himself had termed it in 1915, and what the NWLB had adopted as its guideline for mediating acceptable pay scales: a wage that would "insure the subsistence of the worker and his family in health and reasonable comfort."[6] That is, it was to cover men as well as women and to include allowances for recreation, culture, and education, as well as for food, clothing, and shelter. This, of course, was far more than the most progressive states had legislated.

Largely from personal experience, Walsh believed that the board's first duty was to provide American families with greater economic security. He had known poverty and desperation as a youth after his father, a wholesale grain merchant in St. Louis, died suddenly and left a bankrupt estate. Frank quit school. To help his large family make ends meet, he worked as a water boy at the age of ten and then in factories, became an office boy at fifteen, then moved up to railway clerk and cashier. By then, he was eighteen and a veteran of night schools and a commercial college. At twenty-one, he was a shorthand reporter. In 1887, at twenty-three, he took a job as a stenographer in a Kansas City law firm and read law when he had the time. In the years of his self-education, Walsh was haunted by the poverty that had come with his father's death. After his admission to the Missouri bar in 1889, he worked to spare others from the kinds of conditions that had left him destitute.[7]

Since then, Walsh had neither forgotten the emotional costs of starting with nothing nor relaxed his drive to make life easier for others. As he wrote to a friend early in the Wilson years, his "natural instincts . . . [were] with the 'under dog' perhaps on account of having been one for so long."[8] He was impatient with laws that kept men poor, and he despised the values that deemed poor men to be wicked. As joint chairman of the NWLB, the fifty-four-year-old Missourian agonized about the lifestyle of the common laborer in the summer of 1918. The fixing of a living wage, he told his colleagues on the board, was "as truly saving my country as if I took a gun and a bayonet into the theatre of the European War and killed my quota of the enemy."[9]

Walsh had laid the groundwork for his wartime efforts even before the NWLB began to function. While serving on the War Labor Conference Board, he had worked as unpaid counsel for 100,000 men and women employed in eleven cities by the five great packinghouses. From 11 February until 7 March 1918, he had argued their case in arbitration hearings before Judge Samuel Alschuler, labor administrator in Chicago. "For once," the Chicago *Herald* commented on his performance, "the humble day laborers who exist in the slums of Packington had counsel quite as adroit as that which their multimillionaire employers had been able to acquire."[10]

On 24 March, five days before the WLCB released its principles, Walsh's work in Chicago paid off. Judge Alschuler handed down a ruling that anticipated most of the NWLB's policies, liberally interpreted, and granted the employees almost everything that they had requested. He called the shorter workday beneficial to employers, employees, and the public because it prepared workers for better citizenship. He gave the packinghouses six weeks in which to reduce the basic workday from ten hours to eight and the basic week from sixty hours to forty-eight. He outlawed discrimination against union members and granted women equal pay for equal work. In a radical departure from tradition, Alschuler also ordered wage increases to give the common laborer both a relative and an absolute pay raise larger than that accorded better paid employees. This immediately increased the minimum wage from 27½ cents an hour to 32 cents. The judge further forbade a decrease in daily pay when the packinghouses reduced hours to an eight-hour basis; rather, the minimum should be increased to provide the workers with the same pay at the end of eight hours as they had previously earned in ten. Finally, Alschuler refused to consider the financial ability of the companies to increase wages and suggested that they accustom themselves to profit sharing.[11]

Although Alschuler confessed his inability to define the living wage, he agreed with Walsh that $825 compensation for 300 days' work at 27½ cents an hour was inadequate: "While it might generally be understood to be a wage affording a living suited to one's condition in life, it could hardly be said that if because of an unreasonably low wage the condition in life of the employee sinks low, but that his family manages to subsist thereon, that the condition in life of this family is thereby established, and that the wage paid is suited thereto. A living wage surely imports something more than this."[12] Conflicting statistics presented at the hearing, the judge said, had shown that a family should have anywhere from $800 to $2,000 to live adequately for a year. The 32 cents an hour he assigned in March would become 40 cents when the company reduced basic hours in May. Thereafter, if the lowest paid employee worked two hours overtime at time and a fourth, he would get $4.20 instead of the $2.75 he received before the arbitration. This would give him $1,260 for 300 ten-hour days.[13]

The outstanding thing about Alschuler's award was that it put considerations of equity above the laws of supply and demand. In its aftermath, Walsh told the president of the Chicago Federation of Labor that, if Alschuler was made labor administrator of the United States, "we could all go home, quit our foolishness, and go to work."[14] Later, he wrote that the packinghouse arbitration "furnishes the ground work for everything we do on the National War Labor Board."[15]

As the Alschuler award took effect, labor troubles in Waynesboro, Pennsylvania, attracted the Wilson administration's attention. In that busy industrial town just above the Maryland border, more than 2,500 workers were locked in a struggle with the management of eight machine shops over hours, wages, and working conditions. In May, Clifton Reeves, a Labor Department commissioner of conciliation, abandoned efforts to effect a reconciliation between employers and employees. Yet Reeves feared a strike if the men got no relief, and on 14 May he suggested to his superiors that the NWLB take the case.[16]

The small-town Pennsylvania controversy offered a better test of the board's workability than did the Western Union case. Both the Waynesboro employers and employees admitted the NWLB's jurisdiction from the outset. By all rights, it would also be an easier test. Adjusting wages and hours was hardly as controversial as trying to provide for union rights in an open shop. Even so, fundamental disagreements within the board on substantive issues, so evident in the Western Union case, were sure to complicate its work. The jointly submitted controversy would force the members to apply new principles, this time unanimously, or to admit failure by calling in an umpire. It would hasten the showdown between those members who believed that the NWLB should preserve the existing order and their colleagues who intended to achieve qualitative change.

On Thursday, 23 May, Hugh Hanna, the NWLB chief examiner, took the morning train from Washington to Waynesboro—only to discover that he was too late. Hanna fired off an anxious message on arrival; the workers had gone out. Because regulations prohibited any board action while a strike was in progress, Secretary Jett Lauck sent back a telegram to clarify the NWLB's policy for the strikers. At noon, Monday, 27 May, Waynesboro workers rallied at the opera house to hear two mediators from the State of Pennsylvania read Lauck's message. The men agreed to return to their jobs, and the NWLB quickly scheduled a hearing for both sides in Washington.[17]

B. L. Worden, the shipbuilder, and Fred Hewitt, the editor of the *Machinists' Journal* who occasionally represented the machinists on the board, tried to untangle the facts for the NWLB on 5 June. They heard labor's grievances all morning and questioned management in the afternoon. Worden and Hewitt asked about the causes of the strike, living conditions in Waynesboro, the rise in the cost of living over the past three years, the average wage scale in the community, the merits and demerits of a shorter workday, and the value of an hourly wage as compared with payment for piecework. Essentially, they wanted to know what kind of town Waynesboro was and why it had blown up.[18]

At the hearing that morning, local labor leaders described a unionized industrial community in which every craft was more than 70 percent organized. E. E. Conrad of the local machinists union admitted that laborers had been given a 10 percent raise "some time ago" after the unions had gained strength, but he added that most merchants had then hiked their prices by 20 percent. The cost of living, he believed, had risen 250 percent since 1915. The men worked too long for too little. Some of them on hourly rates made only 22 cents, and they worked fifty-five hours a week. C. H. White, spokesman for the Waynesboro Iron Molders, explained the employees' opposition to piecework. White himself earned a fairly good wage—about $5.25 a day. But he worked eleven and a quarter hours to get it, and he had no time for his family. The employers believed that the piecework system encouraged men to increase their skills because it gave them added incentive. In labor's eyes, however, piecework simply led to extended hours. Because of all these conditions, Conrad implied, the workers had ignored union organizers, who had advised against a strike, and walked out anyway.[19]

The employers told a different tale. They saw the town as a "countrified" community where unions had been organized for less than four months and were still unimportant. Some 60 percent of the workers owned their own homes. Most could stroll to work in twenty minutes, and many went home for lunch to eat food that they had grown themselves. Waynesboro was a "clean, open town" where there were "no foreigners and practically no blacks." Bills were paid promptly; no one had debts; rents were seldom raised; boardinghouses and restaurants were cheaper than elsewhere; the number of bank depositors and the amount of deposits had increased dramatically within the last three years. The cost of living since 1915 had risen perhaps 60 percent, the employers said, and certainly no more than the 70 percent estimated by state mediators. During that time, some employers testified, they had raised pay rates by 70 to 80 percent.[20]

Because of the good working conditions and the pleasing lifestyle afforded by the little town, the superintendent of the Frick Company asserted, men who left Waynesboro for higher-paying jobs usually came back. Only recently a man had come to him from Westinghouse in Pittsburgh saying that he would prefer to work in Waynesboro at lower rates than to live in Pittsburgh with more money. The superintendent added: "This man left our employment a few days ago owing to labor trouble stating that he did not care to get mixed up with more strikes."[21] Why, then, had the Waynesboro workers struck? Said one employer: "When we go through and talk to them we ask, 'What is the matter with wages?' 'Nothing.' 'What do you strike for?' 'I don't know.' And those conditions exist."[22]

Wage statistics presented throughout the day seemed to confirm the existence of two separate towns. The union men testified that their men averaged about half the wage paid for comparable work in Baltimore, where the Labor Department estimated that the cost of living was only 20 percent higher. Waynesboro boilermakers, for example, got 25 to 35 cents an hour; molders earned 36 cents and coremakers, 34 cents.[23] These figures were contradicted somewhat by payroll figures supplied by management. Management, not surprisingly, focused on its highest wages. At the Frick Company, for example, the best paid toolmakers received 49½ cents; machinists, 39 cents; handymen, 29¼ cents; boilermakers, 39½ cents; molders, 48 cents; coremakers, 40 cents; blacksmiths, 39 cents; and carpenters, 33 cents.[24] The employers justified these modest wages at the top on the ground that the workers were mostly local farm boys with few skills. Even so, both Worden and Hewitt knew immediately that the current Waynesboro wages were unacceptable.

What the section could not resolve was how to deal with a special problem that they both perceived. Demands for increased wages and shorter hours were generally common enough, frequently debatable, but rarely controversial. The stumbling block to the Waynesboro settlement was, specifically, the modest demands of the unskilled—those men who worked for 22 cents an hour and now wanted 30 cents. They wanted too little. Thirty cents was nothing like a living wage, nor was that figure likely to satisfy common laborers for very long. Their case was unique in the board's experience. Hewitt thought, under the circumstances, that the board should act in harmony with both the Alschuler precedent and its own commitment to the living wage. To do so, he believed that the NWLB should set a guaranteed day wage for common labor at Waynesboro, with an hourly average well above the 30-cent demand. Worden disagreed. To hand down such an award, he maintained, would lead inevitably to new demands for further rulings from the NWLB. He proposed, instead, that the board declare the current Waynesboro rate for common labor too low. It should then leave the determination of hours to the antagonists themselves and the fixing of rates—for both skilled and unskilled labor—to a local committee of three to five Waynesboro residents. Worden, in other words, thought that the NWLB should abdicate primary responsibility for what happened in Waynesboro.[25]

Under the NWLB's regulations, the disagreement within the section meant that the full board would have to decide the case. When it met on 10 July, no two members weighed the evidence alike. All of them, no doubt, understood the larger implications of the matter before them. If the board refused to assign a minimum for common labor and adopted Worden's plan for an all-powerful local committee, or if it deadlocked and had to call an umpire into the case, it would discard its first great opportunity to deal with the living wage. If, on the other hand, it followed Hewitt's advice to give the lowest paid workers more than they had requested, it would set a precedent for an NWLB-sanctioned, standardized minimum wage. It would assume, in effect, legislative powers.

Members such as Frank Walsh and Tom Savage were in no mood to leave the Waynesboro settlement to either a local committee or a single arbiter. "I want to see some decision made by this Board," Savage said. "I want to see it become a Board that will . . . say that we are not one of those governmental departments . . . so bound up with red tape that it takes a year to get anything and then you don't get it."[26] Seeing the board act was chiefly what Savage had in mind when he agreed to accept 30 cents. That would quell discontent for the moment, he believed, especially if a local board was appointed to deal with further difficulties.[27] In that way, the NWLB would act positively, common laborers would get what they thought they wanted, and the local committee could henceforth deflect the soon-to-be unhappy laborers from the board itself. Not rocking the boat was the board's fundamental unwritten principle, and Savage had followed it. His proposals would not disturb production; they would hardly disturb the status quo.

Frank Walsh was eager, he said time and again that morning, "not to disturb conditions."[28] No one really believed him—especially as he continued to talk. Obviously, Walsh saw the NWLB as a legislative as well as a judicial body. He believed that it could guide the country toward a national wage policy, and he hoped to direct it down that course. Perhaps with that in mind, Walsh balked at any action by the board which would perpetuate substandard wages. The Worden-Hewitt section had estimated a 100 to 114 percent rise in the cost of living in Waynesboro since 1915, yet Walsh was unwilling to accept automatically the standard wage of the past to which the higher cost of living had been added. Perhaps, he suggested, people "were not getting enough to eat at that time." For years certain industries had "shifted the burden of the living wage on the community so that we filled hospitals, alms houses, and jails and kept up boards of public welfare at immense cost to the people of the community . . . [for what] was required for men and women to live upon. So we come right down to the question now in this particular case and it can't be dodged, and so far as I am concerned, I do not want to dodge it."[29] Dodging it, he suggested, would even be counterproductive. If the NWLB denied any worker a living wage, Walsh warned, "it would put us in a condition of chaos that would make the President . . . establish another board, perhaps with teeth in it, that would keep things going and not let employers be on the Board."[30] Tom Savage had said that employers and employees in Waynesboro could "go along in their old-fashioned way if they want to carry on that way."[31] With precedent at stake, Walsh felt no such generosity.

Walsh met the issues in a totally new proposal. In it, he declared that 45 cents an hour was "the lowest a man can live on in Waynesboro." He proposed also to cut the work week by five hours, as the workers had requested, by establishing the basic nine-hour day Monday through Friday and retaining the five-hour Saturday. Employees would earn time and a half for ordinary overtime, and double time for Sundays and Pennsylvania holidays. Walsh had determined that the living wage in the average city amounted to a daily $4.75.[32] If his program was accepted, the Waynesboro laborer could make $4.72½ Monday through Friday if he worked ten hours and $2.25 on Saturdays, almost $1,300 per annum. Clearly the boat had been rocked.

The employer members were stunned and uncooperative. Their most persuasive spokesman, Loyall Osborne, objected to what Walsh was trying to do on two grounds, and he refused to yield even in the face of cost-of-living statistics presented by the staff budget analyst, William F. Ogburn, a professor of sociology. First, Osborne argued that the establishment of a living wage was a matter for the full board to decide, not a figure to be announced by the joint chairman. Second, he believed that the NWLB should set no minimum higher than that established by another governmental agency. The Shipbuilding Labor Adjustment Board, for example, had set a flat rate of 40 cents— minimum and maximum—for common labor. The NWLB should be mindful of that figure and should set no higher wage until all federal adjustment agencies could agree on a proper minimum. Osborne, of course, saw the need for standardization of federal action, as did Walsh. The difference was that the Westinghouse executive wanted some other agency—in particular, Felix Frankfurter's War Labor Policies Board—to initiate the drive toward uniformity. That attitude marked his major tactical difference with Walsh, who not only hoped but also believed that the Frankfurter board would never function.[33]

Professor Ogburn's statistics, part of an exhaustive study on the living wage which he had undertaken on the board's behalf, lent important support to the Walsh proposal. Ogburn had examined earlier cost-of-living studies and probed into recent changes in the costs of food, rent, clothing, fuel, and sundries. His research revealed a national increase of 55 percent in the cost of living from January 1915 to June 1918. Ogburn testified that afternoon that he had arrived at two, five-member family budgets: a minimum subsistence level at $1,300 (later revised to $1,386); and a minimum comfort level at $1,750 to $1,800 (later, $1,760.50).[34] If the NWLB granted Waynesboro common laborers exactly what they wanted, they would earn only a projected $850 in a year. The Walsh proposal, in contrast, would bring their earnings to near the minimum subsistence level, the lowest acceptable figure in Ogburn's estimation.

Yet Walsh was willing to compromise. In order to overcome the employer members' opposition, he suggested the terms stipulated by the Shipping Board: a ten-hour day, 40 cents an hour for the first eight hours, and time and a half for the last two.[35] On its face, the compromise was perfect. It met Osborne's objection against superseding the wage settlements of other boards, but it had not surrendered much. The new terms, however, satisfied neither the employer nor labor members. "That doesn't quite meet with what we would like to see," said Worden, the New Jersey shipbuilder. His Submarine Boat Corporation would need 12,000 to 15,000 new men within the next few months, and he did not want to have to fight for them.[36] Osborne backed him up. The labor leaders now came alive to the real issues. Tom Savage pointed out that another adjustment board had recently awarded machinists' helpers 46 cents an hour. Adam Wilkinson of the coal miners, alternate for Frank Hayes, explained that 500,000 miners had just received an advance of $1.50 a day, making their daily average about $5.00. To compensate for the wage increases, the president had then raised coal prices 45 cents a ton. Why, they asked, could the NWLB not take its cue from one of those actions rather than from the Shipping Board? Their remarks fell on deaf ears. Osborne wanted, by now, no more than 38 cents and categorically refused to go geyond 40 cents. At 4:35 P.M., the frustrated labor representatives called a recess in order to caucus.[37]

Labor, belatedly and somewhat clumsily, decided to return the discussion to matters of general wage policy. When the caucus ended, Tom Savage challenged Walsh before the full board and said that the figure the NWLB needed to determine was "a living minimum wage." Addressing Walsh directly, he continued: "We disagree with your figure. We say that fifty cents is the figure and . . . if . . . it is going to an umpire, I offer as an amendment that the 'fifty cents' be inserted in lieu of forty-five cents."[38] Walsh, who had never intended the 45-cent proposal to determine a nationwide standard, conceded that 50 cents was nearer the mark. Then, when the Savage amendment lost by one vote, he pushed harder than ever to get 45 cents adopted.

In the exchanges that followed, Walsh and Osborne met head on.

Osborne stated his case with determination: "It is either living wage or arbitrary rate. If . . . [the Walsh proposal] is a living wage I decline to vote for it on the ground that I don't know the living wage. If it is arbitrary fixing of forty-five cents I vote against it because I decline without conference with other instrumentalities of government who are fixing wages to fix a wage that I know will create disturbances throughout all industries."[39] Walsh then determined to get to the heart of the matter. He was especially concerned about Osborne's persistent deference to the War Labor Policies Board. Frankfurter had recently asked other adjustment boards to proceed cautiously. "My question," Walsh asked directly, "is do you agree with him you should go slow on wages even where the wages are below the standard of living?" Said Osborne: "I would go slow if that wage that we feel ought to be paid was one that was going to be out of line with that established in every other field of government activity, yes."[40] The Waynesboro controversy, he believed, could be settled with a 30-cent minimum wage. "We are here to settle controversies."[41] When the other employers agreed, the board was bogged down practically as well as philosophically.

In a final attempt to avoid calling in an umpire, Osborne and Victor Olander agreed to work overnight and submit yet another proposal for discussion in the morning. After token debate, their compromise award was approved and promulgated on 11 July. The award retained piecework and the basic ten-hour day, but it provided for time-and-a-half and double-time rates. Among its provisions was an order that no Waynesboro employee should receive less than 40 cents an hour. Common laborers therefore won a significant daily increase from $2.20 to $4.00.[42] Without working overtime, they would make a minimum of about $1,100 per annum.

Only Frederick Judson, the St. Louis attorney who served as Taft's alternate, was genuinely pleased with the award. Osborne and Olander, he said happily, had demonstrated the "fundamental principle that all government is based upon compromise."[43] Walsh, Savage, and even Olander felt no pride in the NWLB's decision. The Waynesboro common laborers had won more than they had asked, almost as much as Samuel Alschuler had granted the laborers in a much larger city; but their minimum compensation remained slightly below the flat standards set by the Shipping Board. In the aftermath of the award, the workers demanded a further increase to 50 cents for common labor, a demand that B. L. Worden had correctly predicted. The Waynesboro employers, too, were unhappy. They asked the

NWLB to reduce the wage award to the 30 cents they themselves had originally refused to grant.[44]

The labor representatives on the NWLB tolerated the settlement only because the award itself provided for the determination of the living wage and for the potential adjustment of the Waynesboro decision. Ironically, the man they had to thank for that provision was Loyall Osborne. To get the award adopted, Osborne had agreed to conclude it with the following statement: "The board hereby announces that it has under consideration the matter of the determination of the living wage, which under its principles must be the minimum rate of wage which will permit the worker and his family to subsist in reasonable health and comfort. That in respect to the minimum established by this finding it shall be understood that it shall be subject to readjustment to conform to the board's decision when and as a determination shall be reached in that regard."[45] Fundamental questions about wages and hours were going to recur often, he said. The NWLB ought to inform itself, discuss the issues, and establish some policies. Speaking for the NWLB employers, Osborne urged the board "to get them settled and not get our cases stalled every time by trying to settle them in each case."[46] Because of what Taft later called Osborne's "blunder,"[47] the board then set aside the last week of July for policy discussion.

When the matter came up on Tuesday, 23 July, Osborne retreated. He needed time, he said, to analyze all the materials that Professor Ogburn had collected for the board members. Osborne did not say how much time he needed, but he bristled when Walsh suggested that he had done no homework in two weeks. Taft remarked impatiently that, if Osborne would only read the available reports, he would know as much as the joint chairmen did. When the Westinghouse executive objected that "nobody on earth can digest . . . [that kind of evidence] in twenty-four hours and have a reasonable opinion about it," Taft acidly gave him "credit for more capacity . . . than you admit." Tired of the weeks of delay on the wage question, Taft, Walsh, and the labor representatives stopped Osborne's filibuster. They decided to discuss the living wage on the following day, 24 July, at 10:00 A.M.[48]

Both sides came in that Wednesday morning prepared to end the internecine warfare, and Frank Walsh opened the talks. Walsh moved to adopt Ogburn's estimated minimum comfort budget as the NWLB standard. The $1,760.50 could be apportioned into equal payments on hourly, weekly, or monthly bases in order to conform to the methods of payment already established within individual industries. But the worker would earn his $1,760.50 without working more than eight hours a day for 300 days.[49] The Walsh wage motion—a subtle attempt to establish also NWLB support for a national eight-hour day—would bring common laborers who came before the board about 73 cents an hour and $5.85 a day.

In the exchange that followed, all the expected arguments were aired. The labor representatives rallied around the Walsh-sponsored 73-cent minimum and even bargained for strength by questioning *its* adequacy. Management thought and spoke as management traditionally thought and spoke. The NWLB employers were troubled about increasing inflation, overpaying their employees, and stifling competition. Behind the emotion-charged debate were the opposite goals of the two groups within the board, which had always made voluntarism difficult. The labor members, perhaps fearful that any NWLB-sanctioned minimum would become a de facto maximum, wanted the board to set a high standard. They felt, too, a particular urgency. Only that month, the president had signed a new law stipulating that no federal money be provided to contractors to pay a wage that exceeded the minimum set by the War Labor Policies Board, unless a higher wage had already been set by law. Many labor leaders blamed employer associations for this "joker" attached to the Civil Appropriation Act and saw the measure as an attempt to hamstring the NWLB. Although no one knew how the law would be interpreted, especially if the Frankfurter board set no minimum wage, it was clearly in labor's interest for the NWLB to act first and fast.[50] The employer members' chief objectives were to prevent definitive action and, at whatever cost, to preserve freedom of action for their fellow businessmen.

The labor members took Ogburn's budget apart that week. Based primarily on a study of shipyard workers in the New York area, it allowed $200.00 per annum for rent; $625.00 for food; $92.50 for a man's clothing; and $87.00 for a woman's. Certain that a family could not get a decent, unheated flat for less than $25.00 a month, T. A. Rickert complained that the rent allotment would house no one in New York "unless it is in the outlying districts and they must be shacks." The clothing budget, the president of the Garment Workers continued, was also unrealistic because the cost of cheaper fabrics had increased while the quality had declined. Shoes and overcoats fell apart while still new. Victor Olander questioned Ogburn's food allowance. Another investigation had "already proved that $607 is too little," he said. "Here $625 is allowed. Isn't that a pretty narrow margin?"[51]

Nor did the labor representatives ignore charges that a family could get rich on the Ogburn schedule. When Worden suggested that four persons within one family could earn a combined income of $7,040 if they all worked at the proposed minimum, Walsh and Rickert described the adolescent wage earner: Wasn't it true, Walsh asked, that, when a boy earned a man's wage, he controlled his own expenses as well as his own income? And did not young men without families frequently support dependent relatives? "My opinion," said Rickert, "is that it equalizes itself. As that boy grows older . . . his expenses become greater to the family, say the boy is 16 and working and gets $6, $7, $8 a week, you will find that boy will demand clothing for his employment . . . and he probably wants to go to some school . . . or learn something that will entail greater expense than is allowed here and that boy . . . would take about all . . . [he earns]."[52]

The little drama within the board eventually took on all the proportions of an old-style morality play. VanDervoort simply meant to be practical when he explained reality as he saw it. He saw the Walsh motion as both a threat to industrial stability and a pipe dream. He thought first of the billions of dollars of unfulfilled contracts that could be endangered by the NWLB's action. He believed, moreover, that wages had kept pace with the rising cost of living. Of course, if the base rates had been originally inadequate, that was unfortunate, but this was hardly "the time to change the entire social fabric of the country." Even if such a course was wise, which by his lights it clearly was not, VanDervoort was sure that it could never achieve the end that Walsh desired. Prices, he believed, would merely go up to accommodate the wage hikes. As for the possible long-range benefits of a higher income on the "lower classes," VanDervoort merely shrugged. "I know that in my own experience," he said, "these laborers, no matter what we do for them, they would herd together, a dozen in a house in spite of us."[53]

For Walsh's purpose, VanDervoort's remarks were almost too good to be true. His were the kind of statements that the joint chairman liked most to attack, the kind of statements, in fact, on which he had built a reputation by attacking. The VanDervoort hypotheses, more than anything else, gave Walsh the opening he wanted. For two hours on 26 July, he flayed the employer members and defended his beloved poor. If underpaid employees left their jobs after only a few days, he reminded the employers, they ought to remember that "a man ill-nourished has more desire to lie down and stretch his muscles than a man like us who is over nourished and keeps away from the work for other reasons."[54] Furthermore, VanDervoort's words—which the East Moline businessman himself later recognized as "perhaps unfortunate"[55]—had betrayed fundamental ignorance: "I believe the way he put it was that he shuddered at the thought of what would happen to the lower classes if they got a living wage. Well, on all the studies upon that question, why he need not shiver or shudder. They will act just like he did and with perhaps this exception. For the difference in financial accumulation or in comfortable living they will work a good deal longer proportionately than he does."[56]

Armed with statistics, Walsh continued the attack when he offered two social reasons for the adoption of the 73-cent wage. First of all, he said, the NWLB should remember that each of the men whose wage was under consideration was "necessary in an industry that is necessary for life."[57] Chicago's pauper budget, corrected to February 1918, allowed $1,076.50 for a family of five. This meant that a man who worked half-days on Saturday had to earn 49½ cents an hour in an eight-hour weekday or 44 cents in a nine-hour day. A ten-hour day on the pauper's budget would yield 39½ cents. "Now our people are not paupers and . . . they cannot be placed upon a pauper's budget."[58] Furthermore, said the impassioned Walsh, a proper wage was the key to America's future. Only one out of three children of common laborers had a grammar school education, and less than 10 percent had finished high school. In four industrial towns recently investigated by the Bureau of Labor Statistics, 75 percent of those children quit school before reaching the seventh grade; more than 40 percent either worked at home or undertook outside employment.[59] A just and efficient society, he implied again and again, demanded more of modern industry.

Throughout the week, the employer members consistently reverted when necessary to their best defense for inaction, the NWLB's limited powers. John F. Perkins, the copper magnate who routinely substituted for Osborne, saw no need to take exception to any statistics. Instead, he opposed the board's fixing any standard wage. "My understanding," he said on the day that the discussions opened, "was that we were to try to see whether such a thing were possible, and the more I think about it, the more it is not possible."[60] Osborne applauded his alternate's sentiments two days later. His own words revealed a variation of his approach to the Western Union case. "I don't believe the Board has a right to do it but I certainly didn't commit myself to a decision on that matter when I made that suggestion [in the Waynesboro proceedings]," he explained. "If we determine that we can't do it that is just as much determination as to determine that we can do it."[61] C. Edwin Michael did not believe that any governmental agency could "govern the minimum rate of wages to be paid for men for their services." He believed instead in "the law of supply and demand," which Osborne then justified through "the fact that we insist upon competitive civilization." The way to win the debate, the employer members had perceived, was not to bargain for a lesser wage but rather to refuse to act. Their solution to the wage problem, in short, reaffirmed American individualism. Each employer member should decide for himself what a living wage was and should, without public comment, apply his personal standard in the cases assigned to him.[62]

By 30 July, both sides had introduced all the information that was germane—and some that was not—into the debate on Walsh's wage motion. It had been a week full of sound and fury, and none of it had changed anyone's mind. Only William Howard Taft was still to be heard. Taft, disturbed all that week by the discord, complained to his secretary that there was "always a wrangle and a row when the whole Board meets;—that's the cost of harmony."[63] Now he came before the hopelessly divided members to remind them that their great public strength lay in unanimity. If it was generally known, he said, how far apart the members were on their own great principle, future awards would likely be ignored. Then, in true deus ex machina form, he offered the only possible solution. He moved that the NWLB continue to assign a wage to fit the circumstances in each case that it settled, being careful not to "seriously impair" the country's economic structure. Almost gratefully, the board accepted Taft's resolution to settle nothing.[64]

What purpose, then, had the debate on the living wage served? And what had it really been about? To answer those questions, one must look more closely at Frank Walsh. It had been Walsh's week from start to finish. The debate had begun and ended on the merits of his proposal. What had Walsh wanted? Obviously, he had tried to persuade the NWLB to adopt a wage standard and thereby provide a basis from which to work in future cases. (Even Walsh admitted that he intended the basis to be flexible and that the "living wage" should be adjusted to fit local conditions.)[65] But Walsh was neither stupid nor impractical, and he must have known that the NWLB would never approve a 73-cent wage when most common laborers in America earned less than 40 cents an hour. He suspected, moreover, that the NWLB employers had agreed in advance not to go beyond 40 cents.

The importance of the debate, in Walsh's mind, must therefore have gone beyond the question of merely setting a wage standard. Given his temperament and experience, it seems likely that he saw the weeklong discussions as a forum from which to generate publicity. Professor Ogburn's report carried the authority of statistical evidence and, to the public, bore the imprimatur of the NWLB. Nor was Walsh above allowing the public to think that the board theoretically accepted the Ogburn minimum-comfort budget as a moral standard to uphold voluntarily. Indeed, he did so after the debate. In that way, he hoped to affect the wages of common laborers whose grievances the board would never hear. The employer members had stopped the adoption of the 73-cent wage, but they could not stop Walsh from advertising it outside the board.

Walsh had also been careful that week to protect his special relationship with William Howard Taft. Before Taft's inevitable charge to the full board, the two men had met behind closed doors, and their private talks foreshadowed Taft's remarks on 30 July. The former president warned Walsh of the "absurdity" of the 73-cent wage standard. The employers of the nation would never accept it even if the NWLB employer members did, and "we would drive away all our business, because employers would not submit to a jurisdiction that would revolutionize business and destroy the economic structure of our community during the war." Walsh bowed quickly to Taft's appeal. The joint chairmen had agreed then that the NWLB should study more statistics and settle more cases before it undertook to set standards.[66] In reality, their agreement spelled the end of the NWLB's official effort at standardization. Theoretically, Walsh had conceded a chance for a firm statement on a poorly understood principle, but it had been a slim chance. In return, he had won increased respect from the man who held the balance of power.[67]

In general, the board's actions on wages in the summer of 1918 encouraged both workingmen and the labor movement to anticipate future benefits from the NWLB. After the debate over wages, expectations of those groups seemed well-founded. The War Labor Policies Board never established a wage standard, and the NWLB staff, through Secretary Lauck and Ogburn, worked with Royal Meeker, United States Commissioner of Labor Statistics, in continuous reappraisals of the cost of living. Many awards were given an effective life of only six months in order that wages could be reviewed periodically. Newspapers throughout the country, to the delight of Frank Walsh, continued to portray the NWLB's awards as boosts to the interests of workingmen everywhere. Conservative observers, in turn, complained to Taft of insidious Marxist influences within the NWLB.[68] All of this enhanced the board's reputation as an instrument of justice.

In actuality, however, the NWLB's awards were not so radical as some believed them to be. The board brought the wages of common laborers who appealed to it up to a level only slightly higher than the average wage of 39½ cents that common laborers earned in 1918.[69] The NWLB's decisions were, nonetheless, advantageous to working people. Most of the approximately 500 awards that the board handed down included new wage schedules, and many of the common laborers who came before it had worked for grossly substandard pay. Although far short of the standard Frank Walsh had urged, the 40 to 42 cents that the board generally awarded did, therefore, significantly raise the standard of living for countless workers. In the absence of a legislated minimum wage in 1918, the NWLB—through awards and publicity—virtually set an unofficial minimum wage, and in that year, common laborers earned a higher real wage than ever before in industrial America. In part, of course, wage levels rose because of a shortage of labor, but the NWLB's awards helped to make the new levels possible.

 A Moderate Advance

> That capitalists have gotten into an unfortunate investment is no reason why working men should not receive the wages justified by . . . the cost of living.
>
> —William Howard Taft, personal correspondence, January 1919

Domestic wage adjustments during modern wars, so the theory goes—especially among marginally-paid workers—are facilitated somewhat by the availability of new money generated by the war economy. Yet the Waynesboro decision, and countless others, indicated that adjusting wages was never easy, not even in private industries where employers enjoyed governmental contracts with cost-plus factors. In a regulated industry, such as the street-railway industry, where operating revenues were fixed, adjustment problems during the war reached astronomical proportions. That industry's difficulties were compounded by the aggressive tactics of the Amalgamated Association of Street and Electric Railway Employees, an AFL affiliate that as early as 1914 had organized over 30 percent of street-railway workers. The union's persistent cry for higher wages appeared justified when street-railway employees brought their grievances before the NWLB. In June and July of 1918, the first of many such series of cases presented Taft and Walsh with fundamental problems: Did assigning a just wage require consideration of the financial status of a company? Or had Samuel Alschuler been right to discount such criteria altogether? What, if any, responsibility did the NWLB have to cushion a precarious industry against financial disaster? What was the responsibility of the public and of the federal government to satisfy the needs of a public-service industry as well as its employees? In answering those questions, the joint chairmen themselves refined the NWLB's wage adjustment policy.

As the NWLB entered private industrial disputes, employees in the public sector clamored for equal attention. The board declined to intervene in municipal affairs when firemen and policemen called for recognition of their unions and for higher wages. But the efficient operation of public utilities, the NWLB decided, was necessary to the conduct of the war. Overcapitalized and hampered by outdated fare-freezing contracts with the communities they served, streetcar companies by 1918 were deeply in debt, and they also paid their employees far less than a living wage. Wages had failed to keep pace with the rising cost of living, not only because fares had remained constant in an inflationary era, but also because even union contracts had been drawn to remain in effect for several years. As a result, the real wages of the average street-railway employee in 1917 were lower than they had been since before 1890. That year the typical employee who belonged to a union earned only 35 cents an hour, and discontent was rife by 1918.[1]

The financial difficulties of the street railways obviously predated wartime labor demands. In the halcyon days, traction companies had expected the heavy volume of short-term riders to compensate for riders who traveled long distances at the same low fare. For a while, they had been right. But in the two decades since most companies had agreed to fixed fares, machinery had become more sophisticated and therefore more costly; riders had continued to expect good service when they dropped a 5-cent piece in the toll box; and railway equipment had been neglected.[2] Throughout the decade before the United States entered the war, the street railways had staggered under a growing imbalance between costs and revenues. By 1917, 44 percent of 1,307 systems reported no surplus at all or admitted to operating at a deficit.[3]

The wartime economy deepened the economic crisis of the street railways, and many companies faced new problems when they asked the municipal or state authorities that regulated rates for permission to raise fares. Public officials were unwilling to alienate their constituents by increasing transportation costs. Antimonopolists demanded fundamental reforms in return for even considering bailing the companies out, and some citizens wanted to punish the transit lines for what they perceived to be long-standing greed and economic stupidity. In June 1918, as Joint Chairmen Taft and Walsh began to consider some twenty-two cases involving demands from 50,000 street-railway employees, the status of the industry was unreservedly grim. Financial reports from 365 electric roads, representing over 60 percent of the total street-railway mileage in the country, showed an 82.4 percent decrease in net income in the first six months of that year as compared with the first half of 1917.[4]

In early June, with landmark cases such as Western Union and Waynesboro pending before the NWLB, Frank Walsh saw an opportunity to generalize testimony about working conditions on the traction lines. Because of the public nature of the railway companies, he and Taft, exclusively, were assigned disputes from that industry. This first series, therefore, provided an opportunity to build a strong case for the living wage. Walsh wired Taft in New Haven on 5 June that cases were being added daily to the list of streetcar dockets. Representatives of the employees, Walsh said, wanted to present five or six expert witnesses to discuss what they considered to be a living wage throughout the country. Both the companies and the employees, he suggested, should be allowed "a limited number of witnesses" to aid in formulating a general policy governing wage hikes within the industry. The problem of the living wage, Walsh explained, was an issue "we are going to have . . . to meet in every street-railway case now under consideration."[5] Taft acquiesced in his colleague's request for a general hearing.

When the hearings began in Washington on 24 June, the joint chairmen especially wanted to resolve one major question: "Under the principles and policies of the National War Labor Board, what is the relevancy, if any, of the questions of the financial conditions of the companies and their ability to pay to the function of the Board in fixing a fair and living wage for the employees?"[6] That, at least, was the question that Frank Walsh had instructed James H. Vahey, attorney for the carmen's union, and top management officials to address. Only nine companies participated in the hearings, but, even as they got under way, the NWLB's press releases stressed the national implications of the testimony.[7] Predictably, representatives for the employees made a cogent case for higher wages. Spokesmen for the companies, in general, agreed that wage levels were inadequate, yet industry representatives denied the companies' ability to make adjustments.[8] Half of the traction lines in the nation, they said, already faced bankruptcy. Thus, by 2:30 on that hot Washington afternoon, Taft and Walsh had begun to seek a way to establish a living wage for street-railway employees without bankrupting the owners.

During the two-day hearing on 24–25 June, the most compelling testimony came from industry spokesmen such as Thomas N. McCarter, chairman of the War Board of the American Electric Railway Association, and Philip N. Gadsden, an attorney who was a member of that board and also chairman of the National Committee on Public Utility Conditions. Both men stressed the multi-faceted contributions of public-service utilities to the war effort. On the first day of testimony, McCarter predicted a "national calamity" if the utilities should no longer be able to provide light, heat, and transportation for war workers. He even cited correspondence between President Wilson and Treasury Secretary William G. McAdoo which emphasized the critical importance of maintaining public utilities at the level of maximum efficiency. State and local regulatory authorities, Wilson and McAdoo agreed, had to be encouraged to "respond promptly" to national needs. If the NWLB increased wage scales on the street railways without assuring the companies additional income, McCarter argued, the board would accomplish exactly what the administration sought to avoid. The NWLB, he added, should therefore act responsibly. The least that it could do in each case was to inform the proper rate-regulating authority of "the exact amount of money" required to effect a wage increase and then recommend that the authority secure "a compensating increase in revenue" for the traction line.[9]

McCarter and Gadsden, however, did not share the Wilson administration's belief that state and local authorities would act responsibly when presented with the facts. Neither man put much faith in a process that, at best, would mean piecemeal administration of additional money secured through voluntary cooperation. First and foremost, these industry spokesmen sought direct relief from the federal government.

Gadsden presented the hard evidence for the president's authority to regulate street-railway income directly. After declaring war on 6 April 1917, he said on 25 June, Congress had directed the president to use the "resources of the Government" to carry America to victory. Since that time, he continued, the government had assumed unprecedented regulatory powers over private industry. No less than eleven congressional acts, presidential directives, and letters from governmental advisers had affirmed those powers and hinted at still more. For Gadsden's purposes, the single most pertinent congressional action, approved on 15 June 1917, permitted Wilson to assume control of any plant whose operations were vital to United States military or naval operations. The Urgent Deficiency Act, as it was called, had since been amended to increase the president's authority. In the language of the amendment, the president had specific power to "take possession of, lease, or assume control of any street railroads, interurban railroad, or part thereof, wherever operated, and all cars, appurtenances and franchises, or parts thereof . . . necessary for the transfer and transportation of employees of shipyards or plants engaged or that may hereafter be engaged in the construction of ships or equipment therefor for the United States."[10] Furthermore, Gadsden reminded the NWLB, the federal government's power to increase fares was independent of the president's authority to assume the management of streetcar lines. Recent congressional rate-fixing measures for steam railroads had been an exercise of necessary war powers, and the legitimacy of such action had not been conditioned upon the government's running the trains. Gadsden concluded simply that the President could increase the rates of fare on the street railways "through such instrumentality as he may designate."[11]

After the two-day hearing, Walsh struggled in vain to frame a letter to President Wilson. Gadsden's statement had impressed both Taft and Walsh as well as the chief counsel for the carmen's union, who had officially concurred in Gadsden's remarks. Walsh, on behalf of the joint chairmen, wanted Wilson to know that and to encourage presidential action in the street-railway crisis. The board's primary responsibility, he and Taft agreed, was to fix a fair wage; but both men worried about subverting the purpose for which the NWLB had been created if, in fixing that wage, they bankrupted the companies.[12] Walsh nevertheless remained cautious about unnecessarily augmenting federal powers and unable to reconcile his hopes for speedy relief to the industry with private doubts about Wilson's constitutional power to raise the fares. In the end, he left his dilemma for the NWLB to resolve on 28 June.[13]

Since the hearing, Taft, too, had weighed the merits of swift federal intervention against persistent qualms about the limits of presidential power. Like Walsh, he doubted Wilson's authority to act without further action by Congress, but legislation would take time, and any financial relief for the companies, he believed, should predate wage-increasing awards. At the meeting of 28 June, therefore, he suggested that the NWLB sidestep delicate questions about the extent of executive war powers. The letter he intended for Wilson would emphasize instead the president's lawful right to impose a federal solution. The joint chairmen could then give the president over a month to act by holding back the street-railway awards until 1 August. If, in the interim, the president's legal advisers ruled against personal intervention, Wilson would thus have time to secure congressional sanction for federal action. Under Taft's proposal, the NWLB would present both the companies' and the employees' positions when it explained the consequences of unrevised fares. The president could then decide what action to take.[14]

Before the meeting ended, the NWLB unanimously agreed to proceed along lines that Taft had suggested, but not before addressing the question that Walsh had originally wanted answered. What troubled Osborne was Taft's implicit "assumption" that ultimately wages should be held to an acceptable standard regardless of the consequences.[15] What Osborne failed to understand was that Taft had assumed nothing. The joint chairmen had set a wage policy for an industry placed by the board itself under their exclusive care. The hearings, apparently, had moved Taft to accept what Walsh had long believed. A proper wage could not be defined according to a company's needs. Under the principle of the living wage, Taft said, the board could not "allow the condition of the companies to affect our findings." After all, "if it were arbitrated with us, how much a coalman ought to get for coal, could we determine what the financial ability of a company was in arbitrating . . . what ought to be paid for the coal?"[16] When Osborne quickly countered that wage increases on the streetcars should be specifically conditioned upon fare raises to match them, Walsh flatly refused to consider the matter and Taft closed the debate.[17]

As the twelve members rallied behind Taft's proposed letter to the president, Frank Walsh murmured to his colleague: "You are making me conservative. Yesterday morning I was trying to write that and tell him he has the power, but it looks too slender, doesn't it?" "Yes," Taft answered, "it does."[18] Only then did it become obvious that the letter to the president was in effect a challenge, meant by the joint chairmen to signal their determination to order wage raises regardless of voluntary or federally imposed relief to the industry.

The NWLB hearings, the joint chairmen's announced intention to set a fair wage, and the union's acquiescence in the companies' request for federal management seemingly pointed toward national operation of the traction lines in the summer of 1918. Indeed, the push for federal intervention closely paralleled the drive that had culminated in federal operation of the steam railroads at the end of 1917. On the steam lines, employees had battled for the working conditions established under the Adamson Act, which, despite approval from the Supreme Court, had yet to be implemented fully more than a year after its passage. Shippers, eager to avoid higher rates, had come to believe that federal controls would lead to greater efficiency without increased costs, and management, when the ICC persistently refused to authorize rate increases, had accepted federal operation as a way to diminish escalating operational costs. The nationalization of the steam railroads, under the directorship of McAdoo, had devolved almost naturally with the full agreement of laborers, customers, and management. The federal umbrella, therefore, had enveloped the rails essentially to end political conflict among interest groups analogous to those affected in the street-railway crisis.[19]

In reality, however, the analogous conditions between the steam railroads and the street railways were so tenuous that the issues of nationalization sparked considerable debate. Unlike the steam railways, the streetcars operated in a mostly local and purely intrastate theater. No federal regulatory authority, such as the ICC, and no federal labor law, such as the Adamson Act, applied to the urban transportation system. In general, state public-service commissions worked in cooperation with municipal governments to regulate the street cars. Federal control of the street railways, therefore, even for the period of the war, would require a reevaluation of the proper relationship between the federal government and the states.

As the debate took shape, the eastern press—particularly the New York newspapers—gave full play to the question of state-federal relations. The *New York Times*, for example, accepted the street-railway network as a legitimate war industry, and an industry in trouble. The NWLB, it explained, had control over only labor problems in such industries and had no jurisdiction over industrial revenues. The *Times* acknowledged that federal responsibility for these intrastate lines was "less clear and close" than for steam railways in interstate commerce. Yet, it concluded, "It is difficult to see why these rates and fares are not as much subject to Federal control as the prices of many commodities."[20] The *Tribune*, antagonistic to federal control, argued that local government needed to solve its own problems lest Washington become overburdened. The clamor for a federal response to this industry's financial stress, it believed, symbolized a dangerous tendency. "This is not a question of Federal regulation . . . as such, to be debated on its merits. . . . The danger already is that the country's affairs will become so enormously centralized . . . that all administrative capacity will be swamped."[21] The New York *Journal of Commerce*, which considered even the NWLB's authority to adjust wages "of doubtful validity," similarly believed that state authorities should do their jobs without interference from above.[22] But the New York *World* was bluntest of all as it decried the fate of American democracy if Washington directed a dole: "If local self-government is assumed to have broken down to this extent, in what possible respect can it longer be assumed to possess any efficiency or worth in our scheme of government where heretofore it has been accepted as the cornerstone?"[23] In short, only the *Times* favored the invasion of states rights, and it did so only reluctantly.

Among the interests directly involved, the street-railway debate generally reflected perceived self-interests more than concern with political abstractions. Joint Chairman Taft, because he had a national jurisdiction to pacify, favored a national solution to uncertainties about rate increases in order to facilitate his own work in adjusting wages. The industry itself obviously wanted to escape the myriad complexities of local politics. The Amalgamated Association of Street and Electric Railway Employees, which considered the NWLB more enlightened than local authorities, was eager to support any measure that made the NWLB's awards feasible. The riding public, as well as state and local authorities, however, was divided. For some, a federal solution would provide a welcome release from unwelcome responsibilities, but for most, federal control spelled an end to long-cherished local autonomy.

That last critical difference of opinion suggested yet a second great weakness in any attempted comparison of the wartime dynamics of steam-railroad and street-railway politics. The kind of consensus that had made the federal assumption of steam railroads possible had failed to materialize among the interest groups concerned with the street-railway industry. That much was evident in June and July of 1918 as the forces for and against federal control went public.

As the matter rested with President Wilson, both the AERA and Joint Chairman Taft branded local authorities as inadequate to perform the task before them. Toward the end of June, the *Electric Railway Journal* emphasized the need for speedy action to avoid an industry-wide panic. But, the *Journal* complained, "The record of local authorities . . . is not such to inspire any confidence that . . . they will deal speedily with utility fare increases unless strongly pushed by the Government." The *Journal* offered a variety of avenues for federal intervention as it begged the Wilson administration to act with vision: "Let their act be the dawn of a new day—not the beginning of the debacle."[24] Echoing the AERA's sentiments, Taft, in one of the editorials that he wrote regularly for the Philadelphia *Public Ledger*, agreed that the existing method of fare adjustment was "a tedious procedure utterly impracticable."[25]

In the interest of national efficiency, and, indeed, in hopes of satisfying the nationwide economic interests that had emerged in the street-railway cases, Taft embraced thorough-going wartime nationalism. Unlike the *New York Times*, for example, which saw the federalization of the streetcars as a necessary sacrifice to be accepted in a time of national crisis, Taft felt no such reluctance to remove local problems from local control. His greatest concern lay not with the health of the industry, nor its potential reform, nor the consequences of setting wartime precedents. Taft simply wanted to see the traction lines operating smoothly and without delay. The NWLB's caseload indicated to him that the street railways were losing skilled operators to better-paying jobs and that workmen who did not change jobs often disrupted the transportation lines in bids for higher pay. Both tendencies, Taft implied, had helped to make the performance of the traction companies unacceptable; and both tendencies could be corrected from Washington. The NWLB, he as much as stated, had a mandate to correct wage inadequacies. Congress, on the other hand, had clear authority to set new fares. In fact, he pointed out, it had done so during the Civil War. In time of war, he wrote matter of factly, Congress could waive the rights of the public to low fares and the rights of the state to sanctify them through local franchises.[26]

In contrast to Taft, William L. Ransom, chief counsel for the Public Service Commission of the First District of New York State, spoke for state authorities who wanted to retain their jurisdictions. Writing in *The Survey* that July, Ransom scored street-railway riders for their "something-for-nothing" attitude, but he trained his heaviest guns on the transit companies themselves. Ransom characterized their requests for federal relief as "a clamor to escape the day of reckoning and readjustment" for mistakes of the past. The urban systems, Ransom said, wanted the same kind of advantages granted to the steam railroads under federal administration. However, he added, they did not want to be embarrassed by the states' suggestions for public protection. "They know that federal action would sweep franchises, contracts, commission orders, state laws, and decisions of state courts into discard, for at least the period of the war. Can you blame them for trying to get away with it?"[27]

In Ransom's mind, the solution to the crisis was for the companies, municipalities, and state authorities to work out long-standing problems over current franchises. The New York State Court of Appeals had already paved the way for fare increases, despite existing contracts, with the mutual consent of both a traction line and the municipality it served. Because of that, Ransom saw a clear opportunity to abolish lingering inequities: "Old franchises, granted in reckless disregard of public rights, as to duration, terms, and the like, may now be put upon a fair, modern basis."[28] To him, federal direction posed an immediate threat to preexisting power and a long-range threat to reformist goals.

President Wilson's decision reflected his essential agreement with Ransom and with the sources most worried about federal encroachment on local authority. Neither the hearing before the NWLB nor the public discussion that followed it had weakened the president's faith in the feasibility of voluntary cooperation among labor, management, and the public. Nor had he changed his opinion that the NWLB could facilitate that cooperation. Federally directed relief for the street-railway industry was not a "wise" policy, he wrote to Taft and Walsh on 9 July, for the state commissions were equipped with firsthand knowledge of transit problems. The commissions, he believed, could provide better solutions than could a federal bureaucracy. "The danger in the present circumstance," Wilson said, "is that we will hasten to erect federal machinery which cannot . . . deal with the complicated questions . . . and which will unnecessarily supplant thoroughly organized and entirely competent bodies already in existence." The president therefore urged the NWLB to exert "its full influence in bringing about a coordination" with existing local bodies.[29]

The reactions of the joint chairmen to the president's decision differed sharply. At Murray Bay, where he relaxed for a few days at his Canadian retreat, Taft had anxiously awaited Wilson's letter, which Walsh forwarded from Washington without comment. Dismayed at its contents, Taft unburdened himself to Walsh. "The trouble with our dear President," he said, "is that he finds it easier to say 'No' to the things he does not suggest himself than to say 'Yes,' and he subsequently has to be driven into it."[30] Walsh, however, remained calm. Local authorities, he assured Taft's newspaperman friend, Gus J. Karger, could perform properly.[31] A member of the Public Ownership League, Walsh worried less than Taft did about the fate of private utility companies. Nor did he believe the president's failure to support federal action would adversely influence the awards that he and Taft would make. Two weeks before any were announced, he even predicted privately to a friend, Harry Tammen of the *Denver Post*, exactly how he and Taft would act: "In practically all [the cases] . . . there will be a swift increase in wages," but the joint chairmen would suggest to rate-regulating authorities "that existing fares be increased to . . . make it possible for the company to grant the increased wages."[32] As long as the NWLB awards augured change, Walsh was more willing than Taft to trust in voluntarism and moral suasion. If he was right, the NWLB could use voluntarism as a tool for social reform, not only in the street-railway cases, but in general.

Taft remained so convinced "that something is going to happen"[33] that the NWLB, at his request, kept the president's letter confidential during the last two weeks of July while more hearings completed the street-railway evidence that the board had been amassing since May. The joint chairmen listened to witnesses in Scranton, Chicago, and Newark. Three-men teams of examiners took testimony in Chicago, New York, St. Louis, and Columbus,[34] gathering data in no less than fourteen cases. At length, under pressure from the Amalgamated Association of Street and Electric Railway employees, Taft and Walsh decided to hand down their awards as scheduled[35]—despite an almost deafening silence from the Wilson administration.

The twenty-two awards of 31 July contained few surprises. The joint chairmen raised wages, significantly, for experienced motormen and conductors according to three general standards: 48 cents an hour in larger cities; 45 cents in second-class cities; and 42 cents in communities with recognizably low costs of living. To common laborers, they generally awarded 40 to 42 cents. Attached to each award, furthermore, was the financial recommendation that Walsh had predicted. Even more important, the recommendation placed the responsibility for raising the fares directly on the public:

> In justice, the public should pay an adequate war compensation for a service which cannot be rendered except for war prices. The credit of these companies in floating bonds is gone. Their ability to borrow on short notes is most limited. In the face of added expenses which this and other awards of needed and fair compensation to their employees will involve, such credit will completely disappear. Bankruptcy, receiverships, and demoralization with failure of service, must be the result. Hence our urgent recommendation on this head.

To underscore their point, the joint chairmen reminded communities that "the history of the relations between street railways and the municipalities in which they operate" was not at issue.[36]

Among the seventeen cities affected by the awards of 31 July, one in particular, Buffalo, remembered the history of its traction line with such vengeance that cooperation between local and federal authorities appeared impossible. The battle in that city between the International Railway Company and taxpayers was well underway even before the NWLB granted experienced motormen and conductors a 41.2 percent advance, which increased their wages from 34 to 48 cents.[37] After the city council gave International tentative permission to raise its nickel fare to 6 cents in May, angry citizens had demanded a referendum. By the beginning of August, with the referendum still three weeks away, the Public Service Commission had not yet ruled on the fare increase. Against that background, the NWLB's award put voluntarism to an extraordinary test at Buffalo. Indeed, the award was unique. Unlike awards affecting other cities, it conditioned the increase in wages specifically on the implementation of the 6-cent fare. In Buffalo, it appeared when the award was announced that the public would not pay war prices to the company, even though the company's many enemies fully supported the NWLB's wage increases to its employees.[38]

The Buffalo Central Council of Business Men's Taxpayers' and Citizens' Associations and its supporters wanted International to abide by the "Milburn" contract, in which the city in 1892 had accorded the traction lines generous terms in return for a nickel fare. In their view, International, which had subsequently absorbed its only two competitors, had taken advantage of the city for years. It had provided increasingly poor service, reduced the number of cars in operation by half since 1913, and, all the while, had paid employees substandard wages and stockholders substantial dividends. Worse still, the traction company had prevailed on the city council to support a fare increase while it enjoyed a healthy surplus. Those surplus funds, said the Central Council, should be used for maintenance and for increasing wages to meet the NWLB's award. The 6-cent fare that the NWLB had written into the award, it believed, would only reward the company's unacceptable performance.[39]

George Clinton, a Buffalo attorney in the forefront of citizen protest, resented the NWLB's attitude almost as much as the company's. For Clinton, the award, when coupled with Taft's well-publicized opinions about federal war powers, in effect asked the city to surrender its contract rights. In three pointed letters to Taft during August, Clinton challenged both the joint chairmen's interpretation of the law and the merits of the award. The Milburn contract, he wrote, secured a fundamental property right of the city, one sanctioned by both state and federal constitutions. To Clinton's mind, Congress could no more "waive" those rights than it could waive the state's right to impeach its own governor. "War," he concluded, "does not override the Constitution of the United States, revolution may." Yet Clinton did not object to a fare increase per se. The people, he explained to Taft, "would cheerfully submit to the payment of any [necessary] fare" as long as the city could shed the current street-railway leadership. Either governmental ownership or a receivership would provide good service to the city and ample wages for the employees. More important, neither of these alternatives, which the award precluded, would infringe upon "the absolute rights of our citizens" or establish a precedent to give the company a postwar advantage.[40]

The only point of agreement between the embattled company and its many detractors during August was on the impracticability of the NWLB's award. Even before Buffalo residents rejected the fare increase by a resounding vote of five to one, International asked the board to reopen the case. The company's president, E. G. Connette, contended that even a 6-cent fare would provide insufficient funds to finance the wage schedules ordered by Taft and Walsh.[41] After the referendum on 20 August, the Central Council of Business Men's Taxpayers' and Citizens' Associations accelerated its own campaign to persuade the NWLB to sanction the wage increases anyway and to award further advances as necessary to keep the men on the cars.[42] Some 160 like-minded railway patrons petitioned the state Public Service Commission to order International to maintain its men and equipment before paying further dividends or to lose its franchise.[43] But the NWLB paid little heed to either side. Its refusal to reconsider the Buffalo case, coupled with the continued activity of local interests working at cross purposes, insured a deadlock that summer.

The stalemate continued into autumn. Then, apparently, the company and its employees determined to get together to get what they both wanted. For twenty-four days, the street-railway workers crippled the city in a strike for higher wages and fares. Staggered by abuse from the Chamber of Commerce, local bankers, and downtown merchants who claimed the loss of half of their business, the Buffalo City Council had little choice but to enter patient but purposeful negotiations with the company. In November, it brought International to its knees. Henceforth, the city would appoint the traction line's board of directors. The company, which already owed $250,000 in back pay under the terms of the NWLB's decision, agreed to abide by the award. Taft and Walsh, in turn, gave International until April 1919 to meet the new pay schedules, and the city council promised in the meantime to facilitate a reconsideration of a fare increase.[44] Thus concluded, the compromise held something for everyone, especially for the carmen and the railway patrons.

The long struggle in Buffalo paralleled a similar standoff in the Deep South, where an ill-conceived award proved racially unacceptable and, in part, financially unsound. The New Orleans Railway and Light Company paid among the lowest wages of any major city line, this because the cost of living in the city was considered low and because many of the company's employees were black. The award of 31 July raised the hourly wage of experienced conductors and motormen from 24½ to 42 cents—a 71.4 percent advance—and increased the wages of other employees across the board by the same percentage, with the added proviso that no experienced worker earn less than 42 cents.[45] What made the award controversial in New Orleans was that the 42-cent minimum applied to black common laborers and that the 71.4 percent raise inadvertently provided a disproportionately high wage to three classes of skilled employees.

The racial implications of the award were especially troublesome. In July 1918, the street railway paid black common laborers 15 to 18 cents, a wage slightly better than that which steam railroads in the city paid to the same class. But the NWLB's award would drastically alter that. The joint chairmen's wage decision meant as much as a 180 percent advance for experienced unskilled blacks, and it meant that those blacks would earn more than newly employed white motormen and conductors, who, during their first three months on the job, would earn only 38 cents. If the award was put into effect, D. D. Curran, president of the New Orleans Railway and Light Company, predicted such high wages for blacks would "bring about demoralization." Because the black workers were "of the same class as Southern farm labor," he told Taft and Walsh, a 42-cent wage would also disrupt "labor conditions in this city and in the agricultural districts of this state."[46] The award, if implemented as written, Curran seemed to be saying, would upset more than the company's social mores. It would also disturb fundamental economic and occupational arrangements that were common between the races throughout Louisiana.

To complicate matters still further, the award quickly became the plaything of politicians in an election year. The New Orleans city administration, unlike its counterpart in Buffalo, had sole authority to raise utility rates and was under no express compulsion from the NWLB to do so. In July, the administration had seemed ready to volunteer a fare increase to accommodate anticipated wage adjustments, but it stalled in August. The city's change of heart reflected the administration's sudden disenchantment with organized labor. From the city's point of view, the street-railway problem by August had become—politically speaking—a labor problem.[47]

The specifics of the NWLB's award apparently had nothing to do with the administration's decision to stand by the nickel fare. "The underlying reason," two NWLB examiners, Arthur Sturgis and Joseph Chiesa, reported after a brief investigation, "appears to be that local politics at present largely govern the city's actions." The administration supported a candidate whom organized labor opposed in the senatorial primary slated for 10 September. Labor had made an issue of the fare hike, and the administration was afraid to do anything controversial on the eve of the election. In this already confused atmosphere, the local president of the carmen's union, in "his individual capacity as a taxpayer," opposed a fare increase. He was a local politician and not even employed by the company. Given all that, key figures in the controversy had admitted to the examiners that the fare would not be raised before the primary.[48] In New Orleans, voluntary cooperation had been scuttled in the transitory search for votes.

Examiners Sturgis and Chiesa, who came to New Orleans in late August, found themselves not only fascinated by local politics but also sympathetic to the company's request for a review of the award. Even before Taft and Walsh ordered wages increased, the company had needed financial relief, and would have ended 1918 with a deficit of $538,000. If the award was effected, the fare raised from 5 cents to 7 cents, transfers abolished, and gas and electric rates increased by 30 percent, the company would still end the year with fixed charges of $165,000 outstanding. The joint chairmen's across-the-board wage advance, Sturgis and Chiesa concluded, had added unfairly to the company's woes. As for the award's impact on race relations, the examiners offered no comment except to affirm that the company already paid competitive rates to blacks. However, the proposed rates for machinists, pipe fitters, and carpenters clearly needed to be "harmonized" with other standards in the city. A chart that they submitted illustrated their point:

	Union Rates	Railroad Wages	Company Wage	Shipbuilding Wage	NWLB Wage
Machinist First Class	68.5¢	68¢	58¢	62.5–72.5¢	99.4¢
Pipe Fitter		68¢	62.5¢	72.5¢	$1.07
Carpenter	50¢	42.5–58¢	50¢	65–70¢	85¢

SOURCE: Letter, Sturgis and Chiesa to Lauck, 31 August 1918.

At the end of August, Frank Walsh quickly agreed that the award deserved review, and he and Taft reworked New Orleans wages in October. As the joint chairmen set about adjusting the pay schedules, Taft pondered lifestyles in the urban South. A Negro, Taft thought, could live "in reasonable comfort" more cheaply than could a white man. In the future, of course, conditions between the races should be equalized, but, he told Walsh, "in the short time during which our jurisdiction lasts, the difficulty of changing is so great that we ought not to make orders based on a reform of an actual racial difference in a manner of life." At first, Taft suggested that the minimum at New Orleans be dropped to 36 cents an hour, among the lowest minimums the NWLB granted throughout the war, for "we could count probably on the living wage for the white laborer being from two to three or four cents higher than that of common labor negroes." In the end, however, he yielded to more liberal sentiments and accepted 38 cents, which meant just about doubling the minimums for blacks.[49] The minimums for motormen and conductors remained the same as those prescribed in the original award. The greatest change, of course, occurred in the adjusted rates for men in the three skilled classifications that the examiners had pointed up. For those men, the joint chairmen assigned a flat 10-cent-an-hour raise.[50] That provided the harmony that the examiners and the company had yearned for and that the union then protested against to no avail.

Ultimately, Frank Walsh's reliance on voluntary cooperation proved as successful in New Orleans as it did in Buffalo. New Orleans was threatened with strikes and violence that November when it appeared that the city would honor its implicit promise of July to raise utility rates. The city did, yet no disturbances followed the city council's decision to grant the Railway and Light Company a 30 percent increase in gas and electric rates or its approval of a 6-cent carfare effective immediately.[51]

In other cities throughout the country, traction companies, city councils, and private citizens reacted to the NWLB's awards and the publicity surrounding them in much the same way as they had in Buffalo and New Orleans. Companies cried for added income; streetcar riders insisted on the nickel fare; and city councils and state public service commissions, more often than not, delayed action until midautumn. There were, however, earlier indications that the public would eventually pay war prices for what it used. Between 1 July and 15 September, street railways in twenty-four cities, excluding interurban lines, received fare increases, 75 percent of them to 6 cents.[52] Although most of those increases came in cities not directly affected by NWLB awards, nonetheless it appeared that Taft and Walsh had begun to affect their national constituency by force of example.

Notwithstanding the random success of voluntary cooperation in the street-railway crisis, both the industry and the NWLB continued the push for direct federal relief. Until October, some hope remained that the administration might yet change its mind. Then McAdoo definitively restated the official position that under no circumstances would the federal government assume the problems of local utility corporations.[53] That left the War Finance Corporation as the utilities' only remaining avenue for federal relief. The WFC, which had $500,000,000 to lend to war industries was, however, of limited value to the street-railway industry. Because loans were available only to companies with good credit, few street railways qualified for assistance.[54] By November, in consequence of the industry's failure to secure federally imposed efficiency, the AERA changed tactics. At their annual meeting in New York, AERA representatives endorsed public ownership of the transit companies as "the most obvious remedy for the perils now confronting the street railway industry."[55] Ideologically, that last response must have pleased Frank Walsh.

Throughout the summer and into the autumn, the problems of street-railway wages caused as many internal problems for the NWLB as it did for the companies themselves. Taft, who was pleased with the standards that he and Walsh had set, told James Ernest King of the Boston *Evening Transcript* that street-railway employees had been "underpaid for years." He also knew that he had displeased the employer members who had selected him chairman. They complained, he observed, that "the Board is constituted of five employers, five trade-unionists, one advocate of the trades-unionists, and one Judge."[56] At the same time, the former president deeply resented the effort that he perceived Walsh and his followers on the NWLB staff were making to paint the awards as even more progressive than they actually were. Like the NWLB employer members, Taft protested, in particular, against the interpretation the Walsh faction gave to the awards of 31 July.[57]

Two NWLB publicists, Charles Sweeney and Hiram Moderwell, clung to the time-honored Walsh approach to reporting—use the press to labor's best advantage. Their estimates of wage increases in the larger cities of 35 to 40 percent and in the smaller cities of up to 65 percent made headlines around the nation.

These estimates also enraged Taft and his conservative supporters. "There is somebody about the Labor Board," Taft wrote to Iowa newspaperman Luther Brewer, "who deliberately exaggerates our decisions in favor of labor and misrepresents them for the press."[58] The average wage increase, he believed, had been from about 40 cents to about 48 cents, or about 20 percent. Such a figure, "in view of the increased cost of living," was nothing more than "a moderate advance," he explained to King. Taft's emotions ran especially strong because he himself had set the rates and Walsh had merely "accepted my suggestions."[59] To counter the publicity, Taft appealed to Jett Lauck: "You will have suggestions advanced that the entourage in the . . . War Labor Board is so prejudiced in favor of the workers' side that even a just statement of what's done cannot be made, and thus create a settled prejudice against the Board that will greatly interfere with its usefulness. For this reason, please look up the matter, and if it is Sweeney, who is responsible for it, let him see this letter."⁶⁰ Taft's main objective, therefore, was that the board create a more conservative impression, not that it make more conservative rulings.

Sweeney, who saw the letter, was indignant. In a comprehensive defense of the staff analysis, he explained the origins of the statistics reported and refused to legitimize Taft's complaints. First, he told Lauck, he had not "emphasized," "enlarged," or "exaggerated" the real gains that the workers had secured in the awards, and he could not be responsible for the attention the joint chairmen's decisions had received in the newspapers. "It is true," he continued, "that the Board's decisions up to date have, in almost every case, been decidedly in favor of the men. The news value of the decisions has been found invariably in what the men have gained." Second, Frank Walsh had approved the text of the entire report. In the absence of verbatim copies of the awards, Sweeney and Moderwell had sat up until four o'clock one morning trying to analyze the wage hikes accurately. Taft had been out of town, but Walsh had worked with the reporters on their analysis. Walsh himself had calculated the 35 to 40 percent advance reported for larger cities.⁶¹

The report was controversial, in part, because it analyzed the advances awarded to beginners. Sweeney justified using those wage levels as the point of analysis because of the heavy labor turnover in the industry. In any event, there was room for misunderstanding regardless of what level the reporters had chosen. Pay scales in the industry traditionally had been graduated variously, according to experience; the NWLB had accelerated and unified the pace of advancement as well as the pay schedules for each rank. While the body of awards thus helped doubly to standardize working conditions, it also made analysis difficult. The awards had been meant to eliminate the wide discrepancies in preexisting conditions throughout the industry. Therefore, there was no general correlation between the percentages advanced to beginners and those awarded to experienced men. However distorted the report may have seemed to Taft, Sweeney contended, any other kind of analytical summation suitable for general readership in the newspapers would have been no less incorrect.⁶²

A glance at the awards themselves indicates that Taft was simply wrong. Wage increases for beginners were not consistently higher than for more advanced employees, as his complaint implied. Furthermore, his belief that wage hikes nowhere amounted to as much as 65 percent was nonsense. Beginners in Galesburg, Illinois, and experienced New Orleans men clearly had been awarded that much.

Finally, the joint chairman's assertion that 40 cents an hour was the general average pay in the industry before the awards was also incorrect. Only street-railway workers in Detroit, after a year's service, and in Omaha, after the fifth year, had received a 40-cent maximum.[63]

In retrospect, it seems that the real truth about that battery of street-railway awards lies somewhere between Taft's estimates of his own work and the Walsh-Sweeney-Moderwell analysis. That becomes clear when one examines broadly the impact of the awards on the wages of experienced workers. Until those awards were handed down, experienced street-railway conductors in the twenty-two cases received an average pay of 34 cents. The average wage advance for those men amounted to 33 percent, but the New Orleans award, the only decision in the South, distorted average calculations. In Missouri, Illinois, Kansas, Ohio, and Michigan, thirteen streetcar awards resulted in a 29.5 percent wage increase for experienced employees and an average maximum of 45 cents. In Pennsylvania, New York, and New Jersey, eight awards provided an average 23.8 percent wage hike and a 44-cent average maximum.

Although the awards of 31 July were controversial, the patterns established in the submission, investigation, and disputation of the twenty-two cases prevailed in subsequent street-railway cases that the joint chairmen settled. Before the end of May 1919, the board handed down about 100 such awards, settled 40 strikes, and diverted 98 threatened walkouts, while it increased wages on 110 lines. The wage advances that it ordered directly affected 78,730 employees and added $30,000,000 to street-railway operating costs. In all but three cases, the employees were organized, and in those three, the board assumed jurisdiction because employees who had tried to join the Amalgamated Association of Street and Electric Railway Employees had been fired. In most cases, employees demanded and received, in addition to wage increases, the right to bargain collectively, the right to organize, and the abolition of individual contracts. In fifty-six cases, the awards made financial recommendations on behalf of the companies; and about half of the time those recommendations spurred fare increases to help ease monetary burdens, which the wage increases had, of course, compounded. Minimum wages assigned to beginners and common laborers averaged 42 cents, with the highest minimum at 44 cents and the lowest at 36 cents. Maximums, for experienced men, ranged from 40 to 65 cents, the single most common figure being about 45 cents. The greatest similarity among the street-railway cases, however, lay in the remarkable degree to which voluntarism actually worked. Almost all of the disputes were submitted jointly by employers and employees, and almost all of the awards ultimately took effect.⁶⁴

Much of the continuity implicit in the awards after 31 July resulted from the efforts of Charlton Ogburn, whom Jett Lauck appointed to lead a special division of street-railway examiners within the NWLB staff. Ogburn, a lawyer from Savannah, Georgia, and brother of the NWLB's cost-of-living analyst, gathered evidence for the joint chairmen and routinely tabulated the results of awards as they came down. More than anyone else, he understood the impact of the NWLB's settlements. Like Charles Sweeney, Ogburn believed that the real news of the awards lay in the wage advances themselves. Unlike Sweeney, however, Ogburn was unable to convince himself of the magnitude of those advances. Like Taft, he believed that the keynote of the NWLB's work was moderation. In May 1919, as he summarized the board's awards, he concluded somewhat reluctantly that the financial plight of the industry, although officially disregarded in determining wage schedules, had made an unofficial impact on the joint chairmen's judgment. The NWLB-sanctioned wages were "rather low." The "true wages," he maintained, "that is, wages defined in terms of purchasing power, have not increased at all, but the wages have increased only as the cost of living has increased."⁶⁵

The street-railway crisis in 1918 put the dynamics of voluntarism to its most sustained test in the NWLB's experience. The body of awards for that industry reflected fundamental refinements of the NWLB's principles, which the joint chairmen developed and applied consistently in the face of initial opposition from their business colleagues. The joint chairmen saw the NWLB's chief responsibility in street-railway disputes to be the maintenance of order through the preservation of justice. To encourage cooperation, when they did what they had determined to do, they agreed with industry spokesmen and union officials that the federal government should, in effect, subsidize the crippled traction industry. When the government did not, Taft and Walsh based their wage awards solely on the NWLB's commitment to a living wage. The riding public, in turn, often agreed to absorb some of the costs. The Amalgamated Association of Street and Electric Railway Employees, whose leadership put its hopes in the NWLB throughout the war, maintained a fairly cooperative attitude toward inevitable delays in the mediation/arbitration process. The joint chairmen's attitude, the frequent increases in fares, and the union's patience combined to facilitate the healthy wage increases that became the hallmark of the board's work. Despite Taft's belief that the advances were only "moderate" and Ogburn's conclusion that wages remained "rather low" even after the awards, street-railway workers in 1918, in large measure as a result of the NWLB's work, averaged a 3 percent increase in real wages. By 1919, again largely because of the NWLB, their real wages increased another 11 percent, which brought their purchasing power in that year to its highest level since 1905.[66] Although street-railway employees failed to win the kind of dramatic advances in real wages that some common laborers enjoyed at the hands of the NWLB, their reliance, by default, on voluntarism brought positive gains.

 # Meeting the Government's Necessity

> If the Government makes a gun, the people will work eight hours and if some contractor makes that gun for the Government, it may be the same gun, the Government does not insist that eight hours be the work day. Now, then, labor feels that that is not fair. It is not right and it is the cause of unrest and strife all over the country.
>
> —T. A. Rickert, NWLB meeting, 11 July 1918

Among the NWLB's principles, none was more difficult to interpret than the statement on hours of labor: "The basic eight-hour day," said the board, "is recognized as applying in all cases in which existing law requires it. In all other cases the question of hours of labor shall be settled with due regard to governmental necessities and the welfare, health, and proper comfort of the workers." In the context of 1918, that principle meant almost anything one wanted it to mean. NWLB employer members, eager to protect existing conditions in private industry, interpreted the hours principle even more narrowly than they had the principle on the living wage. The representatives of organized labor, conversely, considered the general adoption of the basic eight-hour day among their highest priorities. The opposite aims of the two groups on wage policy also colored the debate over hours. The business representatives, for example, maintained that labor's enthusiasm for "basic" hours was nothing more than an ill-disguised grab for higher pay. The difficulties within the NWLB over hours were further compounded by the inability of other governmental agencies to define "existing law." Persistent lack of unanimity within the NWLB resulted for the first time in the use of NWLB umpires—private citizens appointed by the president to act as sole arbiters on behalf of a divided board. In that capacity, men such as Henry Ford and Walter Clark became powerful forces in defining the NWLB's policy on hours and reinforced, in the process, the fragile vitality of wartime voluntarism.

In the first year of the European war, the eight-hour day movement in America was embryonic. Hours legislation had long been on the statute books. Mechanics and laborers "employed by or on behalf of" the United States government had been granted the eight-hour day as early as 1868, but this first federal legislation had been largely ignored because it lacked penalties for disobedience. Subsequent congressional measures in 1892 and 1912 had strengthened the eight-hour law, the latter imposing a fine of $5 for each violation of the act.[1] State governments, too, had begun to set the standard workday for public employees at eight hours in the 1880s. Organized bituminous coal miners negotiated eight-hour settlements after the turn of the century, and between 1907 and 1913, fourteen states put miners on eight-hour days. During those same years, eight states passed eight-hour acts for certain classes of railroad employees.[2] In 1915, however, the movement began to accelerate as 171,978 additional American men and women had their hours reduced to eight.[3]

Organized labor won a major breakthrough in hours legislation in 1916, which seemingly augured well as the preparedness drive got underway. Under threat of a general railroad strike, Congress adopted the Adamson Act that year, which provided the basic eight-hour day for some 400,000 members of the railroad brotherhoods.[4] (The basic day, with its provision for overtime pay rates, was far more to labor's liking than the actual day that merely limited hours.) By then, increasing support for hours legislation, especially in hazardous industries and on governmental contract work, had begun to generate momentum for more regulations. In 1916, 180,000 anthracite coal miners began working an eight-hour day. By 1918, 116,000 machinists, largely employed by firms with government contracts, had secured eight-hour schedules. From June 1917 until 1 July 1918, about 600,000 more workers from shipyards and packinghouses to lumber mills and harness factories earned the basic or actual eight-hour day through the efforts of cabinet members, private manufacturers, federal arbitrators, governmental adjustment boards, and powerful labor leaders. All told, so the Bureau of Labor Statistics reported, 1,440,532 American laborers had their basic or actual workday reduced to eight hours between January 1915 and June 1918.[5]

War necessities, clearly obvious in early 1917, suddenly invested the basic day with greater appeal from the federal government's point of view. As early as March, an amendment to the Naval Appropriations Act permitted the president to suspend the federal eight-hour law of 1912 in times of national emergency. Because of the need to expedite production, Wilson then issued an executive order suspending the actual eight-hour day in favor of the basic eight-hour day, thereby authorizing federal workers to exceed eight hours on the job with time and a half for overtime.[6] The executive order indicated that the president remained committed enough to the eight-hour concept to require that workers in federal employ be rewarded for working longer. Nothing else was clear. The war had changed everything when it made the government an employer in production areas long considered the bastion of private industry. Neither the amendment nor the executive order, however, altered the provisions in the act of 1912 that delineated who were government workers and who were not.

By the time that the NWLB began to consider the implications of its hours principle, both the War Department and the War Labor Policies Board had already grappled with problems concerning the now-ambivalent status of many employees. Central to the actions of both agencies was Felix Frankfurter. In January 1917, Frankfurter had successfully argued before the Supreme Court the constitutionality of Oregon's ten-hour law, which also permitted three hours of overtime daily.[7] After America went to war in April, Secretary of War Newton D. Baker asked Frankfurter to interpret the federal hours law —as altered by the war and the executive order—for the department's use in its relations with civilian employees at home. The report that Frankfurter submitted to Baker at the end of September 1917, spelled out the kinds of contracts that the law excepted, the limitations to those exceptions, and the best means that Frankfurter could devise to comply with the law.[8]

Even on subcontracted jobs, Frankfurter concluded, mechanics and laborers were to be paid time and a half after eight hours. But the law of 1912 applied only when the raw materials could be identified with the product earmarked for governmental purchase. It excepted from hours regulation the manufacture of tools and machinery that were used to fill governmental contracts because the tools would be used thereafter on nongovernmental products.[9]

Certain kinds of governmental work and even certain kinds of products being custom-made for the government also fell outside the perimeters of the hours law, said Frankfurter. Persons engaged in the transmission of intelligence, levee maintenance, and flood control, for example, had no recourse to its provisions. Nor could persons who worked in the manufacture of goods normally available on the open market generally take advantage of the hours law. If, however, those goods were altered sufficiently because of governmental specifications, the men and women who made them could fall within the terms of the law. For those people, Frankfurter decided, the classification of materials was all-important: The "species of wagons or arms should be considered rather than the general class or genus. Thus 'revolvers' or 'ambulances,' as the case may be, instead of 'arms' or 'wagons,' seems the proper division to be applied."[10]

In Frankfurter's view, the government's own record of manufacture limited the exemptions from the hours law. If the federal government ordinarily produced certain products, or had a history of producing them, the law specified that private production of those same products for governmental use must obey the basic eight-hour scheme. Because of that, Frankfurter explained, the federal government could not evade its own statute by farming out contracts to private industry for supplies such as cannon powder and ammunition for small arms.[11]

The wage stipulations of the basic day, as applied now to that law, meant that firms whose employees fell under the provisions of the law could continue to pay piece rates if that was their normal means of payment. The firms that objected to establishing general hourly wages could pay what amounted to piece-and-a-half for overtime hours, or they could establish a standard hourly pay scale and then give the worker the option of taking that, including time and a half for overtime, instead of his piecework earnings. The one thing a firm could not do was to raise the flat rate for piecework in order to pay for work to be completed after eight hours on the job.[12]

As comprehensive as the Frankfurter report was, it was difficult to translate into practical usage. Standard application of the hours regulation for employees working for federal governmental projects also lagged because agencies outside the War Department were free to follow different guidelines. This general lack of consensus within the government itself inevitably led to a broad-based attempt to unify federal application of the basic eight-hour day as required by law.

On behalf of the federal government, therefore, the War Labor Policies Board, which Frankfurter led, undertook the coordination of federal hours policy in June 1918. That month a policies board committee recommended new criteria for regulating the hours of work on government-contracted projects. Samuel Rosensohn, counsel for the committee, pointed out the major problem:

> In many cases workers in the same factories engaged on different articles needed by the Government were treated differently. In more numerous instances workers in adjoining factories engaged on Government work, by reason of the nature of the articles manufactured, were treated differently. These rulings,

which in light of present conditions would seem arbitrary to the workers (whatever historical justification they may have), have created in the workers a sense of injustice and of unfair discrimination which has been responsible for a great many labor troubles.[13]

Rosensohn concluded that blanket enforcement of the executive order on all work done for the government would indeed alleviate one of the country's most serious labor problems.

Rosensohn's proposed solution to the problem, however, dripped with caution and rejected some of the earlier Frankfurter recommendations. Blanket enforcement of the basic eight-hour day on all work done for the government, Rosensohn believed, would disturb conditions in the factories, upset their "well-developed organization," and prevent maximum efficiency. He also upheld two major objections that private employers raised against extensive application of the executive order. First, it could create a precedent for private industry after the war; and second, most employers did both private work and government-contracted orders. If the basic eight-hour day became mandatory on all governmental jobs, the employers would be forced to pay the same wages for purely civilian work. Rosensohn therefore recommended that all mechanics and construction workers *directly* employed by the government be assigned the basic eight-hour day, with time and a half for overtime. By strict interpretation of the law, employees on subcontracted work were not protected by the hours legislation; nor should they be, Rosensohn argued, until the War Labor Policies Board committee could negotiate with manufacturers under governmental contract in order to determine the feasibility of adopting the basic eight-hour day during the war.[14]

The Rosensohn report was intended to do more than point up the difficulties in determining governmental hours policy. Fundamentally, it was meant to centralize all further decisions in the War Labor Policies Board. To achieve that, the report urged other federal adjustment boards to award the basic eight-hour day and overtime only when specifically required by law; and to insure uniform action, Rosensohn recommended that any other board refer to his committee when it needed an interpretation of the altered law of 1912 or of the executive order of 24 March 1917 to help to settle a labor dispute.[15]

The NWLB, not surprisingly, decided to act independently of the War Labor Policies Board and to formulate its own application of the executive order. That meant that it had also to define its own broad statement on hours,[16] which had been written to satisfy the widely divergent goals of the NWLB's business and labor representatives. As in the living-wage discussions, both prior actions of other adjustment agencies and data collected by Lauck's staff would help to shape the board's ultimate rulings, but the undercurrent of personal distrust and disagreement within the NWLB itself would also color its decision making.

The fundamental difference between the actual eight-hour day and the basic eight-hour day played no small part in predetermining the NWLB members' positions. The American Federation of Labor traditionally opposed straight eight-hour legislation because limited hours decreased, at least temporarily, workers' earnings. The basic day, however, as established in the Adamson Act, the executive order, and the packinghouse awards, avoided that pitfall. The National Industrial Conference Board, antagonistic to those measures, understood full well why labor applauded them. Overtime became "operative at the end of an 8-hour work period without shortening the actual hours of work." A measure such as the executive order, therefore, changed "an hours-of-service [act] to a wage statute."[17]

The board's first major encounter with the implications of its hours principle came simultaneously with its debate over wages in Waynesboro in July. Although an NWLB section had already put certain employees in the newsprint papermaking industry on the basic eight-hour day,[18] the board had yet to put an entire plant in any industry on that schedule. The test case came when the employers and laborers of the Worthington Pump Company jointly submitted two disputes. In Buffalo, the employees asked merely for the basic eight-hour day, but in East Cambridge, Massachusetts, they demanded a wage hike as well. Loyall Osborne and Fred Hewitt, who were assigned the Worthington cases, appealed to the full board for help on the afternoon of 9 July. They could agree on a suitable wage in East Cambridge, they explained, but not on the proper hours to award at either plant.[19]

Hewitt was ready to put both plants on the basic eight-hour day and found his rationale therefor in the board's own words. The NWLB's principle allowed its members to weigh "governmental necessities," a phrase that he interpreted more broadly than had Osborne. In the Worthington cases, "governmental necessities" appeared to Hewitt to be the key phrase. Because the men in the Buffalo shipyards and, indeed, in shipyards all along the Great Lakes worked a basic eight-hour day, to deny the Worthington men—who performed essentially the same duties—the same pay scale would likely interrupt continuous production. The Worthington men, Hewitt suspected, would not stay at their jobs while better terms remained so clearly in force elsewhere.[20]

Osborne, in turn, maintained, with strict technical accuracy, that the federal hours regulation did not apply to private establishments such as the Worthington firm. The Buffalo Worthington plant, he explained, had agreed to supply materials for the Emergency Fleet Corporation on that very understanding. Furthermore, he pointed out, the judge advocate general had interpreted the law in favor of the company's position. Osborne's firm grasp of the limits of the law was due, in part, to his familiarity with governmental work at his own Westinghouse Company. Westinghouse, unhampered by governmental hours restrictions, produced engines for the Fleet Corporation such as those produced by Worthington in Buffalo and giant turbines for the Navy, as did the East Cambridge Worthington plant. Because the Worthington plants had undertaken war production on the assurance that the basic eight-hour day would not be necessary, he concluded, "I can't see why there should be an imposition of that . . . now."[21]

The Worthington debates that followed seemed tailor-made for the NWLB's members to develop their preconceived ideas about how to translate principle into action. Catch phrases in the body of principles peppered the remarks of Walsh and the labor members, who argued that "maximum production," "the health and reasonable comfort" of the workers, and "governmental necessities" all demanded the application of the basic eight-hour day in this and untold other future cases. For Osborne and the employer representatives, consideration of the "custom of localities" and the NWLB's pledge to uphold "existing conditions" took precedence. Osborne also knew full well that the Worthington Buffalo employees intended their case as a test— one that would enable other Buffalo workers, if the Worthington men won, to push for a basic eight-hour day in every private shop throughout the city. Osborne, who was determined to prevent their winning, objected to the idea of precedent as much as anything else. The NICB appointees dismissed the "health and comfort" rationale that the labor members fell back on as a moot point. The employees at Worthington did not seek shorter hours in order to gain time to spend with their families or to improve their minds. They only wanted higher wages for the same hours that they currently worked.[22]

Beneath all the rhetoric, more than an hours policy was actually at stake. Perhaps without knowing it, the NWLB's members were debating the government's role in regulating American industry and the NWLB's place in governmental leadership. Privately, the employer members worried about governmental concessions to labor. The labor members, in turn, questioned the employers' emphasis upon procedure and their adherence to a fundamentalist interpretation of the NWLB's principles. Thus, like the debate on the living wage, the debate concerning hours prompted emotional outbursts from the labor leaders, intransigence from the employers, and few concessions from either side.

The debate, again like that on the living wage, took on the trappings of a personal duel between two iron-willed opponents: Loyall Osborne and Frank P. Walsh. Again, Osborne emerged as the acknowledged leader of the employers, a very capable spokesman who denigrated the NWLB's ability to act when it suited his purposes. While Joint Chairman Taft continued to conceive of a strong and independent agency, free to depart from the dictates of other agencies, Osborne carefully painted the NWLB as a meek and humble instrument. Walsh, of course, still wanted to set the standards that other agencies would follow and counted among them an unswerving commitment to the basic eight-hour day.

On the afternoon of 9 July, as the debate began, "governmental necessities" became first prey to the communications gap that split the board down the middle. As members of the War Labor Conference Board, the business and labor representatives had worked in separate rooms when they devised the compromise statement on hours. Both sides, of course, had agreed to the published principle, but the NWLB as a whole had never discussed what it meant.[23] For Osborne, who had his own opinions, "governmental necessity" was something for others to decide. Whatever it might be, he refused to recognize that the NWLB should identify or try to meet it. "If," he said, "the governmental necessity requires eight hours, then *they* should take some steps to give the eight hours."[24]

The labor representatives, shocked by Osborne's logic, demanded a liberal interpretation of the NWLB's powers, and Victor Olander could only sputter that the National War Labor Board was part of the government![25] T. A. Rickert found an analogy to show why the board should standardize the hours in plants that outfitted the American fleet. In his own clothing industry, the War Department had significantly stabilized labor conditions by putting all factories with which it dealt—factories that had worked disparate hours—on an eight-hour basis with time and a half for overtime. The Worthington cases, he believed, had come before the NWLB only because neither the Navy nor the Emergency Fleet Corporation had followed the War Department's example,[26] which had followed Frankfurter's conclusions on interpreting the federal hours law. Fred Hewitt, arguing similarly for the NWLB's right to make substantive decisions, believed that "some governmental agency" would be asked "to step in and decide this question." Said Hewitt: "I don't know any agency better qualified to do it than this Board."[27]

More important, the labor members maintained that the NWLB's commitment to encourage maximum production was best served by an intelligent, standardized, reduction of basic hours. They cited case studies that showed that men produced more in eight hours than in ten. They argued that, because employees with shorter work schedules were more content, those employees tended to strike less often and to change jobs less frequently. In particular, Victor Olander reminded his colleagues of Judge Alschuler's award in the packinghouse cases. Labor turnover at one of the Armour plants had been reduced by 26 percent in the first twenty days following Alschuler's imposition of the basic eight-hour day. "You know," Olander said, "how that affects . . . production."[28] Machinist Tom Savage told the board that the establishment of the basic eight-hour day throughout the war industries would, as Samuel Rosensohn had written, solve more labor troubles than any other single governmental action.[29] Rickert agreed. Employees felt that subcontractors who failed to pay time and a half for hours worked beyond eight were "scabbing" on the government. "Why," Rickert asked, "should the contractor who is making money off the government be given any privilege the government don't ask for itself?"[30] In sum, labor's most telling arguments against Osborne's complacency linked efficiency with worker morale.

When Frank Walsh entered the debate, he sounded like the former social worker he was and drew Osborne out. Walsh ignored tactical matters and got to the humanitarian concerns that shaped much of his thinking: the physical and mental health of America's working class. An eight-hour day would permit the men to be fresh on the job every morning, Walsh began. Furthermore, he felt so strongly about the merits of shorter hours that he threw his support behind the actual rather than the basic day. Only in an emergency, he insisted, should an employee be allowed to work long hours.[31] By changing the nature of the issues, Walsh not only freed himself from the cause of organized labor but also gave the business members an opening to strengthen their argument against hours limitations. "It isn't proposed in this case, Mr. Walsh, to actually cut the hours down to eight hours, that isn't the point," Osborne explained. It is "a wage question with those men to get . . . overtime."[32] Then Osborne continued foolishly. The introduction of the basic eight-hour day, he said, could not "help but to produce a bad effect" because "the men won't work more than eight hours."³³ With his inconsistent argument, Osborne had tagged himself an opponent of innovation, a label that Walsh and the labor members saw no reason to challenge.³⁴

Between the opposite views of Walsh and Osborne, a moderate employer attitude emerged. B. L. Worden, for example, agreed that at his shipyard the men often produced as much in eight hours as in a longer day. He saw, however, some ill effects in the wage provisions attached to the basic day. Time and a half, if not restricted, sometimes caused men to skip regular work days and concentrate their hours at the end of the week in order to collect weekend overtime. That kind of activity obviously interrupted the smooth operation of a plant.³⁵ Frederick Judson, who in Taft's absence acted as Walsh's counterpart, even called the basic eight-hour day the wave of the future, but Judson cautioned against the NWLB's dealing with things as they ought to be. It was the board's duty, he explained, to adjust labor problems according to existing law and local custom, not to anticipate things to come.³⁶

This moderate attitude put the labor members in a more difficult position than had Osborne's recalcitrance even while it provided some hope that the NWLB could reach at least a theoretical consensus. As Olander observed, labor had officially abandoned the right to strike because of the creation of the NWLB. If the board could agree about what should be done, but nonetheless was forced to follow local custom and existing law to such a degree that it could not encourage what ought to be, Olander complained, then agents of change such as the strike must be permitted to operate as usual.³⁷ Against that background, Walsh made a striking breakthrough. Under his prodding, Osborne and Judson agreed that hours should be shortened in cases in which it could be demonstrated conclusively that shorter work days facilitated war production. Satisfied that the members had reached agreement on at least one point, the joint chairman relaxed. "I think we understand the principles all right," he said as the meeting ended. "What I was afraid of was that we were going back to the old question of the status quo ante."³⁸

When the NWLB reconvened to settle the Worthington cases on the morning of 11 July, Frank Walsh brought hard evidence that a shorter workday would speed production in the East Cambridge plant. Production there had ceased after nine hundred impatient machinists building parts for two hundred destroyers had walked out. Walsh clutched in his hand a day-old copy of the *New York Times*. Shaken by a story he had read in his room at the Cosmos Club the night before, he read it in full to his colleagues. The striking workers comprised almost 90 percent of the East Cambridge plant. The president of the Worthington Corporation had telegraphed Secretary of the Navy Josephus Daniels to ask Daniels' aid in ending the strike. Worthington officials were also fearful that the NWLB's decision "would establish a precedent for every manufacturer of war essentials." Before yielding the floor to Savage, Walsh—with help from T. A. Rickert—made it clear that he wanted the precedent set without delay.[39]

Savage paused briefly to defend the striking machinists, who were members of his union, half sighing that "it does seem that that is the only way to get action." He had a point. The NWLB's greatest visible fault lay not in its decisions but rather in the time that it took to make them. The Worthington cases, for example, had been on the NWLB's docket for a month. Yet, for the moment, the crisis in Massachusetts was ended. The striking Worthington employees had gone back to work that morning, personally threatened by Savage with expulsion from the union if they did not. The situation, of course, remained volatile, and Savage, apologies ended, suddenly became shrewd. He called the immediate imposition of the basic eight-hour day at East Cambridge necessary for two reasons. First, the Boston area had been adopting that standard as its normal workday; even former Massachusetts Governor Eugene Fox, a long-standing opponent of the eight-hour day, had begun to operate his business on an eight-hour basis. Second, the Navy Department had not given Savage "a bit of peace" in days. Navy spokesmen frankly could not understand why the NWLB quibbled over hours at East Cambridge. If the case was released to the Navy's jurisdiction, they had insinuated to Savage, the basic eight-hour day would probably be put into effect within forty-eight hours.[40]

The Navy so urgently wanted the Worthington works at East Cambridge restored to a smooth operation that Louis Howe, Franklin Roosevelt's assistant, had written Savage a strong letter on the previous day:

> I have laid the matter before Mr. Daniels and he has instructed me to inform you that the Navy Department is a strong advocate of the eight hour day and believes it to be not only the proper basis for working hours from the standpoint of the employees but also that . . . [a] high rate of production can be accrued better under an eight hour day than any other way. We have always recognized in all our settlements the basic eight hour day

> as a fair basis of adjustment. . . . I have just learned that your Board is taking up the whole situation and am sending this over by messenger rather than waiting till Mr. Daniels returns from the Cabinet meeting to sign the communication himself. The Department wishes to urge upon your Board the vital importance of getting the work going once more at the Worthington Pump Co. They are almost our only source of supply for pumps needed for the destroyers and every hour's delay in production of these pumps will mean just that much longer before our destroyers will take the seas. . . . We cannot urge too strongly the adjustment of this case . . . at the earliest possible moment as it is not putting it too strongly to state that the lives of thousands of soldiers may be jeopardized by further cessation of work at this plant.[41]

The letter made its point, even though the strike for the moment had been quelled. With it, Savage at length satisfied the employer members. He had shown that the change in hours would uphold "existing conditions" and the "custom of localities" in the Boston area, but only the written plea from the Navy Department assured the employers' cooperation with the labor representatives. Here was "governmental necessity," identified implicitly, at least, by an important agency of war.

Because of the Howe letter, the employer members limited their objection to the resolution that Walsh introduced to end both Worthington disputes. The resolution announced an "emergency" in the two plants. Walsh called for the imposition of the basic eight-hour day because "direct information from the Secretary of the Navy" indicated "that even a short delay" would imperil production of U-boat destroyers and consequently endanger the American Expeditionary Force and United States coastal cities.[42] Osborne wanted the resolution to make clear, however, that the NWLB had acted because it had been asked to act. "I would suggest, Mr. Walsh," he interjected, "that where you say 'upon the direct information from the Secretary' that we also say, 'and upon his recommendation.' He does. He recommends it."[43] That tiny objection, so seemingly unimportant, dissolved whatever consensus had begun to develop within the full board.

The semantic dispute that followed was neither a debate over protocol nor a battle over style. It was, instead, symptomatic of the fundamental disagreement that kept the NWLB in turmoil. The discussions of the living wage and the basic eight-hour day sprang from the same mold. In both cases, the employer members saw the NWLB as the caretaker of established industrial practice. The labor members, on the other hand, wanted a bold board, one that would take responsibility for independent action. Osborne's small objection would preclude that. If the Worthington awards rested on the sanction of an outside agency, the employers would demand similar permission on every hours case. The NWLB as judge would succumb to the NWLB as bureaucrat.[44]

As in the wage debates, the inevitable compromise gave labor the larger share of victory, actually and symbolically. The rationale for the award as finally approved contained only one change in Walsh's draft resolution. The "emergency" at the Worthington plants became a "governmental necessity." Significantly, the board failed to make clear who had determined that necessity.[45] The press termed the Worthington decision a monumental gain for American labor, much as it praised the Waynesboro award—issued the same day—as a major boost to common laborers. Gilson Gardner, a prolabor reporter, called the "adoption" of the basic eight-hour day the "most important" of the Labor Department policies being refined by Secretary Wilson, Louis F. Post, Frankfurter, and the Taft-Walsh board.[46] That adoption was sure to be considered by the NWLB because the Worthington decisions, like the Waynesboro award, contained a rider: "The board hereby announces that it has under consideration the matter of the determination of the proper working day and the decision here may be subject to modification when and as the board comes to a determination in that regard."[47] While more thoroughgoing debate within the NWLB pended, Taft and Walsh then ordered the basic eight-hour day imposed at the St. Joseph Lead Company in Herculaneum, Missouri, and at the Sloss Sheffield Steel and Iron Company in Russellville, Alabama.[48] Those actions by the joint chairmen lent some credence to Gardner's remarks.

From mid-July through August, Walsh and Osborne worked continuously to convert important agencies and persons to their viewpoints. In July, the War Labor Policies Board gave Walsh an apparent advantage when it adopted the NWLB's "general principles and policies governing the relation of employers and labor" as "part" of its own guidelines.[49] Regardless of the repercussions for wage policy, Walsh determined to encourage the policies board to act decisively on the hours question. Should the policies board follow Frankfurter's predispositions toward the feasibility of widespread implementation of the basic eight-hour day, the joint chairmen would overcome the employer members' most valid objection against it. On 15 August, therefore, Walsh dictated a message to Frankfurter: "There can be no possible objection to the War Labor Policies Board's at once putting into effect the basic eight hour day in all industries in the United States. The doing of this would not in any way conflict with the principles and policies contained in the President's Proclamation creating the National War Labor Board."[50] The War Labor Policies Board refused, however, to provide Walsh with a blanket ruling. Came the reply:

> In a word, we followed the general policy of the Administration that the drastic imposition of the eight-hour day upon industry generally is not the wise thing to do, but that such extension should be made where the conditions of any specific industry or a given industrial center call for it. . . . Of course, our resolution recognized the governmental policy in regard to the eight-hour day, but seeks to work it out step by step, which I understand is the way you are proceeding.[51]

While Walsh negotiated unsuccessfully with the Frankfurter board, Osborne vied uncertainly for Taft's support. Taft was vacationing in Canada that August when the rest of the NWLB began to deal with a report on hours submitted by Lauck's staff. The report, clearly in sympathy with labor's wartime goals, traced the history of the eight-hour day movement, cited case studies that demonstrated the efficiency of the eight-hour day, and presented the traditional moral arguments in its favor.[52] At the end of the month, Osborne mailed his absent chief a copy of a nineteen-page brief that he had presented to his colleagues to refute the labor member-staff conclusions. Osborne's brief rejected moral considerations because, he correctly observed, the basic eight-hour day would in no way insure the reduction of working hours. More important, perhaps, the brief introduced a legal argument calculated, no doubt especially, to appeal to Taft.[53]

The legalisms that Osborne employed were inextricably bound to the NWLB's role as an agent of voluntarism. As members of the War Labor Conference Board, he pointed out, the NWLB employer representatives had rejected the adoption of the basic eight-hour day as a war-labor principle. Certainly the nation's employers had not since agreed to have the basic eight-hour day imposed upon them by a board that took no responsibility for economic losses. Therefore, Osborne wrote, the sudden push to include the basic eight-hour day among the NWLB's policies was "incompetent, irrelevant, and immaterial." The principles themselves referred to the basic eight-hour day only once, when they empowered the NWLB to uphold the law. If the board now imposed the eight-hour day generally, it would not only act "in contravention of its stipulated principles, but ... attempt ... to exercise broad executive and administrative functions for which no sanction whatever exists in the charter from which the Board derives its powers." The NWLB's limited legal authority and its inability to use coercion made it clear to Osborne that "no power lies anywhere to compel the employer to observe that which is exempt from the operation of the law."[54]

In an accompanying letter to Taft that same day, 29 August, Osborne elaborated further. His brief had objected to the basic eight-hour day as a general policy, but the letter objected to the board's awarding it "here and there" in individual cases:

> It seems now as though our employee friends are stressing the point of Governmental necessity. They are assuming that because men are striking . . . to force the eight-hour day, that that in itself indicates a Governmental necessity. . . . I feel so strongly on this point that I am invoking your great influence, if you feel you can do it, to support my contentions that the Board is not justified in changing hours, either to increase or to decrease them, except for the specific and categorical reasons stated in our principles.[55]

Osborne, who criticized the labor members for wanting to write a "new" principle only because it benefited their side, wanted Taft's help in leading the employers toward the same end.

Taft, as usual, struck an independent course between the extreme positions advocated by Walsh and Osborne. As usual, he also interpreted the NWLB's hours principle in the spirit in which it was written. He declined to lend "his great influence" to restrict the NWLB to following only the letter of the law. Taft wanted neither sweeping acceptance of a policy never intended as one of the board's principles nor complete rejection of the board's role as an agent of progress. "I don't agree with you," he wrote Osborne, "that it is without our jurisdiction to fix an 8-hour day, if we think it is the right day to fix in a particular case." For example, he and Walsh had given street-car conductors working a night shift ten hours' pay for eight hours' work because it had been the "fair" thing to do. The NWLB, he insisted, had a "duty" to call the eight-hour day proper when it believed it was proper. At the same time, the joint chairman resented the NWLB labor members' efforts to lead the NWLB toward "making rules for present controversies which are to be used in the future as a step in achieving that which organized labor seeks . . . as a permanent policy." Above all, Taft shrank from destroying the board's basis for power, the respect and voluntary cooperation of all segments of the industrial world. He wanted the NWLB to remain unhindered by both precedent and prejudice in order to judge substantively each case on its individual merits. In his own way, therefore, Taft accepted Walsh's belief that the NWLB had quasi-legislative functions.[56]

Such divisions within the board, of course, precluded the determination of the proper working day for American laborers, just as it had prevented the establishment of an official "living wage." Yet, like the awards that dealt primarily with wages, those which assigned hours piecemeal built toward generalization. Ironically, the NWLB's inability to agree on an hours policy accelerated the trend. Before the end of summer, a deadlocked board would be forced to release three jointly submitted cases to umpires. All three men would assign the eight-hour day, thus legitimizing what had begun in the Worthington awards of 11 July.

One of the most publicized disputes that came before the NWLB—a massive controversy in Bridgeport, Connecticut—involved the workers' request for a basic eight-hour day in fifty-four (of a city-wide total of fifty-six) factories. The management of those fifty-four factories and their sixty thousand workers appealed to the NWLB to end the turmoil that continuously retarded the making of munitions, but the board remained as divided as the Bridgeport employers and employees. NWLB umpire Otto M. Eidlitz—a builder from New York who was director of the Bureau of Housing and Transportation of the Department of Labor, president of the U.S. Housing Corporation, and a member of the National Civic Federation—made the decision on behalf of the NWLB to put all fifty-four factories, essentially the entire city, on the basic eight-hour day. Forty-five of the firms that had submitted to the NWLB already used that work schedule, and Eidlitz justified his hours award on the basis of majority rule.[57] That part of the decision seemed to satisfy Osborne and his colleagues because the basic eight-hour day had been imposed in Bridgeport in a logical fashion. Osborne even termed the award "wholly in accord with our views."[58]

Yet, two more cases, from the Wheeling Mold and Foundry Company, stumped the NWLB on the same day Eidlitz handed down his award. In the West Virginia foundry, machinists worked a nine-hour basis to prepare tools for unskilled laborers who worked an eight-hour basic day. The company was under contract to the War and Navy departments and subcontracted to the Emergency Fleet Corporation. Although the work schedule followed the policy suggested to the War Department in Frankfurter's report, the machinists nonetheless demanded the more advantageous schedule of the common laborers. The molders at the foundry, whose grievances constituted the second case, wanted an *actual* eight-hour day. Tom Savage and W. H. VanDervoort, the section assigned to settle both disputes, disagreed. Savage believed that the NWLB should interpret the federal hours law to include the machinists, and he thought that the molders deserved the straight eight-hour schedule because of the nature of their work. His reports, tailored to effect those ends, went down to defeat before the full board in tie votes.[59]

When the board surrendered the Wheeling cases on 28 August, hope that its members had learned to deal with the hours question all but vanished. The Wheeling discussions read like a transcript of the Worthington debates, only this time no federal agency came forward to define governmental necessity. The employer members had ignored all arguments based on matters of health and comfort, and they had refused to vote to alter the hours at the foundry without a written statement from an unimpeachable source proclaiming governmental necessity, legal proof that the law required a change in hours, or documented evidence that the proposed schedule changes were wholly compatible with local customs.[60] Their inflexibility at every turn mandated the selection of two more umpires.

The distinguished men who served as sole arbiters in the foundry cases put the Savage recommendations into effect. Henry Ford, who granted the machinists their eight-hour basis with time and a half for overtime and double time on Sundays and holidays, spoke as a man concerned primarily with good work habits. Walter Clark, chief justice of the North Carolina Supreme Court, agreed with the molders' request for shorter hours in the interests of social justice. Their combined decisions rescued voluntarism from lethargy.[61]

Ford's award was brief. The NWLB had asked him, he announced on 30 October, whether the machinists should have what they wanted. His response: "I, the said Henry Ford, do hereby answer the said question, Yes." The rest of Ford's remarks told the NWLB what he really felt: "My experience, and also my reason, teaches me that very few emergencies ever exist in a manufacturing business justifying the practice of exceeding 8 working hours per day. . . . I can not dwell too much on this. For the good of the men, for the good of the employer, and for the general results, I would admonish those interested to adhere to the straight 8-hour day."[62] Ford saw no need to explain his reasons for awarding the basic day unless the board requested them.

Walter Clark, on the other hand, wanted his award and his reasons for granting the molders a straight eight-hour day understood, and so did Frank Walsh. On 16 September, Clark wrote Walsh a personal letter. The opinion that prefaced the award, Clark said, had been finished and was "about 2,400 words—a little longer than you suggested."[63] The preface cited legislation, quoted President Wilson, and praised Samuel Alschuler's decision in the packinghouse cases. Clark wrote that molders' work produced "fatigue and exposure to noxious and dangerous fumes." Similar conditions had already led to the limitation of hours as a matter of course in dangerous industries. But Clark wondered, since the free countries of the world "were on their way" to adopting an eight-hour day, why American employers did not "frankly accept it" and settle the "question, once [and] for all." Hazardous conditions or not, said the jurist, it was "the consensus, as President Wilson stated, of students of the subject that the maximum production is to be had by the adoption of the 8-hour day, and that the preservation of the health and the lives of the employees will be promoted by that limitation."[64] As to the award itself, Clark ruled that wartime adjustments to the federal hours law of 1912 did not require laborers to work longer than eight hours. He therefore specifically prohibited a longer day for the Wheeling molders unless sanctioned by three members of a four-man committee that he ordered established and composed equally of foundry employers and employees. Only if they approved—because of emergency conditions—could molders at the plant work more than eight hours in a twenty-four hour period, and even then the molders could work only at time and a half.[65]

Clark's award was by far the most comprehensive statement issued by the NWLB on behalf of hours limitation, and Clark's rationale delighted Walsh. In particular, Walsh liked the way in which the North Carolinian had given foundry employees an equal voice in the determination of essential policies. With a "deep sense of gratification," the joint chairman thanked Clark for furthering his hopes "that much good is to come to us all through the frightful experience of the present war." The introduction of a democratic production committee in such a large factory would be "at once understood and appreciated . . . by all students and workers in the cause of industrial and economic regeneration, and ultimately by us all."[66]

Like Walsh, Clark wanted the Wheeling molders' award to influence a broad audience. The significance of the decision could transcend the settlement of a specific case, he believed, if the award received sufficient publicity within the legal community. The "legal profession is . . . reactionary" and difficult to reach, he wrote, "because we rely so much upon precedent and think that the opinion of the Judges who lived 100 to 400 years [ago] is far better . . . than the statute law of today." For that reason, Justice Clark asked Basil Manly of the NWLB staff to mail 235 copies of the award to the nine U.S. Supreme Court justices, to the chief justices and attorney generals of 53 states and territories, and to the deans of 120 law schools. They "*might* read an article of this kind coming from a member of the Bench," he told Manly.[67]

Whatever their effect on the legal profession, both Wheeling decisions encouraged labor's loyalty, made an impact on industrialists beyond the board's jurisdiction, and influenced the NWLB's future awards. On 5 October, *The Nation* termed Clark's award, along with an AFL pledge to organize the steel mills, instrumental in the United States Steel Corporation's decision to change its basic day from ten hours to eight.[68] During and immediately after the war, the NWLB itself earned a reputation as a strong proponent of the eight-hour day. It did grant the eight-hour day, basic or actual, in 151 cases. Yet the board's decisions evolved without benefit of a clear-cut hours policy and followed Taft's ideal of judging each case individually. The NWLB sometimes refused to change hours, sometimes awarded a nine-hour basic day, and sometimes left the determination of hours to the discretion of shop committees, which it ordered established for that and other purposes. On occasion, the NWLB even awarded forty-eight hour basic weeks in order to prevent abuse of overtime.[69] All in all, however, postwar analysts concluded that the NWLB usually supported the basic eight-hour day. In November 1919, the Bureau of Labor Statistics went so far as to attribute the eight-hour-day movement's "very considerable headway" during the war to "the position taken by the War Labor Board."[70] Yet without the decisions of Justice Clark and Henry Ford, it seems safe to say, the NWLB position would have been considerably weaker.

7 Democratizing Industry

> The old idea that when everybody votes you have a democracy—that is pretty much exploded. . . . Political democracy is a delusion unless built upon and guaranteed by a free and virile industrial democracy.
>
> —Frank P. Walsh, "Democracy or Destruction," August 1918

As the NWLB shored up the right to organize, raised wages, and shortened hours, pointed demands for "industrial democracy" began to overshadow all others. "Industrial democracy," to most workers who thought of it, meant an end to "autocratic" rule by management. The phrase captured the spirit of labor's war aims. It meant the right to organize, of course, but also included collective bargaining between representatives of workers and employers. The wartime concept of "industrial democracy," therefore, built on the idea advanced by the AFL and theoretically supported by the National Civic Federation since the turn of the century. Because of the NWLB's principles and a severe shortage of labor, the workingmen's drive for power seemed more likely to succeed than ever before. Their cause was aided by the general attitude of the Wilson administration and by wartime rhetoric aimed against "autocracy" throughout the world. Organized labor echoed the high-sounding aims of American war policy in its own campaign for equal rights. For the NWLB, the most important repercussions of labor's campaign followed assaults on long-standing employment practices at Bethlehem Steel and the General Electric Company. The board stepped into serious disputes at those companies and painstakingly translated the right to bargain collectively from principle to practice. Under firm leadership from Taft and Walsh, a reluctant NWLB sidestepped the Supreme Court once more and rescued voluntarism from inertia.

"The work of the War Labor Board is mounting up to the skies," Frank Walsh wrote to a friend at the end of August, "and I am almost encouraged to say that it is going to be a success." Walsh was especially proud of a series of recent awards that had begun to put teeth into the NWLB's principle on the right to bargain collectively. An award of 31 July for the Pittsfield, Massachusetts, works of the General Electric Company had broken new ground because the NWLB, for the first time, had specifically banned individual employment contracts until the war ended. By 21 August, three awards—including the one at Pittsfield, one for the Bethlehem Steel Company, and a third for the Smith and Wesson Arms Company of Springfield, Massachusetts—had provided procedures through which employees could elect representatives to deal in committees with management. With those awards, Walsh believed, the NWLB had finally "established precedents along the lines of justice covering almost every conceivable proposition under our principles."[1]

The establishment of shop committees such as those ordered by the NWLB seemed almost a natural consequence of a war being waged on behalf of democracy. Indeed, the President's Mediation Commission had directly criticized the strain on democracy at home inherent in common industrial practices. "American industry," the commission concluded, lacked "a healthy basis of relationship between management and men" because of "the insistence by employers upon individual dealings with their men." Too many employers also actively opposed labor organizations. Together, these conditions insured a failure "to equalize the parties in adjustments of . . . industrial contests," which the commission identified as "the central cause for our difficulties."[2] The way to resolve the problem was obvious: "Some form of collective relationship between management and workmen is indispensable . . . and should form an accepted part of the labor policy of the nation."[3]

While the commission labored over its conclusions, *The Survey's* preeminent labor analyst, John Fitch, undertook a private study of existing forms of collective relationships in open-shop companies. Among them were the employee-representation schemes at William Filene's Sons Company in Boston and at the Colorado Fuel and Iron Company. Since the turn of the century, Filene's had enjoyed a solid reputation as a progressive employer and had permitted the operation of an employee organization so powerful that it could veto management decisions. At the Colorado Fuel and Iron Company, John D. Rockefeller, Jr., had introduced a committee system following the strikes and violence that Frank P. Walsh investigated through the Commission on Industrial Relations. The Filene organization represented the very best in shop committees, while the Rockefeller Plan of 1915 was more controversial. Yet at neither company would management deal with representatives of organized labor, and this was what intrigued Fitch the most. For all of their theoretical responsibilities, the employee committees at both concerns were dependent for their very existence upon the whim of company officials. Without the continued support of management, the workers at these open shop establishments remained completely powerless.[4]

The Rockefeller Plan was interesting, in part, because it was designed to quiet unrest in a tumultuous industry. The scheme also revealed an obvious attempt to make unionization unnecessary. Rockefeller himself admitted as much. Labor organizations, he confided to the Denver Chamber of Commerce, pitted labor against capital. On that ground, he justified his refusal to recognize the United Mine Workers as it moved into his Colorado works. Even so, the Federal Commission on Labor Difficulties in the Coal Fields of Colorado had praised the Rockefeller committee system as "a new departure in the United States." The "underlying principle" of the plan —"cooperation"—seemed to anticipate much of Woodrow Wilson's formula for wartime harmony at home.[5]

When Fitch visited the Rockefeller mines in 1917, he came away with cautious optimism about the new cooperation. True, "a wonderful improvement" had taken place in Colorado, for the plan was "a radical break with the past, apparently . . . being administered . . . in good faith." The armed-camp atmosphere of a few years earlier had disappeared. Visitors even walked about unchaperoned by company marshals. Employees openly joined the UMW. But something made Fitch, like a character in a "B" Western, sense that things were too quiet. How, he wondered, did it benefit anyone to join a labor organization when the company was sure to ignore its presence? And why did every employees' representative whom he interviewed recount the flawless operation of the system? The new atmosphere itself fed Fitch's gnawing feeling that something was wrong. He was suspicious of people who claimed to be so completely satisfied. In general, he concluded, they were either currying favor with superiors and had become "company men" or they were afraid to speak their minds.[6]

Even as Fitch wrote, he understood that the men were not satisfied and why. The UMW reported that 90 percent of the employees were organized, and management admitted to 50 percent. Not only that, but the members of the labor organization had so bitterly resented the company union Rockefeller introduced that they had boycotted camp elections and staged counter meetings of their own. A large percentage of the employees, therefore, had sullenly ignored the procedures through which their representatives were chosen. More important, the union had threatened to strike in the summer of 1917, some two years after the introduction of the Rockefeller Plan, if the company continued its refusal to recognize the UMW. Even though the threat had died, the underlying frustration of the organized employees lingered.[7]

Those men had earned Fitch's real sympathy. The threat of strikes would grow stronger, he warned. The fatal flaw of the system, no matter how smoothly it appeared to work, was that it could never succeed as long as it alienated the bulk of the workers. The alienation, in part, had developed because the employees had no independent voice; company officials managed the elections, and employee committees met in the presence of management spokesmen. Nor were such vital concerns as wages and hours subject to negotiations under the committee system. "No system," concluded Fitch, "devised and wholly controlled by the employing interests, as this one is, can either command the confidence of the workers or be counted upon to administer justice."[8]

For the NWLB, bound to preserve both open shops and the workers' rights to organize and to bargain collectively, a shop-committee system offered a means to both ends. The board's essential task was to devise a bargaining plan that protected both unionized and nonunionized employees. For that reason, Newcomb Carlton's plan for Western Union employees had been unacceptable; his refusal to deal jointly with workers if they organized was contrary to the NWLB's principles. Since Carlton had eluded the board, no system had yet been devised under the auspices of the NWLB when the board entered a major controversy at Bethlehem Steel.

When the NWLB demanded and got an official request from the Labor Department to come into the Bethlehem case on 11 May, discontent had raged in the steel mills of the Lehigh Valley for almost a month. In mid-April, many of the 21,000 machinists—2,000 of them unionized—at Bethlehem Steel's Bethlehem, Pennsylvania, plant walked out complaining of unsatisfactory wages and hours. Specifically, the machinists protested against two things: the Bethlehem bonus system, a pay method so complicated that no one could understand it; and the unique application of the basic eight-hour day in machine shops under governmental contract. Although the machinists returned to work when federal and state labor mediators effected a temporary settlement, they walked out again in early May. This time they conditioned their return on the right to bargain collectively.[9]

On Friday, 10 May, two federal mediators came from Bethlehem to testify before the Taft-Walsh board. For three weeks they had tried to resolve the steel controversy, and now they dismissed further Labor Department efforts as "fruitless." In their judgment, only the NWLB could effect a lasting settlement. Circumstances at Bethlehem were indeed grave. Not only were five thousand machinists from three shops still out, but also the position of the electrical workers, said one of the mediators, had become "very delicate." Since the end of March, when the company had refused their wage and hour demands, the electricians had been "very uneasy." They had stayed on the job because governmental agents and union officials had begged them to do so, but they would strike if the NWLB hesitated to take up the case. Coupled with the machinists' strike, an electricians' walkout could cripple the plant.[10]

The mediators explained to the board what had already happened. The machinists' first walkout, one said, "could hardly be called . . . a strike, or hardly a lockout." The men, who worked straight eight-hour days, were told to report for ten-hour shifts on 16 April. Expecting to be denied overtime on the new schedule, they came instead at their regular hour, later than orders dictated. Locked out by company officials, they struck. Bethlehem President Eugene Grace attributed the incident to a misunderstanding. Grace had assured the mediators that the machinists would get their time and a half after eight hours; the law demanded it. He had also implied that the men might present their grievances through shop committees. Soothed by Grace's promises, the machinists had cooperated with the new hours, but when their grievance committees, which refused to renounce the machinists' union, were refused interviews with plant superintendents, they had returned to the streets.[11]

The electricians had continually threatened to strike over wages and hours during the last few weeks because their standards were lower than those of electricians in government-run shipyards at nearby Bristol and Hog Island. Among other things, they worked longer than eight hours and with no overtime pay. Unlike the machinists, the electricians did no production work, only repairs and maintenance and were therefore not under governmental contract and not guaranteed a basic eight-hour day. Like the machinists, however, they believed that their problems could be resolved only through joint dealings with management.[12]

After the NWLB entered the controversy on 11 May, Tom Savage and Herbert H. Rice, the section assigned to frame the award, worked toward a fast settlement. Never was maximum production so crucial to the war effort. Bethlehem Steel was the largest ordnance-producing company in the country. Between 80 and 90 percent of its work was under contract to the War and Navy departments, and the munitions it manufactured were "absolutely necessary to the success of the American Expeditionary Forces."[13] But the settlement would not be easy. Steel was among the staunchest of open-shop industries, and the Bethlehem company had long considered the treatment of its employees a private matter. In 1918, the company denied discriminating against employees who organized; it could not deny its treatment of employees as "individual contractors with whom an individual bargain must be struck."[14]

The section brought the case unresolved before the full board in New York on 1 June. After a one-day hearing, the two men had agreed on only one issue, that the wage and hour demands of the Bethlehem electricians deserved reexamination by company officials. On the machinists' demands, the section was stymied. The stickiest problem was the bonus system. That, along with confusing data that Grace had supplied on collective-bargaining methods, portended a long and tedious meeting.

Only Tom Savage came to New York with a finished report on the machinists' grievances. In four months, the International Association of Machinists official would be dead, a victim of Spanish influenza at thirty-one. This meeting brought forth his finest service on the NWLB, when he slowly and logically unfolded the issues in perhaps the board's most complicated case.

For Savage, a bonus system could stimulate production. Unfortunately, however, the Bethlehem system had so many disadvantages that it was a major source of discontent. The machinists could only guess the standards upon which the bonus would be based from day to day. Furthermore, a man who spoiled materials in his race for a bonus had their value deducted from his pay. Worst of all, on governmental contracts, a bonus in effect denied a man his overtime wages. All of these factors, Savage argued, retarded production. The Bethlehem bonus system, he concluded, was therefore at odds with the NWLB's principles.[15]

Savage knew why his fellow machinists had struck at Bethlehem. Eugene Grace had been wrong to speak of a misunderstanding. The first revolt in the machine shops had been stimulated by a change in the company's policy. Before the change, the machinists had earned a base hourly rate when they worked eight-hour shifts; but for each hour an employee exceeded the requisite output, he had received an extra sum—a bonus for outstanding efficiency. Under the new ten-hour schedule, a machinist could still earn a bonus, but when he did, he received only enough pay for his two hours of overtime to bring the day's total wage into conformity with federal law. If his bonus equaled the value of prescribed overtime wages, the overtime pay was withheld completely. The men had walked out, Savage insisted, not because they were confused, but because they refused to accept—with no hope of bargaining for more—the same wages for ten hours' work that they had previously been able to earn in eight.[16]

Savage knew, too, that the Bethlehem controversy need never have been referred to the NWLB. Although the application of the bonus system had initially triggered the walkout, only the refusal of management to meet the men had precluded a settlement. The machinists' dissatisfaction could have been "very readily cleared up," Savage told his colleagues, had Grace conferred with a committee of his "own employees."[17] The federal mediators who had given up on the controversy had reached the same conclusion. They had begged Grace to explain the pay system to a "carefully selected" committee of his machinists, "a committee not composed of Firebrands, or boys who were inclined to be radical and lose their heads, but fellows who were cool-headed and [would] sit down and reason with him."[18] Grace's refusal had been in keeping with company tradition. Even within the last few years, the Bethlehem Steel Company had dismissed men who objected to working conditions if they objected collectively.[19]

By the spring of 1918, Eugene Grace had apparently learned to use collective bargaining as a weapon. While the machinists were on the streets, Grace had met a group of electricians employed by the company, with a leader of the local electricians' union serving as group spokesman. Explaining his denial of like treatment to the strikers, the steel company president clung stubbornly to his prerogatives. He called himself "always willing and ready to receive an individual employee . . . or a group of individual employees," but he would not deal with a committee that "in its formation in any way savored . . . of organization." Neither the committee of machinists nor the committee of electricians had asked for recognition of the union, but only the machinists had been asked to renounce union affiliation. Why, then, had Grace met with unionized electricians? Savage could only speculate that the electricians had been rewarded for staying on the job. Unionized employees were acceptable at Bethlehem, it appeared, only as long as their organization behaved.[20]

Section partner Rice, a General Motors executive from Detroit, turned his corporate mind to business as he heard the Savage report. Appointed alternate for W. H. VanDervoort, Rice had never before served on a section and proved to be a mediocre choice. Rice did little homework for this meeting, and he made no formal report, partly because he still weighed the evidence. Tom Savage had stated the facts well, Rice said.[21] Nevertheless, he rallied to Eugene Grace and sought shelter for the steel giant under the protective cloak of the NWLB's principles.

The unique application of the bonus system to the basic eight-hour day in the Bethlehem machine shops was entirely "within the law," Rice told his colleagues.[22] Grace had letters from government officials which proved it. Nor did the revised form of payment violate the NWLB's ideals as far as Rice was concerned. The fairness of the system was inherent—the men could not "have their cake and eat it, too." The basic eight-hour day guaranteed time-and-a-half pay for service beyond eight hours in one day. That payment was a right of employment of men under contract to the government, but a bonus was not. A bonus was a reward for efficiency. Under the new system, when a machinist's bonus exceeded his guaranteed overtime pay, he received the bonus instead. For Herbert Rice, the NWLB could maintain only an "academic" interest in the way in which Eugene Grace paid his machinists if they earned the equivalent of time and a half for overtime hours.[23]

Rice even offered a feeble defense of the company's policy on collective bargaining. Both the machinists and the electricians were unionized, he reasoned, but the machinists had recently stopped production in the Bethlehem plant while the electricians had cooperated with management. Thus, Rice seemed to imply, members of the machinists' union had seduced loyal company employees, had nurtured their discontent, and had encouraged their strike. To deal with returning strikers who refused to deny their union affiliation, he insinuated, might be to extend tacit recognition to an organization responsible for stopping production. None of Rice's remarks, however, obscured the obvious fact that Eugene Grace had compromised NWLB-sanctioned rights to organize and to bargain collectively, and to do so free of discrimination.[24]

As they heard the section's diverse remarks that morning, the joint chairmen formed a joint response to what they heard. Bethlehem Steel's actions pleased neither Taft nor Walsh, and both men discounted Rice's effort to harmonize them with the NWLB's principles.

Taft was both troubled and frustrated at the Rice-Grace position on the bonus system. How, he wondered, could the steel company and Rice justify making an employee's pay for extra hours dependent upon a mediocre performance during the first eight? How could a man be denied time and a half because his supplemental pay during the regular day surpassed its value? How could the company claim to pay overtime wages if a man could not also collect his earned bonus?

Putting it simply, Taft imagined a fictional foreman, in conversation with his imaginary laborer, saying, "'If you will . . . do better work in . . . eight hours . . . we will give you more [money.]' After that eight-hour day is over, [the foreman] says, 'But I can't get through this work and I need two hours more of your time.'"

"Now," Taft asked, "by what process of reasoning can you take away from" the laborer "that which he has earned under the agreement? That is what I don't understand." And that was what H. H. Rice had not explained.[25]

Both of the joint chairmen knew, too, that the distinction that the steel company president made between a "group" and a "committee" of Bethlehem employees was specious. For Grace to insist that he would meet only with a group and not with a committee that "savored of organization" was nonsense. The men "couldn't very well have a committee unless they organized," said Taft.[26] Indeed, Rice and Savage had both confirmed what Taft and Walsh feared. As long as a union organized actively at Bethlehem, as the machinists had done, Eugene Grace would continue to demand disclaimers of membership in that union from potential spokesmen for employees. Furthermore, the steel executive had told Tom Savage that if management was to deal with a committee, then management would "have to have something to do with the selection of that committee." It worried Walsh that Grace had admitted interest in the Rockefeller Plan.[27]

When Walsh took the floor, he was determined to see that no tinsel democracy would be established at Bethlehem Steel under the guiding hand of the NWLB. In an emotional speech, he begged for a bargaining system fair to the common laborer. Walsh had seen workers like those at Bethlehem, he said. "They have been engaged in digging iron out of the mud and they are uncouth of speech. They haven't the habit of consecutive thought," he reminded the employer representatives, and unlike a "man whose mind was trained and whose educational advantages had been such as to meet you on common grounds," a typical steelworker could be tricked into a poor settlement. The Rockefeller Plan, Walsh had decided, afforded insufficient protection to uncouth men who dug iron out of the mud.[28]

Democratizing Industry 117

When the session ended at noon, the Bethlehem controversy was so far from settlement that the full board decided to send special examiners to Pennsylvania with orders to return with clear recommendations. Discussion of the issues that morning had generated nothing like consensus within the NWLB. Grace, moreover, remained an enigma. Although cordial and cooperative thus far with the NWLB's personnel, he had hardly embraced its policies, and his smiling noncompliance with whatever decision the board might reach could prove more difficult to counter than Newcomb Carlton's open defiance of its authority.

Secretary Jett Lauck and Chief Examiner Hugh Hanna arrived in Bethlehem in mid-June only to find several serious situations threatening to become worse. The company was three months behind in its arms production, and War Department representatives were already there making preparations for nationalization of the plant if necessary.[29] The NWLB men nevertheless took testimony from both management and men in closed sessions, but before they could return to Washington, new disturbances grounded on similar complaints came to Lauck's attention. The machinists' and electrical workers' unions had become controversial elsewhere in the East.

General Electric, a company that allowed plant managers to set labor policy, had become the target of organizers from both unions. At the Pittsfield, Massachusetts, plant the 7,000 employees chafed at "yellow-dog" contracts requiring them to present grievances individually. Employees at the Schenectady, New York, General Electric plant could bargain collectively, but the 21,000 employees there, supported by the machinists' and the electrical workers' unions, threatened to strike for increased wages, the basic eight-hour day, and equal pay to women for equal work.[30]

Conditions in Schenectady, in particular, alarmed Lauck, and after two days in Bethlehem, he sped to New York. Late on the night of 19 June, he penned Taft an urgent note from his hotel room. Schenectady faced nothing less than a general strike. The foundry workers at a locomotive works had considered a walkout. Streetcar employees had gone out, but come back to work after assurance that the joint chairmen would hear their grievances. At the General Electric plant in Schenectady, a strike had been averted only because Lauck had wired the employees that Taft and Walsh would take their case, along with that of the transit workers, on 22 June. He explained that he had promised the employees that the joint chairmen personally would listen to them because he "had to." Another NWLB section, he told Taft, "would not have carried enough prestige."[31]

At Pittsfield, Lauck had calmed a charged atmosphere by inviting the General Electric workers to come to Schenectady to tell their problems to the joint chairmen "informally." Those employees were especially restless because another NWLB section had investigated their case weeks earlier but, like the Bethlehem section, had deadlocked. So Jett Lauck furthered a developing trend and bought employee cooperation by volunteering the good offices of Taft and Walsh. No other section had interpreted the NWLB's policies so consistently to the advantage of the workers. For that reason, the NWLB's most important awards—those effecting policy decisions or settlements in major industries—would all, eventually, come from Taft and Walsh.[32]

Because Schenectady's problems took the entire day of 22 June, the Pittsfield workers came before the full board in Washington on 28 June. The meeting was decisive. The NWLB ordered the General Electric Company to eliminate employment contracts at Pittsfield, and it ordered Taft and Walsh to take over the case and to devise a collective bargaining system for the plant. The board also directed Jett Lauck and his staff to submit an election code through which the employees could choose their committeemen. Taft then assured the employees that he and Walsh would do whatever "we, in justice, think should be done to secure proper representation for the men." The employees, confident at last, left for home after promising to stay on the job.[33]

Friendly Massachusetts newspapers hailed the NWLB's action as the greatest victory for labor "since the government began to mobilize industry to win the war." The importance of the board's ruling against individual contracts was "far-reaching," said the Springfield *Republican*, for the "Official Bulletin specifically states it is the first of its kind made by the board and will act as a precedent." With apparent ease, the NWLB had dealt with a General Electric plant as Frank Walsh had wanted it to deal with the Western Union Company. This time, it seemed, the Boston *Advertiser* had good reason to proclaim, "New Ruling to Be in Effect Throughout Period of the War."[34]

The inevitable subliminal comparison between the Western Union debacle and the General Electric controversy, however, was strained. For one thing, the Pittsfield management had submitted to the jurisdiction of the board. It had since agreed to meet grievance committees if the open shop was preserved and had therefore emasculated its own contract policy. Furthermore, the idea of a shop-committee system at Pittsfield was not even new, for management had already allowed the workers to elect fifty fellow employees to a cumbersome general works committee.³⁵ Finally, the NWLB decision had been only slightly less than inevitable. By now, the NWLB's employer representatives must have sensed that a majority would never support a measure that denied employee rights.

While the Pittsfield proceedings made headlines throughout the country, the problems at Bethlehem Steel continued unabated and drew special attention from a radical source. Someone at the Lauck-Hanna hearings had leaked snatches of testimony to the New York *Call*, and on 21 June, that socialist newspaper published the story about five thousand gun makers who had been on strike for two weeks. The *Call* also charged that the company had made no substantial effort to normalize production levels. "So far," it barked, "patriotic speeches have been delivered by company officials, and officers have been hired to terrorize the men."³⁶

The *Call* even revealed Lauck's recommendations on the bonus system before the NWLB secretary indicated his own formal conclusions: "The system whereby a president can collect $1,000,000 bonus and a vice-president $500,000 in one year, with smaller amounts going to . . . other officials, while the toilers constantly work themselves out of theirs, must be changed, the investigators declare."³⁷

Finally, the *Call* reported company discrimination against men who joined a union, a precise violation of the NWLB's principles. At the hearings before Lauck and Hanna, the *Call* told its readers, more than fifty unionized workers had complained of being forced from the company. Some claimed to have had their piece rates cut without explanation, by as much as 50 percent, to make them quit. New men hired in their places, they testified, had been hired at higher rates. Others had been transferred to shops run by foremen so tough that they knew they would be dismissed. Most of the fifty men were machinists, and their alleged maltreatment had followed their participation in the strike.³⁸

As the *Call* exposé hit the newsstands, Frank Walsh received a confidential memorandum from the man who had probably leaked the story. William P. Harvey, former managing editor of the Kansas City *Post*, was one of two special field representatives for the NWLB. Like Walsh, who had appointed him trouble-shooter for the labor members, Harvey was a dedicated crusader, and, like Walsh, he believed in telling the truth as he saw it loudly—so loudly that military intelligence reported him as a possible agent of the International Workers of the World. His "Dear Frank" report of 20 June read like a schoolboy's speech for industrial democracy.³⁹

The Bethlehem Steel Company, Harvey said bluntly, was a menace to the war effort. While America sacrificed "a generation of its best men," company executives devoted themselves "to strategic moves to perpetuate feudal control of labor after the war." The company itself presented "a front of frozen greed." Eugene Grace had no conception of the needs of his laborers because their complaints never got beyond the petty bosses in the shops who earned their own bonuses by cutting labor costs. Employees were therefore victimized by every level of authority. Within the last year, Harvey continued, dissatisfaction with wages and corrupt supervisors had generated an incredible labor turnover. Fewer than 1 percent of 57,500 new hands had stayed on at Bethlehem. In the machine shops especially, Harvey believed, the "evil" aspects of the bonus system reached "past any results that might affect mere wages." Only the introduction of collective bargaining and the resultant "democratization of the industry would spell the end of bosses sharing in wage savings." Until then, with their profits at stake and their powers unlimited, even lower-echelon management representatives would remain the "deadly enemies of organization."[40]

The report that Jett Lauck and Hugh Hanna distributed to the NWLB members on 9 July confirmed the conditions at Bethlehem as disclosed by Harvey and the *Call*. Among the many recommendations of the two staff members were those most often advocated by the workers and their supporters, the abolition of the bonus system and the establishment of some kind of bargaining system—specifically, whatever shop-committee plan Taft and Walsh devised for the General Electric plant at Pittsfield.[41]

By the time the NWLB considered the report almost three weeks later on 30 July, Loyall Osborne had formulated a familiar rebuttal. This Bethlehem discussion coincided with the NWLB's debate on the efficacy of setting a standardized minimum wage. It was therefore doubly important to Osborne to emphasize the board's limitations. At every turn, he did so.

Osborne's best argument lay in jurisdictional technicalities. He was quick to point out that Grace, like Newcomb Carlton, had not submitted to the NWLB, and an official award was therefore impossible. Osborne suggested that the NWLB recommend how the company might pacify the employees and that it volunteer its conciliation services and those of the Ordnance Department. The board, for example, could advise that both the "processes" and the "feeling" at the steel company would "be greatly improved" if the company adopted "some method" of collective representation for the men. The board could also suggest that the company eliminate unsatisfactory elements in the bonus system, but without making "any definite suggestion" because the system was too "technical" for the NWLB members to understand. Finally, the Westinghouse executive believed that the board could denounce company discrimination against union members, but no more than that. "We can only reiterate our own principles in that respect," he said, "and accept the company's word in good faith that it is not doing it and insist that it shall not do it." In sum, Osborne's proposed action was almost an apology to Eugene Grace for having questioned the way he ran his company.[42]

Frank Walsh resented the jurisdictional obstacles that Osborne regularly erected in the path of NWLB action. Often when a case was submitted by one side, he explained, the other side would agree to come in at some point in the negotiations. Then he became impatient, as the impact of Osborne's words became clearer. The "continued question of jurisdiction" had been a matter of "embarrassment if not harassment to the operation of this Board," he said. One or both sides at Bethlehem could reject the NWLB findings since the case was not yet an arbitration, but the rejection must be dealt with only if and when it came. "I think," he concluded, "we have passed the point of jurisdiction in this case and that we should proceed with it."[43]

No one was more eager to proceed that morning than Joint Chairman Taft. The Bethlehem investigation had dragged on for two and a half months, too long to suit Taft. Since the 1 June meeting, his convictions about the motives of the company president had become firm. He was ready to vote because the evidence in the case was full and the "equivocation of the company" was obvious. Grace, Taft said, had "really refused to comply with our principles and on the other hand didn't want to say so." The steel company had denied government-sanctioned employee rights, and Taft wanted the NWLB to "express ourselves emphatically on that subject."[44]

Impatient with Osborne's tactics and ideas, Taft came down firmly in accord with Frank Walsh. Osborne's use of procedural arguments, in this case on the matter of jurisdiction, was part of his overall strategy to confine the NWLB. His suggestion to share responsibility with the War Department for what happened at Bethlehem was calculated to serve the same purpose. Taft, however, had consistently urged the board's strong autonomous stance on matters properly before it. Now, he quickly dismissed what he called "the troublesome or not troublesome question of jurisdiction." Taft also dismissed Osborne's unwillingness to deal directly with the bonus system, calling it immaterial that the pay method was "technical" and insignificant that Grace had governmental approval for the way he handled overtime pay. "If any governmental official has held that you can by giving overtime reduce the bonus that has already been earned," he said, "that governmental official needs some more information on general principles with respect to the meaning of the term." Nor did Taft have kind words for Herbert Rice, who had at length submitted a tardy report of his own. The General Motors executive, said Taft, had "slurred over" the issues. "I am used to weighing evidence," Taft concluded, "and if there ever was a case on the record that shows evasion it is by this President of that Company, Mr. Grace, in . . . complying with our principles. Now we can make a finding. If they don't choose to obey it, that is all right, but we ought to give the moral effect of our order concretely now."[45]

Taft therefore supported Lauck's recommendations. He agreed that the bonus system should be abolished and that the Pittsfield plan of collective bargaining should be applied to Bethlehem Steel regardless of whether Grace appeared cooperative. Since Taft held the balance of power, not even Osborne objected to his motion that two labor members and two employer representatives draft an award for consideration by the full board the next day. The award Taft expected was obvious.

In the end, the Bethlehem award, as well as the two General Electric awards, came on 31 July from the pens of Taft and Walsh. The steelworkers got almost everything they wanted; the electricians received increased wages; and the machinists, the promise of a revised or eliminated bonus system and a minimum hourly wage rate that conformed with wage scales applied by the War and Navy departments. The shop-committee system devised by the joint chairmen provided for both minimal interference from management and maximum protection of minority rights, be the minority union or nonunion workers. To insure fairness, elections would be held outside the plant "in some convenient public building." An examiner, authorized to report to the NWLB any cases of discrimination by the company against union men, would supervise the annual elections and would devise a means to protect minority rights by limiting the number of candidates that each voter could support to a number less than the total number of representatives to be elected.[46]

As instructed, Taft and Walsh had designed the Bethlehem committee system to conform with the system they established at Pittsfield.

The powers and responsibilities of the committees themselves, however, differed. At Pittsfield, departmental committees could adjust disputes between lower level management—shop foremen and division superintendents—and the General Electric workers. From there, unsettled problems would be taken by a three-man committee of appeals, selected from within the departmental committees, to higher officials in the company. The Pittsfield committees were, therefore, merely grievance committees, while at Bethlehem, the shop committees were expected to assume a role in policy making.[47]

The Bethlehem award specifically left important refinements of wage and hour policies for shop committees and management representatives to decide. The award, for example, generally left the determination of piece rates to those groups, who would have the counsel of an NWLB-selected expert. Additionally, the award provided time and a half for overtime and double time for holidays, but left the standard workday in occupations that fell outside governmental-contract work and the designation of official holidays to committee-management determination. Instead of a committee on appeals, as at Pittsfield, the joint chairmen created a local mediation board at Bethlehem, with three of its seven members to be selected by the employees and three by the company. The seventh member, the chairman, would be chosen by the secretary of war. The local board, which would not be paid for its efforts, would settle "disputed issues not covered by the award." Appeal from its decision was directly to the NWLB.[48]

Thus, by the end of July, the board had banned "yellow-dog" contracts in a single firm statement: "The practice of making individual contracts of the restrictive character in evidence before this board is prohibited."[49] It also had authorized a bargaining plan adaptable to every kind of industry. The NWLB's plan minimized the opportunity for management intimidation of employees, which was so often present in company-union schemes like the Rockefeller Plan. The NWLB's committees would also have more independence and responsibility than those provided for in many prewar shop-committee systems. Most important, NWLB committees would have recourse to a governmental agency that stood squarely behind collective rights for workers. The end-of-July awards were therefore compatible with the way in which conservative labor defined "industrial democracy." Because labor now had the unencumbered right to organize, nothing remained to stop labor from controlling the elected committees.

In August, however, the new awards failed to impress an eastern pistol manufacturer under contract to the War Department. Douglas Wesson had no use for industrial democracy. The conflict between men and management at the Smith and Wesson Arms Company of Springfield, Massachusetts, demonstrated that business interests still required more than force of example before yielding long-standing policies that ran counter to the NWLB's principles.

Events at Smith and Wesson closely followed the Bethlehem scenario. Douglas Wesson, who had used "yellow-dog" contracts since 1904, dismissed men who joined the machinists' union and then, as a committee, tried to bargain collectively with management. The inevitable strike in mid-July prompted inevitably unsuccessful efforts by the War Department to persuade Wesson to reinstate the discharged employees, eliminate individual contracts, and allow collective bargaining. In anticipation of a settlement, the machinists had come back to work and then, inevitably, gone out again when no settlement came. After a month of frustration, the War Department had deferred to the NWLB on 13 August.[50] The board had then inevitably assigned the case to the joint chairmen, who within a week applied the policies devised for Pittsfield and Bethlehem to Smith and Wesson.

The easy extension of precedent to cover Smith and Wesson was more apparent than real. Difficulties arose because William Howard Taft played no part in the decision. While Taft vacationed at his Canadian retreat, Frederick Judson acted in his place. Although Judson came into the Smith and Wesson controversy intending to speak as Taft might speak, he was almost completely unaware of the evolution of Taft's attitude since serving on the NWLB, and he, therefore, approached the case prepared to interpret the NWLB's principles strictly. "There is a right difficult question presented by this case," he said, namely, the Supreme Court ruling in the Hitchman case. Taft, Judson insisted, would not encourage an employee to break a legal contract. The Pittsfield award as precedent was thereby jeopardized before the very board that had sanctioned it.[51]

Because Taft's absence threatened to roll time back, a curious transformation occurred in the behavior of Frank Walsh. In his appearance before the NWLB on 13 August, Walsh wore two hats. He played Taft's familiar role as well as his own; he became both moderator and agitator. As moderator, Walsh painted the Pittsfield award as a conservative ruling, telling his colleagues what few of them seemed to know and what most of the press had apparently misunderstood: The award prohibited only those individual contracts made at Pittsfield after the promulgation of the NWLB's principles, and even then it said nothing about the legality of those contracts. Taft had insisted on those conditions, he said. At Pittsfield, the joint chairmen had thus upheld the NWLB's principles and, at the same time, had neatly sidestepped the Hitchman decision.[52]

Then Walsh as agitator told the board about how things ought to be. The Pittsfield award, he maintained, had been but a first step toward justice. Walsh believed that every restrictive contract regardless of when effected was "immoral and void" despite the Hitchman ruling. He had wanted the board to say so even before the Pittsfield award, and he wanted the board to say so now. At Pittsfield, Walsh confessed, he had compromised "far beyond what I should have done."[53]

After that, Frederick Judson was relieved when Walsh agreed to an award for Smith and Wesson which ordered only the reinstatement of the men, the introduction of the Pittsfield bargaining system, and an end to individual contracts.[54] The relief blossomed into triumph when Walsh signed a statement that Judson drafted as the private opinion of the joint chairmen. The opinion admitted both the legality of individual contracts and the right of a company to discharge employees who violated those contracts, and it stipulated that, "of course," the NWLB could apply its principles only to the "future conduct of corporations and their relations to their employees."[55]

On closer inspection, the statement—which was an in-house paper for Jett Lauck to file away—also legitimized the Pittsfield and Bethlehem awards as viable models for future dealings with antiunion employers. It reiterated what Taft and Walsh had already concluded. It was, in fact, a pledge to uphold labor's right to organize regardless of the law. The statement specifically affirmed the board's right to condemn individual contracts whenever effected: "It does not follow, however, that the Board cannot recommend . . . that the exercise of such legal rights should be waived, or even prohibited in the term of the war." Judson's triumph, from that perspective, merely assured that the NWLB could never hide behind "legality" to excuse inaction. Walsh as agitator had gotten exactly what he wanted.

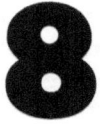

The War Labor Board in Autumn

> The War Labor Board is a bunch of radicals and
> I.W.W.'s. The only man who represents us is Taft and
> he is nothing but a jelly fish—never was anything
> else. Walsh is the worst appointment that the admin-
> istration ever made. The labor situation is too
> damned serious to have an agitator of his stamp in
> charge. We have got to have conservative business
> men in authority at this time, particularly after
> the war ends.
>   The War Labor Board has the unprecedented nerve
> to openly support unionization. . . . Furthermore
> they are trying to bluff employers into thinking they
> have the power to demand that we . . . unionize our
> works. . . . They haven't got the power. All we've
> got to do is sit tight and tell them to go to hell.
>
> —Remarks overheard by Stuart Chase in the smoker
> of a Pullman car, Autumn 1918

By all rights, the NWLB should have had an easy time in the autumn of 1918, for the battery of summer decisions should have made subsequent work almost routine. Instead of the easy application of summer precedents, however, the board faced mounting difficulties in the autumn. As the impact of its decisions began to filter through the economy, newly defined war-labor policies helped to polarize employer and employee interests. Manufacturing associations and local business concerns became increasingly hostile to federal intervention in their affairs. Employer associations in New England, the Midwest, and the South, for example, evaded or denounced NWLB action. Important companies that had already been directed by the NWLB to alter policies moved to effect awards with less than deliberate speed. Organized labor, on the other hand, continued to view the Taft-Walsh board as an influential friend who could be ever more helpful. As a result, tensions ran high in the weeks before the Armistice. Inevitably, the primary responsibility for maintaining cooperation among private interests devolved on the joint chairmen. Not surprisingly, Taft and Walsh discovered that cooperation had been easier to maintain while war-labor principles were but cloudy statements of contradictory intentions.

From early September until after the Armistice, Taft and Walsh guided the NWLB's actions in conformity with their summer rulings. The joint chairmen had defined NWLB principles only after hard-fought battles among their colleagues; and, although hundreds of new cases were referred to the board that fall, few new issues were raised. Autumn brought a new series of streetcar awards, revised shop-committee plans, increased minimum wages, and sporadic efforts to curb employees' abuse of overtime-pay provisions. But those awards generally refined principles already set out. The summer had been a time of policy making, newspaper headlines, and general praise. Autumn was a time for administration, for meeting the consequences of earlier decisions, for combating snipers from the outside. It was a tedious time and a difficult one.

Cooperation suffered that fall partly because American employers saw NWLB awards in two broad categories that might now be merged. Wage and hour awards were potentially hostile to employers' immediate profits but posed little threat to the control of company policies. Such awards, therefore, had been generally, if grudgingly, accepted. But collective bargaining awards—such as those devised for Bethlehem Steel, General Electric at Pittsfield, and Smith and Wesson—alarmed employers. Those awards invited union inroads that could long outlast the war. At the very least, they demanded that management share power with employees. For these reasons, the collective bargaining awards were in themselves unpopular. More important, they generated employer misgivings about future NWLB action. Nothing was to stop the board from recommending a shop-committee plan for any firm in which wage and hour controversies threatened production. Consequently, many employers began a more or less automatic retreat behind the prewar rhetoric of individualism.

Conservative spokesmen attacked the NWLB's right "to come into a man's own property and tell him how to run it."[1] In Minneapolis, that sentiment emerged when industrial leaders flatly denied the board's right to settle a series of local disputes and urged the intervention of the state conciliation agency instead.[2] Elsewhere, subtler but likeminded businessmen determined to control the limits of collective action. The Louisville Employers' Association, for example, suggested that its members volunteer to meet with employees, thereby "avoiding the necessity of . . . making arrangements through United States conciliators." Each employer should "be sure that the shop committee is of your best employees and not a committee appointed by outside agencies."[3]

Management spokesmen also complained bitterly about organized labor's refusal to honor the open shop and the NWLB's refusal to protect it. "The right of workers to join a union is not questioned," Walter Drew wrote on behalf of the antiunion National Erectors' Association, "but . . . the 'right of workers to organize' and the right of . . . [the Bridge and Structural Iron Workers' Union] to institute a country-wide attack in war-time upon peaceful establishments . . . are two very different things."[4] *Iron Age*, which until September 1918 had reported NWLB decisions with little editorial comment, suddenly stiffened. "It cannot be proved," said that weekly journal, "that the closed shop brings better co-operation between employer and employee. Why then in such abnormal times disturb the *status quo ante* or continue to introduce such controversial matters as the National War Labor Board has done in its Bethlehem, General Electric, Smith & Wesson and Bridgeport awards?"[5]

The "country-wide attack" that Drew condemned had come principally from the Midwest and had been engineered by John Fitzpatrick and William Z. Foster of the Chicago Federation of Labor. Both men had worked the packinghouses before Judge Alschuler's groundbreaking rulings in March 1918 and had then begun to organize the steel industry. In support of their efforts, the American Federation of Labor had instructed its executive council that June to "plan and carry into effect the most intensive campaign of organization within its power, and urge and aid all international, state and central bodies to do likewise." In September, the month that *Iron Age* exhibited a markedly changed sentiment, the National Committee for Organizing Iron and Steel Workers went to work.[6]

The chairman of the committee was Fitzpatrick, president of the Chicago federation and good friend of Frank Walsh, and the committee eventually boasted the membership of twenty-four national unions, among them the machinists, the electrical workers, and the bridge and structural iron workers. The committee itself had been established in Chicago by fifteen unions on 1 August, the day after the NWLB issued the Bethlehem and Pittsfield awards.[7] Even then, organized labor had seen the uses of the NWLB's shop-committee plan.

Samuel Gompers, titular leader of the steelworkers' organizing committee, was realistic but optimistic in the September issue of the *American Federationist*. There could be difficulties, Gompers admitted, "in the most effective use of their ballots by these workers only now industrially enfranchised." But with help from the outside, the Bethlehem steel workers could use the shop committee to organize themselves as thoroughly as management was organized. "A shop committee for the Bethlehem steel workers," Gompers believed, "may mean the beginning of industrial freedom." Shop committees established in other companies, he implied, could bring more workers the same benefits.[8]

That September, industrial freedom was the theme of Frank Walsh's Labor Day message. Walsh's buoyant remarks, which received wide notice, could hardly fail to enhance the NWLB's already prolabor image. The World War was teaching Americans what democracy really meant, Walsh wrote. Democracy meant that people could control the conditions of their lives; and with the "aggressive assistance" of American laborers, democratization would continue "until there will remain not one wage earner in the country deprived of full voice in determining the conditions of his job and consequently of his life."[9] Another piece, which Walsh wrote for the *American Federationist*, left no doubt about the kind of assistance the joint chairman meant: "You must continue to organize your unions, strong and liberal, fearless and far-seeking."[10]

That kind of rhetoric evoked a flurry of denunciation of Frank P. Walsh in the conservative press. The Spokane *Spokesman-Review* called his Labor Day press release a "Bolshevik utterance." Were Walsh "not a member of a government board," the Butte *Miner* sputtered, "his remarks would not even be considered." The joint chairman seemed "afflicted with that peculiar notion sometimes manifested by those of the agitating coterie. . . . Class hatred preaching, industrial disruption and opposition to any and all industrial progress without offering even the slightest substitute plan of any value, is the peculiar trend of their minds."[11] The New London, Connecticut, *Day* discredited Walsh by claiming not to understand his remarks. What does he mean, it asked, when he predicts that wage earners shall have a "full voice" in determining the conditions of labor? "Possibly if he had known he would have told us." A lot of people, the *Day* concluded, were being "tragically misled" by an abundance of "hot air" and "have come to have an eager expectation that the millenium will begin about 1920, or 1921 at the furthest. They will be bitterly disappointed."[12] Such editorials, coupled with the praise that prolabor reporters heaped on the "new" Taft that September, generally served to redouble labor's trust in the NWLB.[13]

Labor's trust in the board, however, did not prevent what *Iron Age* called the "outlaw strike" in Bridgeport—the only pre-Armistice strike called in protest of an NWLB award. The Bridgeport men and women whom NWLB member William H. Johnston addressed on Labor Day had already been bitterly disappointed, and Johnston did little to change their sentiments. He told a standing crowd sweltering in the hot September sun in Seaside Park that they "hadn't had a square deal." The machinists' president also told the working-class audience other things that they had come to believe—that the war effort depended on the small arms and cartridges that Bridgeport's ten thousand machinists and toolmakers made, that they deserved to be partners in industry, and that human rights were paramount in the war experience. At no time did Johnston tell the members of the errant machinists' local to end their strike against sixty-five shops. On the contrary, the union president implied that the body denying the strikers a "square deal" was the NWLB itself, and he tacitly encouraged the six thousand strikers to stay out. "You have been robbed and exploited all your life," Johnston said. "You will be robbed and exploited for the rest of your life if you don't get together and act together."[14]

In Washington that week, Frank Walsh anguished over the Bridgeport strike, in part perhaps, because he had inadvertently helped to cause it. For once, his enthusiastic support for the workers' position had proved counterproductive. On 23 August, ten days before Johnston's speech, Walsh had gone to Bridgeport and averted a threatened strike by winning the confidence of five thousand workers assembled at the Bridgeport casino. Before the wildly cheering workers, he had pledged that the award expected in a few days from umpire Otto Eidlitz would be just. Because of Walsh's words, morale and expectations had soared.[15] "There may be strikes against the policies of the National War Labor Board as Frank P. Walsh outlined them," the Bridgeport *Labor Leader* reported on 29 August, "but they will not be strikes inaugurated by labor."[16] The following day, the Bridgeport machinists struck. The Eidlitz award, issued at Washington on 28 August, had brought too little too late.[17]

At the root of the problem were money and union standards, and for a time, it seemed that the workers had got what they wanted. Before the NWLB came into the case in June, the Ordnance Department had made a city-wide settlement that, among other things, classified trades and granted a minimum wage rate to each class. Bridgeport employers had then objected that the kinds of work being done there made classification into trades impossible. At their behest, the Ordnance Department settlement had been withdrawn, and the NWLB had inherited the case. When the board deadlocked on classifications and minimums, the dispute had gone to Umpire Eidlitz. Eidlitz upheld the Bridgeport employers by refusing, for the time being, to classify trades.[18]

In other respects, the award was a clear victory for the employees. Eidlitz raised wages across the board, imposed a 42-cent minimum for unskilled labor, granted the basic eight-hour day, outlawed discrimination against union members, and ordered shop-committee elections. In Bridgeport, those provisions could transform working conditions. Wages and hours varied drastically from plant to plant; men who joined unions were often dismissed, then blacklisted; and collective bargaining was almost unknown. In short, Eidlitz had brought the NWLB's version of "industrial democracy" to an entire industrial community. For skilled workers such as the machinists, however, the new wages would continue to vary and would remain well below union scales. The Eidlitz award, therefore, was unacceptable to them.[19]

On Friday, 6 September, when their strike was a week old, the machinists petitioned President Wilson to commandeer the companies at Bridgeport, classify trades, and increase wages again. Almost alone, a Bridgeport newspaperman defended the strikers. For months, he wrote, the government had done nothing but build hope while the men patiently waited for action, and that hope had been dashed. Eidlitz's award was "only the last straw, that straw which has been breaking camels' backs for centuries." Caught up in spiraling inflation and faced with inequities now perpetuated by the NWLB, he implied, the Bridgeport machinists had no time for democracy.[20]

While the Bridgeport strike continued unabated, the Smith and Wesson Company in nearby Massachusetts awaited news from the War Department. The arms company had become the second employer to reject an NWLB award. Rather than reinstate the men who had broken their individual contracts and then establish shop committees, Smith and Wesson wanted the department to assume control of the company for the duration of the war.[21]

At the end of August, George P. Chapin, secretary of the Smith and Wesson board of trustees, explained at length to the NWLB why the company "respectfully declined to accept" the Judson-Walsh recommendations. First of all, Chapin pointed out, the company had never submitted to the NWLB's jurisdiction. Then, he attacked the NWLB's policies: "If the closed union shop is to remain undisturbed," Chapin insisted, "there is just as potent reason why the closed non-union shop should remain undisturbed." Citing both state and federal court decisions, Chapin went on to call the award logically unsound, economically unnecessary, and legally untenable. Collective bargaining, he continued, was not bargaining at all unless freely consented to by both sides as specified by the Supreme Court in the Hitchman case. Wartime, he further lectured the NWLB, was no time "under the guise of settling labor disputes, to substitute a social and economic theory, at best of doubtful value, which could by no possibility be imposed upon the business world in normal times, for established lawful methods of known practicability and proven efficiency." The Smith and Wesson Company, therefore, saw no reason "to abandon its lawful and legitimate method of doing business . . . for the fantastic method" recommended at Washington.[22]

Other New England manufacturers closed ranks behind the Massachusetts gun maker in early September. Smith and Wesson blamed its recent labor troubles on an infamous "campaign of agitation started by outside labor organizers," and eighteen firms in Hartford, Connecticut, rose to defend the open shop. On 7 September, the Hartford manufacturers asked Secretary of War Baker to allow Smith and Wesson to "disregard" the NWLB and predicted "industrial chaos" if the board was permitted to erode the "sanctity of contract." They especially deplored the idea of collective bargaining and shop committees at Smith and Wesson and praised instead the efficiency of autocratic management.[23]

The Hartford manufacturers were hardly subtle in their efforts to sway Baker. They evidently believed that a proper response from the War Department could shelter many industrialists from both the NWLB and outside labor organizers and therefore compared an industrial plant to a military contingent. The secretary of war, the Connecticut employers wrote, "would not tolerate . . . soldiers' committees in the army which should negotiate with the commander-in-chief as to when and on what terms they would fight." Like an army, they suggested, an industrial plant reached its highest productivity when controlled exclusively by one man. They even obfuscated the issues at Bridgeport in order to illustrate their point: When the manufacturers of that city agreed to Eidlitz's directive to establish shop committees, production almost ceased; in contrast, one-man rule at Smith and Wesson had kept production ahead of schedule.[24]

For Frank Walsh, those early days in September were "awful."[25] For almost a month, he had shouldered the responsibility for the NWLB's work while Taft vacationed at Murray Bay. Within the last few weeks, he had moved his wife and most of his eight children to Washington, and now he was spending almost every day hard at work on matters that defied easy resolution. Neither he nor concerned labor members of the board had been able to quiet the dissidents at Bridgeport. Walsh was also powerless to end continued recalcitrance from the Smith and Wesson Company, and he knew it. He was tired—and despondent.

On 9 September, however, Walsh recovered his fighting spirit. On that Monday morning, he lent his son Frank, who was studying naval aviation at the Massachusetts Institute of Technology, a bit of fatherly support: "You will come out all right, old man; never have a fear. And, if you don't, well, then you know the family motto: 'To h———l with them.'" As for himself, Walsh wrote that despite recent frustrations, he had his "teeth sunk into the hindquarters of the job" and was "hanging right onto it." He was certain, he said, that the board could overcome its troubles "no matter how hard the struggle may be." The joint chairman's sudden high spirits reflected his relief at Taft's return from Canada. Taft, in fact, was due at the office even as Walsh dictated his letter to Frank. "So I hope," the father confided to his son, "the worst of my troubles is over."[26]

By 13 September, it was. On that day, the War Department seized Smith and Wesson as though putting down a local rebellion, announcing as it did so that the department intended to uphold the decision of the NWLB.[27] That was not the kind of takeover the company had wanted. Simultaneously, President Wilson dealt just as firmly with the machinists at Bridgeport. The Smith and Wesson Company had "flaunted" the decision of the NWLB and, on his order, had been punished, the president told the men. "Having exercised a drastic remedy with recalcitrant employers," Wilson continued, he was obligated "to use means equally well adapted to the end with lawless and faithless employees." The machinists had acted with "disloyalty" and "dishonor," and he was ordering them back to work. If they did not return, he added, he would bar their employment during the next year in every war-related industry, and he would lift the draft exemptions granted them because of "alleged usefulness on war production." Patently, they must work or fight.[28]

Both of the administration's actions that day gave ironic credence to wartime "voluntarism." The *New York Times* and the Newark *Times* rejoiced in the reinvigorated NWLB and predicted that other groups that defied awards would receive the same treatment accorded Smith and Wesson and the Bridgeport machinists. Frank Walsh also celebrated and enthusiastically confided in his son that the president's action had fixed "the status and power of our Board beyond all question." Significantly, Walsh gave much of the credit for the president's bold stroke to William Howard Taft.[29]

Taft had often stressed the board's duty to uphold its principles, and now he had acted with Walsh to insure that, once rendered, the NWLB's decisions would be obeyed. The president's letter had been designed "to show both sides that they had to carry out the principles laid down by . . . our Board." Walsh knew that, he explained to Frank, because he and Taft had drafted the letter and suggested that the president send it. Wilson, in turn, had "followed it almost literally." The fatigue that had plagued Walsh in recent weeks had given way to unfettered exuberance and unqualified admiration for his Republican colleague. "It is a joy," he concluded, "to have that man around. He helps over all the rough places, and has such a sane, clear, and honest view about everything, that it certainly lightens up my work."[30]

In Bridgeport, however, the NWLB's problems were far from over. The machinists, as instructed, agreed to return to work and to seek adjustment of the award through the board's own machinery, but the employers refused to reinstate the returning strikers until the president intervened once again, this time to order management to take the men back.[31] Almost immediately afterward, Taft and Walsh scheduled a new hearing at Bridgeport on 23 September in order to "straighten out . . . [some] knotty issues." Their confidence in the board restored, Bridgeport labor leaders predicted that the visit of the joint chairmen would mean the revocation of the odious provisions of the award. They were almost right.[32]

At the county courthouse in Bridgeport, the meeting of the joint chairmen with the local representatives of labor and management lasted twelve minutes. Taft told the three hundred people assembled in the civil superior court room that the NWLB's examiner, Alpheus Winter, had full authority to interpret Eidlitz's award. Winter then announced his rulings on nine points at issue.[33] Among the most important was his decision to institute collective-bargaining procedures without interference from either side. The examiner also authorized the local mediation commission—identical to the one devised for Bethlehem Steel—to "create specialized craft or other boards to work out specialized craft problems such as classification and minimum rates of pay." Finally, Winter gave returning strikers a full voice in the election of labor's representatives on the local commission, thus clearing the way for the machinists to achieve goals that had not been realized in the award itself.[34] Swiftly, Taft then adjourned the meeting. It would be a sheer waste of time, he added, to extend the discussion.[35]

By then, the NWLB had become involved in a third General Electric case, one that it had inherited in August from the Massachusetts

Board of Arbitration. Except for inevitable local colorations, the issues were all too familiar. A strike of ten thousand employees at the Lynn, Massachusetts, plant had left the plant manager apparently perplexed. The men had just walked out in July, he complained, giving no reason for the strike. In turn, the strikers had declared their confusion when management would not readmit them to the plant to hear their grievances. They had quit work because the manager ran a closed nonunion shop and had dismissed sixteen employees who became active in the electrical workers' union.[36] Both management and men had expressed a willingness to meet collectively. Management, however, privately leaned toward adapting the Rockefeller Plan and working with delegations of older men; many employees, on the other hand, wanted to disregard the rights of unorganized workers. The Massachusetts board had surrendered jurisdiction in the interest of a speedy settlement and because, frankly, the strikers objected to its tedious procedures, which first required an investigation by the company.[37]

The Lynn award of 24 October followed precedent closely enough. It ordered the election of shop committees "forthwith" under the supervision of an NWLB examiner and "in conformity with" a board-sanctioned plan. The award also ordered the reinstatement, with their former seniority and back pay, of eleven of the sixteen men who had been dismissed. One of the men had since joined the service, and Taft considered two to be personally undesirable and unworthy of reinstatement. The other two men whose dismissals were allowed to stand had urged sit-down strikes by fellow workers after company foremen had directed them to get to work or leave the shop. Sit-downs, held Judge Taft, were not legitimate union activity.[38]

The elections at Lynn were the first to be held under a general election procedure initiated by the employer members and adopted by the board on 4 October. In two respects, the new code modified the Pittsfield plan. It permitted elections inside the plant, and it omitted special safeguards for minority representation. The employer members believed that outside elections catered to the unions. The new code only partially satisfied them, as it provided for balloting "in the place where the largest total vote of the men can be secured, consistent with fairness of count and full and free expression of choice."[39] Selection of that place was left to Jett Lauck and Hugh Hanna. Although the plant was the logical choice, they remained free to follow the Pittsfield method of voting in "some convenient public building."[40]

Taft considered the new code "reasonable" and so assured Loyall

Osborne. At the same time, he gave the Westinghouse executive a lesson in diplomacy. Tom Savage vehemently opposed in-shop elections, Taft explained, and there might be cases in which he was right. However, the joint chairman said, all of the NWLB's examiners thought that elections should be held in the plant except "in rare cases." Jett Lauck had gone as far as to say that voting should always be held in the shop, Taft pointed out, and since Lauck could decide the matter, "we have accomplished our purpose." Gradually, he believed, the custom of in-shop elections would develop automatically. It was "just as well," therefore, to leave Walsh and the labor members "a convenient ladder . . . to come over to our side without making the surrender too obvious."[41]

The surrender was so subtle that it was no surrender at all. The code protected elections from interference by management regardless of where held. The examiner in charge of each election would continue to use employees to help officiate and would continue to bar company officials from the polling places. W. L. Stoddard, the examiner who had administered the Pittsfield award and was now assigned to Lynn, was pleased with all of the modifications in the code. Pittsfield employees had so resented management that they had vowed to sit out any elections held within company grounds, but outside elections had required balloting after hours, and Stoddard confirmed a low percentage of voters. Stoddard had also observed at Pittsfield that safeguarding minority rights was unnecessary. Unionized employees did not corner the elections and shut out the nonunion minority, but rather, the minority supported union candidates. "Most elections," he wrote later, "were unanimous." No part of the new code, therefore, could be expected to hamper a well-organized campaign to elect union candidates to committees.[42]

By October, some American employers had written off the NWLB as an unregenerate tool of organized labor. A New York friend of Taft's attempted to warn the former president about what was happening, but when he informed Taft of his "great concern for the strangle hold which labor seems to be getting on the employers," the joint chairman merely observed "a good deal of indurated prejudice on both sides."[43] The New England manufacturers who continued to react to the Smith and Wesson award made Taft's point nicely. The NWLB's decision was "the rawest deal ever given an honest business concern," "The Voter and His Employer" announced; the employer members of the board should have resigned in protest when the president ordered the arms works commandeered and the award enforced. The solution to such abuse, continued that Worcester, Massachusetts, publication, was to elect a Republican Congress in November, which would relegate the National War Labor Board "to the rear."[44]

Even the National Industrial Conference Board, the employer organization responsible for half of the NWLB's membership and much of its statement of principles, joined the opposition. The NICB's Ninth Yama Conference that October sharply criticized war-labor policies. In particular, the conference attacked the basic eight-hour day and wage increases, and it warned that "unless promptly changed after the war, the prevailing high rates, short working schedules, and low work efficiency in American industry" could hinder foreign trade. The NICB members also echoed Newcomb Carlton and Douglas Wesson by calling for protection of the closed nonunion shop. They endorsed collective bargaining, but with severe limitations.[45]

Nothing more clearly drew the line between the NICB and the NWLB than the businessmen's views on this matter of bargaining, the issue on which they most nearly accepted governmental directives. The employers, for example, even objected to the phrase "collective bargaining." They preferred to use "co-operative representation" because that term minimized, in their minds, any implication of "fundamental disagreement or strife" between employer and employee. Then, they stated the terms under which they would tolerate such cooperation. In an election held within company gates, a majority of all employees entitled to vote should first request a committee system. If they did so, any attempts by committees to adjust wages and working conditions should be contained within individual departments of a plant. As for the NWLB, the Yama conferees conceded that the board could conduct an election to determine if employees wanted shop committees, but they resisted further direction from Washington. No governmental agency, they agreed, was "within its rights" when it imposed a plan without first securing the consent of both labor and management. Having made shop committees difficult to establish, and having then designed a weak and fragmented committee system, the Yama Conference had ultimately denied the NWLB's powers to implement a collective-bargaining plan without employer approval.[46]

In New York that month, Scott Nearing—economist, teacher, former chairman of the antiwar Peoples Council of America, and Socialist candidate for Congress—read the temper of the times warily. Workers were enjoying temporary gains, he told a gathering of Italian laborers, but labor's position was weak, and wartime complacency would yield peacetime defeat. "The bosses are organizing," he warned, "organizing more effectively than ever before. In a few cases, such as the Smith and Wesson company . . . they have even gone so far as to defy the war labor board. During war time that is manifestly impossible, but when peace comes and there is no longer a war labor board, these bosses will have something to say again."

Almost daily, Nearing noted, the New York *Call* printed extracts from businessmen's newsletters that deplored the strength of American labor and reminded "the masters to take care." Labor interests, he predicted, would survive the peace only if the workers were "well organized, intelligent, and awake to their opportunities."[47]

While Nearing campaigned in New York, employers in Minnesota organized against the NWLB. Some fifty cases from Minneapolis and St. Paul were pending before the Minnesota State Board of Arbitration that autumn. Although the employers were amenable to potential state action, labor leaders in the twin cities wanted the Taft-Walsh board to take over the disputes. On 30 September, labor's cause was strengthened when the Minnesota board wired Jett Lauck that one case, that of the machinists versus the Minneapolis Steel and Machinery Company, was "a controversy for your board." Lauck read the message as a waiver of jurisdiction, even though the state agency had earlier claimed jurisdiction over all wage and hour disputes. The steel company and other companies with labor problems viewed the NWLB's interest in the case with alarm.[48]

Tensions ran high in Minneapolis as the city awaited a visit from the joint chairmen on 10 October. Local industrialists stacked their arguments against the NWLB's intervention. The Citizens' Alliance of Minneapolis swelled the resistance with emotionalism and hate and publicly praised the Smith and Wesson Company, calling the company's attitude toward the NWLB "clearly" indicative of the sentiment of major employers. "Actuated by the War Labor Board's stand on unionism," an Alliance pamphlet declared, "all the agitators of the country have been turned loose . . . to organize every industry in the United States. They have overplayed their hand."[49] Minneapolis labor leaders, nonetheless, smelled victory in an inevitable showdown with the Alliance. "The Employers expended their every resource to keep the Board away," wrote R. D. Cramer of the Minneapolis *Labor Review*, "but we have evidently won the first round . . . for the Board is to be here."[50]

The battle stemmed from the obvious conflict in state and federal labor policies. The wartime policies of the state arbitration board, like those of the NWLB, had been endorsed by representatives of both sides. They had been written in April—less than one week after the creation of the NWLB—by the executive council of the Minnesota State Federation of Labor and the same Citizens' Alliance that now vilified the NWLB some six months later. Like the NWLB, the state board forbade strikes and lockouts and pledged the maintenance of existing conditions, but the Minnesota board read "existing conditions" literally. Furthermore, its interpretation of the term was beyond dispute. Governor J. A. A. Burnquist had given the new principles the force and effect of orders of the Minnesota Commission of Public Safety, which, in turn, had announced that strikers would be jailed.[51]

The Minnesota board's commitment to existing conditions was underscored by a blunt statement in the arbitration principles in which "employers and employees agree(d) in good faith to maintain the existing status, in every phase of employment, of a union, nonunion, or open shop."[52] The state board also failed to guarantee the rights to organize and to bargain collectively. The omission of this guarantee effectively denied the rights and consequently set the labor policy of the state in opposition to that of the NWLB. While the NWLB's principles forbade using coercion to change the character of a shop, the Minnesota principles in effect forbade asking for a change. As the closed nonunion shop was among the existing conditions to be preserved, it is little wonder that Minnesota employers preferred the jurisdiction of the state board or that labor leaders looked to Washington.[53]

By summer, organized labor had lost faith in the state's machinery. The arbitration board had done virtually nothing for employees. (Indeed, its overall record was so bad that it had failed to satisfy even the employers in its most important case, a street-railway dispute.) In July, the state federation of labor voted in convention to recognize the Taft-Walsh board as the only agency to which disputes might be referred. Thereafter, when the Minnesota board tried to achieve recognition as a subsidiary of the NWLB, the federation denounced the action as a ploy by Governor Burnquist to redefine federal labor policy to conform to his own. In protest against this, the labor federation ordered its representative on the state board to resign. After St. Paul played host to the AFL convention that summer, unionization spread rapidly through the twin cities, unionization that was carefully designed to follow federal guidelines and built "on the basis that . . . demands . . . would be adjusted by the National War Labor Board and no strikes were necessary and would be not countenanced in any event."[54]

In September, trouble was imminent. Minnesota miners organized the Mesabi range, and Minneapolis labor leaders worked day and night to keep newly organized workers from bolting the shops. Vernon Rose of Kansas City, an NWLB investigator and a friend of Frank Walsh, reportedly kept "the lid on" the mills, cereal works, and rapid-transit lines in the Twin Cities only by promising employees a speedy hearing from the NWLB. On 26 September, Arthur LeSueur of the Nonpartisan League called the labor situation in Minnesota a powder keg and predicted that strikes in the Twin Cities would produce a statewide revolt, especially in the mines. Low wages were the major ostensible grievance, but LeSueur informed Walsh of the men's deeper resentment of the "pernicious activities of the Minnesota Public Safety Commission and the officials of those companies in discriminating against union men."[55]

Joint Chairman Taft entered the fourth-floor court room of the Minneapolis federal building on 10 October with a cheery good morning to the capacity crowd. Then he got down to business, casting "red tape to the winds." He and Walsh, he cautioned counsel for both sides, wanted to hear only the facts, no legal technicalities. Specifically, the joint chairmen were in Minneapolis to decide whether to assume jurisdiction in the steel case. That decision, Taft explained, would determine the NWLB's action in most of the fifty other cases pending before the state board, which included disputes in almost all the machinery plants in the Twin Cities. At issue, then, was the labor policy of the state. If the NWLB took up the steel case, Minneapolis employers could no longer expect the state to protect them against union organization. If the NWLB declined action, labor organizers would continue to be branded as outlaws.[56]

At the hearing that morning, Frank Morrison, secretary of the AFL, appeared with Arthur LeSueur and other officials from the Nonpartisan League and leaders of the state federation of labor to encourage the NWLB's intervention. LeSueur, acting as chief counsel for all unionized employees, and the steelworkers' counsel, T. E. Latimer, came prepared to demonstrate that the NWLB's principles had been ignored in Minneapolis. Latimer, a former Socialist congressional candidate, brought hard evidence that the Minneapolis Steel and Machinery Company had dismissed men for joining a union.[57]

As counsel for the steel company, Pierce Butler, future justice of the Supreme Court, based his case on jurisdictional matters. Butler, who held the floor most of the morning, denied any controversy between the Minneapolis Steel and Machinery Company and its employees. He also objected to what he considered an attempt by the NWLB to force owners of open shops to treat with union officials at the hearing. The point of his carefully-prepared remarks was simply that no arbitration was necessary. If a genuine controversy developed between the company and its employees, he argued, the company was bound to submit the dispute first to the War Department, to whom it was under contract, and then to the state board of arbitration, which was the only duly constituted authority to settle labor disputes in Minnesota. Butler, in short, resolved a potential conflict between state and federal policy by claiming superiority for the state.[58]

Taft came to labor's defense. In so doing, he refined his own thoughts about the rights of union labor in an open shop and the right of employees to adequate representation before the NWLB. "Where men seek to bargain collectively in an open shop," he told Butler, "their employers may refuse to deal with any but their own employees. In other words, it's a family arrangement. But the War Labor Board has never laid down the rule that . . . it would not allow unions to represent their members who happen to be members of that family."[59] From the joint chairman's remarks, it must have been obvious what action he and Walsh would propose in Minneapolis.

When the NWLB assumed jurisdiction in all the Minneapolis cases on 22 November, Ambrose Tighe, counsel for the Minnesota Commission of Public Safety, was courteous. He acknowledged "an apparent variance between the state and national program." Unlike the NWLB, he implied in a letter to Taft, the authors of the Minnesota policies "thought they could not ignore the closed non-union shop and still preserve the *status quo* in Minnesota, so they included it." Given that, Tighe admitted, the Taft-Walsh board could hardly have refused to intervene unless it believed that it could act only in the complete absence of state arbitration machinery. "I do not believe this position was possible," said Tighe, "because it would make the national board's intervention so sporadic as to defeat the purpose of its creation."[60]

Minneapolis employers were not so ready as Tighe to accept the displacement of state authority. Yet rather than defy the NWLB as the Smith and Wesson company had done, they asked that the full board overrule the joint chairmen. When that tactic failed, the employers gambled that time was on their side and won. As peace returned to America, the NWLB's rulings lost their urgency and, indeed, their moral force. The Minneapolis awards, issued in the spring of 1919, upheld the employees' rights to organize and to bargain collectively, but they were rarely enforced. Moral suasion meant little to the Minneapolis Steel and Machinery Company and other companies in the Twin Cities.[61] What counted was that the threat of governmental takeover in the interest of war production had passed. With it had gone the NWLB's ability to impose its awards upon unwilling employers.

The Mothers of the Race

MARGUERITE MARTYN: Well, do you think street car conductoring and traffic officering and such jobs are suitable women's work?
ANNA HERKNER: I think the only question as to what constitutes woman's work is, given certain work, does she do it as well as a man?

—Interview with NWLB Examiner Herkner, October 1918

In the 1960s, two federal steps against sex-based discrimination—the Equal Pay Amendment to the Fair Labor Standards Act and the Civil Rights Act—brought victory to the heirs of the women who had fought for both equal pay and equal employment opportunities during World War I. The NWLB had stood behind the demand for equal pay but equivocated on the right of working women to continue to enter new occupations, and, in the end, left a checkered legacy. For a variety of reasons, application of the equal-pay principle proved difficult. Throughout the war, the board also remained trapped by the protective language that people then used, often in good faith, to control women's economic opportunities. After the Armistice, the most the NWLB could offer working women was moral support for their right to retain, at equal pay, the specific jobs that they had been able to secure during the emergency.

The NWLB's principle on equal pay for equal work when women worked at jobs ordinarily filled by men pleased both feminists and the labor movement. In 1918, women earned only one-half to two-thirds as much as men, and frequently less than boys not yet eighteen. Part of the wage imbalance had developed because women worked in industry's lowest paying and least prestigious jobs; yet, even when they performed similar tasks in jobs usually held by men, they remained underpaid. Traditionalists rationalized the disparity by holding that a woman's pay was "personal" or supplementary and that family considerations mandated the higher wage-scale for men.[1] In these circumstances, the unregulated introduction into the war industries of 1,500,000 women, many of whom performed as efficiently as men, caused problems. As early as March 1917, therefore, the

American Federation of Labor had joined the women's wartime fight for equal pay.² Eight months later in convention, the AFL urged women to organize and announced that only through organization could the sexes effect wage quality.³ Elated, feminists had united with labor to protect men's wage levels and to prevent women from superseding men by underbidding them.

The NWLB's promise of equality suggested a status for working women that the protective legislation of the prewar years had militated against. The minimum-wage legislation passed in twelve states after 1912 had never reached most working women, either because it was drawn too narrowly or because it was ignored. Nor did the legislation ever imply equality. None of the laws, for example, ordered women's pay scales raised to the level normally accorded men, whose wages remained unregulated. Furthermore, their value to those women whom they did help was diminished by the reasoning that generally sanctioned protective laws. Justice Brewer in the Muller decision, for example, had approved the invasion of a woman's contract rights because something in her "disposition and habits of life" prevented her full assertion of them. Even if a woman stood, "so far as the statutes are concerned, upon an absolutely equal plane with her [brother]," Brewer explained, she was "so constituted" that she relied upon his aid. Beyond that, "her physical structure and a proper discharge of her maternal functions—having in view not merely her own health, but the well-being of the race—" justified state action on her behalf.[4] Hours-limitation laws, while rarely sustained for men when Brewer spoke in 1908, were thus acceptable for women because women had little bargaining power, and more precisely, because women were considered inherently unequal.

Yet, the wartime government's measures to protect working women reflected those prewar values. As Jett Lauck later remarked, "Women are the mothers of the race . . . and can not be dealt with on the same terms as men workers."[5] Although the NWLB itself merely cautioned against allotting women tasks "disproportionate to their strength,"[6] the War Labor Policies Board debated "what kinds of work women should perform, how they should best be introduced, under what conditions they should be employed, and what work should be prohibited." That board even barred women from certain hazardous work and from places of employment for which they were "clearly unfit," like saloons and poolrooms, and it bound their employers to existing protective measures.[7]

The NWLB's detailed explanation of its pay principle revealed a similar inability to break free of accepted conventions about women's roles and a potentially troublesome indecision on the permanent status of women in industry. First, it went a half step beyond the protective legislation by accepting the feminist cry for "abstract justice." Women, it asserted, deserved payment commensurate with service. Then, it slid into traditionalism by saying that many women deserved consideration because they temporarily took "the place of some man" in supporting a family. Finally, the NWLB virtually admitted that the real purpose of the principle was to protect working men by keeping women at home: "It is not economically sound or socially desirable that women should be brought into industry at a faster rate or in greater numbers than the needs of production actually demand, and the only check is to make it no more profitable to employ women than men."[8]

The application of the principle, the board soon discovered, was "not so simple as it looks."[9] In matters unrelated to pay, it awarded women equal rights with little publicity and few internal disagreements. Women, like men, gained shorter workdays and the right to join unions—when the unions would have them—but when the board set wages, it sometimes made women's pay only three-quarters equal. Only if an unassisted woman performed the same tasks in the same time as a man was equal work irrefutable. To provide for instances when that was not the case in the summer of 1918, the board in four of the five awards that called for equal pay also set women's minimums at 30 to 33 cents an hour, some 10 to 12 cents below the minimums it fixed for men in the same plants. The lower minimums were meant to apply when women either produced less than men or worked at tasks categorically unequal, that is, at jobs that men had never held. The awards gave men about $21 a week, and women about $15,[10] a figure Taft and Walsh considered a living wage for a woman in a small city and without dependents.[11] Thus the NWLB only amended convention. A woman needed a smaller wage than a man with a family, unless of course, she broke tradition by holding a man's job. Even then, when it offered the alternative of lower minimums, the board unwittingly offered unscrupulous employers a means to evade the principle altogether.

Nevertheless, the NWLB set far higher standards than either state and local regulators or the federal government. In early 1919, eight months after the board had begun to translate principle into policy, the average minimum for adult, experienced women in states that regulated women's rates was just $10. Only the District of Columbia, at $16,[12] came close to meeting the $16.50 that Frank Walsh considered a living wage for women in large cities.

One case that overrode federal standards made news throughout the country. As Taft and Walsh drafted the award for the General Electric plant at Schenectady, Taft noticed that the scrubwomen there, who worked four hours a day between the hours of 5:00 and 9:00 A.M., earned a mere $5 a week. That meant that they worked the rest of the day in Schenectady laundries to supplement their income. Although the scrubwomen were outside the board's jurisdiction because they had made no complaint, Taft ignored legal technicalities and became their "knight errant" when he suggested a wage increase of more than 100 percent.[13] The new $10.50 weekly minimum was of special importance, the Newark *Ledger* reported, because the charwomen for the executive departments in Washington earned less than $8.75 a week for a six-hour workday beginning at 7:00 A.M.[14]

Meanwhile in New York mail rooms, so a newspaperman disclosed to Walsh, women earned $8 per week addressing envelopes for the Committee on Public Information.[15] Their superintendent's apologetic explanation that $6 or $7 was average for such work in New York "almost put me to bed," Walsh told public information director George Creel as he urged Creel to raise the wages to $16.50. The federal government should "set the mark in decent wages and conditions," Walsh wrote angrily, but the government was itself "the worst offender in this respect." Creel's New York subordinate had parroted the argument "offered by private employers every place." The incident, Walsh wrote in disgust, "made me remark, for the millionth or two time, 'what's the use?'"[16]

To raise the standard of living of women who were frequently unaware of their rights obviously required more than chance discovery and correction of inequities. In August, therefore, the NWLB created two women's divisions within its staff. Elisabeth Christman of the Women's Trade Union League came from Chicago to lead a team of field investigators who, like the men investigators already at work for the employer and labor representatives, were to counsel their clients in advance of board hearings. Marie Obenauer of the War Department became the chief examiner of the Division of Women Administrative Examiners and would direct eight women in studies of conditions at the plants.[17] Their greatest contributions, like those of men examiners assigned the same duties, could be in recommending and administering awards.

While Christman's investigators moved smoothly into the NWLB's bureaucracy, Marie Obenauer and her examiners challenged it. Obenauer wanted to administer awards so that standards set up thereunder would have "a cumulative influence" on industries that employed women. Although she recognized the difficulty of determining equal work,[18] she nevertheless meant to apply the equal-pay principle systematically and to improve the means generally used to set women's wages in plants affected by NWLB awards. A capable labor analyst, Obenauer moved quickly to give female industrial workers a role in wage determination. In early September, one of her examiners arranged a special settlement at the General Electric plants in Schenectady and Pittsfield—which had been directed that summer to pay women equally but had also been provided with alternate lower minimums. The examiner's ruling specified that women would receive the piece and hourly rates given men working at the same jobs. Reasonable deductions for "additional assistance" or "special equipment" were to be decided by agreement between NWLB-ordered shop committees and committees representing the plant managements. Simultaneously, at Obenauer's suggestion, the NWLB ordered the election of a proportional number of women to the shop committees.[19]

Obenauer was also quick to criticize awards that had been issued since the precedent-shattering decision at Waynesboro. Nowhere had the Waynesboro award called for equal pay, but because it made no distinction between male and female employees, the 40-cent minimum for common laborers had applied to both sexes. To Obenauer, the board's subsequent establishment of lesser minimums for women in larger towns where the cost of living was higher had been ill-conceived. Furthermore, apprenticeship and age qualifications attached to those minimums had sometimes provided experienced workers with lower wages than older, inexperienced women.[20] Such infelicities prompted Obenauer to try to professionalize the data upon which awards were based through local cost of living surveys, budget analyses, and careful scrutiny of working conditions.

Above all, Marie Obenauer demanded freedom of action and broad investigatory powers for her division. The division could be a catalyst for change, she believed, only if she maintained a virtually autonomous organization within the staff. Lauck, however, intended a different role for Obenauer's small force. As coordinator of the board's 250 employees, he wanted an integrated, cohesive staff directed by the chiefs of existing divisions—Hugh Hanna of the Division of Examiners and E. B. Woods of the Division of Administration of Awards. Failing to understand that the grievances of the women examiners were symptomatic of the problems of working women, Lauck was both unwilling to restructure the staff and eager to avoid a direct confrontation with the fiery Obenauer. On 9 September, he asked for her opinion on the best method of procedure following his impending abolition of her division.²¹ Her response made future cooperation between them impossible.

Determined to salvage the plans Lauck had "wrecked so suddenly and unexpectedly," Obenauer prefaced her reply with a stinging statement of ideals that boldly set forth her differences with the NWLB secretary. She was most angered by Lauck's conclusion that the NWLB had no more need of women examiners than of Negro or Indian examiners. With "the extended draft on man power forcing thousands of women to take the places of men both as producers in the factory and providers in the home," she wrote, and "with the thoughts of men centered principally upon the effect of this woman invasion upon the status of men in industry, a woman problem and not a negro or an Indian problem has been created." An "intelligent consideration of the resulting difficulties which confront women," she continued, "demands that women as well as men shall be on the force of examiners." Her examiners, she insisted, should be allowed to confer with Christman's investigators and representatives of women workers and management in order to clarify unanswered questions during board hearings. They should also be given the same opportunities as men examiners to discuss the contents of pending awards with board members.²²

Lauck's persistent refusal to clarify the responsibilities of the women examiners, coupled with his veiled threat to eliminate their jobs, hampered the division's work for several weeks. On 25 September, following a conference with Lauck, Obenauer realized that her function was to reflect, not to make, policy. She was to "keep in close touch with" Woods concerning the administration of awards and to get prior approval from Hanna for all first-hand investigations by women examiners. Although her staff could continue to analyze briefs and testimony, an informal order from Lauck to send women examiners to no more hearings until "procedure was settled" diminished the sources for analysis. As Obenauer complained, this new directive stymied her work: "Although a number of cases involving women are now set before men examiners, I am unable to get the data required as a basis for an appropriate award for women."²³

On 28 October, Lauck officially abolished the Division of Women Administrative Examiners, but Marie Obenauer refused to be silenced. In early November, she sought a conference with the NWLB secretary and, at the same time, clung to her convictions. Although "keenly disappointed" that he denied women a voice in defining policies that affected women, she wrote on behalf of her staff, "'the girls'" felt no personal hostility toward him. Indeed, they wanted to prevent "*needless*" destruction of friendships.[24] Lauck's willingness to confer, however, resulted only in Obenauer's reiteration of her demands for independence and for equal time before the board. To help control the growing conflict of interest she perceived between men and women workers, she asked further for appointment to Lauck's Committee on Awards.[25]

Lauck's rejection of Obenauer's ultimatum ended the women's struggle for equal status on the NWLB staff. Any woman examiner who agreed to work as an integral part of Woods's force, Lauck promised, would be "given the fullest opportunity to be of service," but under no circumstances would he permit the continuance of Obenauer's division. Her repeated attempts to distinguish the duties of the women from those of the men examiners, he wrote on 13 November, had "been our chief cause of trouble and misunderstanding in the past."[26] Her purpose defeated, Obenauer and three of her colleagues resigned, leaving behind a condemnation of the board's attitude and a bitter expression of democratic hopes dashed. Cases involving women were "submitted, heard, decided, and administered" without her knowledge; awards were sloppy; and Lauck's orders resorted to "the old method of securing harmony by making woman's work absolutely subordinate to the man's viewpoint."[27]

During Marie Obenauer's protracted battle within the staff, women from the outside had launched a campaign for the appointment of two women to the NWLB itself—and understandably so. Women already served on community war-labor boards, and representatives from the Women in Industry Service of the Labor Department met regularly with the War Labor Policies Board. Mary Harriman Rumsey of New York and six others organized the Temporary Committee to Urge Representation of Women on the National War Labor Board. Among Rumsey's confederates, Margaret Dreier Robins, president of the National Women's Trade Union League, was a Chicago confidante of both board member Victor Olander and Elisabeth Christman. Mary Dreier, Robins's sister and another committee organizer, was a leader of the Women's Joint Legislative Conference of New York.[28] The temporary committee used publicity well and found champions both in women trade unionists dissatisfied with widespread abuse of the equal-pay principle and in organizations eager to enhance generally the cause of women's rights. In September and October, the committee's supporters flooded the NWLB with telegrams, letters, and resolutions.

From the University of Wisconsin, John R. Commons asked the board to give women representation. From New York, Theodore

The Mothers of the Race   149

Roosevelt endorsed the idea, and Rabbi Stephen S. Wise offered a candidate for the post. Cornelia Byrne Pinchot, Gifford Pinchot's wife, told Secretary Wilson that the appointment of women members was a "matter of vital importance," and her brother-in-law, Amos, asked William B. Colver of the Federal Trade Commission to nominate *her* to the NWLB. "If, as he says, Mrs. Pinchot would back you up," Colver noted as he passed Amos Pinchot's letter on to Walsh, "I am for her. I am for anybody that will back you up."[29] The New York *Public* also lent its voice to the women's push for recognition on the NWLB.[30] The Conference of Trade Union Women, called in October by the Women in Industry Service, wanted a woman on the board to redress wage grievances. Like Marie Obenauer, it also anticipated that women employees would need job protection in the postwar era.[31]

Among NWLB members, Walsh alone approved of the addition of women representatives, and he repeatedly promised his strong support when the issue came up for discussion.[32] Both the employer and employee members opposed the modification of the board's "conventional character," Taft wrote to Theodore Roosevelt, while he himself denied its power to augment its membership.[33] Then, in unanimous action taken while Walsh was out of town, the NWLB without comment referred the question to its founding fathers, the National Industrial Conference Board and the American Federation of Labor. With that action, Walsh knew, his colleagues intended an end to the matter, but on 30 October, he asked President Wilson to intercede.[34]

Walsh's letter to Wilson might have been written by Marie Obenauer. Women who had taken jobs in war-related industries had been met with hostility from their co-workers, he began, and those unaware of their rights had been abused by their employers. When cases affecting women came before the board, moreover, the female employees were poorly represented by the male examiners, partly from ignorance and partly from prejudice. "I feel sure," he wrote two days after Lauck abolished Obenauer's division, "that our board could act with much more intelligence if we had the advice and cooperation of two women who could act with us in the settlement of controversies constantly coming before us in which conditions surrounding women workers are among the principal issues." Accordingly, he asked Wilson to intimate to the presidents of the NICB and the AFL that "if the nominations are not promptly made you may, on account of the urgency of the matter, feel compelled to make the appointments by executive order." In response, President Wilson promised to give the matter his "most serious consideration without further urging." No women, however, were appointed.[35]

If the NWLB had a policy on women before the Armistice, it was a policy of convenience, as the women's demands for higher wages had neatly dovetailed with the goals of organized labor. Private employers frequently found ways to avert equal pay, and their representatives on the board had made little issue of the principle. Furthermore, the board had excluded women altogether from policy making. Its confusion about women's status after the Armistice arose because its earlier awards had been drawn to accommodate the two interest groups represented within its membership: organized labor and management. As the nation began its transformation from war to peace, the needs of those groups changed, and women were caught in the cross fire. The NWLB floundered.

Appeals from women streetcar conductors who faced summary dismissal that fall put squarely before the board the critical question that Marie Obenauer, the Temporary Committee to Urge Representation on the National War Labor Board, and the Women in Industry Service had all anticipated: Did women have a basic right to work once the war emergency had passed? The equal-pay principle, read strictly, applied only in cases in which it had become "necessary" to hire women to do men's jobs.[36] Did the principle really mean that women had the right to fill those jobs only as long as no men were available to assume them?

The answer from the street railways, where women conductors did undeniably equal work, depended on whether locals of the Amalgamated Association of Street and Electric Railway Employees agreed with the AFL statement that women should be organized. In Kansas City, for example, men conductors had welcomed women into the union, supported their demands for equal treatment, and united with them against the Kansas City Railways Company. The NWLB's settlement of their case in October had reflected the harmony between the sexes by granting absolute wage equality, uncompromising and direct, in language it had never used before and would not use again. Women conductors, whose hours were limited by state law and who had been guaranteed only $60 a month, were to receive the same $75 monthly minimum accorded men. Every other "adult employee" was to get a 42½-cent hourly minimum and under no circumstances was "he or she" to be denied that rate.[37] In Cleveland and Detroit, however, the men conductors had barred women from the union locals, insisted that "necessity" be interpreted literally, and demanded that the women conductors be removed.

In Cleveland, 150 women conductors had been hired in August and September because the NWLB sanctioned the employment of women in the absence of qualified men.[38] A Labor Department investigation, initiated at the company's request when the men threatened a strike, had persuaded the department to order the women replaced by 1 November. There was no shortage of men in Cleveland, the investigators found, provided the company lowered its standards "somewhat."[39] Instantly, the local press denounced the investigators' conclusions. Rose Moriarty, a feisty young lawyer who had fought for women's rights in Ohio for almost twenty years, organized local suffragists and the Cleveland Chamber of Commerce in a campaign to reverse the removal order.[40] A. L. Faulkner, Cleveland's Commissioner of Conciliation, was unable to reconcile the department's decision with the reported 4,000 advertised vacancies in Cleveland industries and asked Secretary Wilson for a reconsideration of the matter.[41] Then, when the women conductors complained that the investigators had given them no hearing, the NWLB on 31 October ordered their retention on the cars until it could review the facts.[42] Five weeks later the 2,400 men on the Cleveland railway walked out while the women conductors awaited the NWLB's decision.

On 3 December, the day the men struck, the mayor of Cleveland appeared before the board to demand action. The men had grown tired of waiting, he said, and both he and the city law director wanted the Labor Department's ruling enforced immediately. With six hundred unemployed men recently back from the front, with thousands more expected, and with increasing layoffs prompted by the termination of war contracts, the men in Cleveland needed the women conductors' jobs. "Quite a number" of the returning soldiers, the mayor testified, had worked on the street railway, and the women could return to whatever they had done before the war. As for the NWLB, the union had promised to ignore any award that contradicted the Labor Department's decision.[43]

In the absence of the joint chairmen, who were closeted privately on Walsh's last day on the job, the board groped for an answer. Taft appeared only long enough to regret that, legally, the women had no case;[44] the labor members argued for the first time against the interests of fellow employees; and the employer members watched labor's strained logic unfold. Behind the logic lay unspoken fears. Organized labor had sometimes resented women on the cars, where they received equal pay, because it was believed that women rarely agitated for increased wages. Labor worried, too, that the women's presence would influence arbiters to believe that conducting was "woman's work" and that wages were thus already adequate.[45] Therefore, Fred Hewitt and William Hutcheson intimated that the company had had no right to hire the women, indicating that the Labor Department investigation had made this clear.[46]

Loyall Osborne proposed the award that was intended to end the dispute. The women had been wronged, he explained, by the Labor Department and by the company that called it in. For the labor members, self-interest and fear of setting precedents had destroyed principle. "I have sat here for nine months and heard great arguments about the rights of employees," Osborne chided. "Just because these people are women, you are not giving them rights." Having thus embarrassed labor, he deserted the women and hid behind "necessity."[47] The board at his suggestion considered the employment of women conductors an obsolete war measure. Men were "becoming immediately available by virtue of the reduction in the forces of industry in Cleveland and the return of men from the camps." The board ordered that the women be paid their December wages and replaced by 3 January.[48]

The award prompted considerable public criticism. It was denounced in Congress; the New York *Telegram* printed the order side by side with excerpts from a presidential address on the equality of women, asking if the president had no influence with the NWLB; the Washington *Times* predicted serious new industrial adjustment problems;[49] and *The Nation* suggested that it might now become necessary for women to fight "simply for the right to work." The Cleveland decision, *The Nation* implied, was part of a campaign by labor unions to "oust women from war-time positions . . . through the Labor Department and the War Labor Board." Already, it pointed out, Frank Morrison was talking about "the problem of disposing of women in overalls and in uniform," and W. D. Mahon, president of the Amalgamated Association of Street and Electric Railway Employees, reportedly had declared, "Women's place is not on the street car."[50]

In response to various pressures, the board at its meeting on 19 December overcame the labor members' opposition and assigned the case for reconsideration to Taft and to Walsh's successor as joint chairman, Basil Manly, the former director of investigation for the Commission on Industrial Relations. *The Survey* attributed this startling action to the public outcry,[51] but other forces had been at work. On reflection, Taft had questioned his tacit acquiescence in the ruling of 3 December.[52] Lauck, too, had been affected by pleas from groups such as the National Women's Trade Union League.[53] He was especially moved by the reaction of Mary Van Kleeck and Mary Anderson, both in the Women in Industry Service, who had been disturbed enough by the award's import to write him a personal letter. The case

The Mothers of the Race   153

must have been settled, they wrote, "with reference to immediate local needs rather than in the light of its far-reaching implications," for it directed the "dismissal of an entire group of women from an occupation as a means of settling an industrial dispute."[54] Throughout the country, Lauck suddenly understood, women had interpreted the Cleveland order as an NWLB statement on reconstruction.[55]

The Cleveland case, along with the similar case pending before Joint Chairmen Taft and Manly at Detroit, became a cause célèbre among persons committed to women's economic advancement in the postwar era. Each dispute provided the opportunity for a clear-cut governmental statement against sex-based discrimination, and the Detroit controversy attracted attention as dress-rehearsal for the second Cleveland decision. In Detroit, the lines of conflict were sharply drawn. The Detroit United Railway, unlike the Cleveland Railway Company, operated under a closed-union shop—one of those existing conditions that the NWLB's principles bound it to uphold.[56] After the Armistice, the Detroit carmen's union had not only protested against the continued service of the women conductors whose employment it had sanctioned in September, but had also reneged on its promise to issue them union cards. The union, therefore, was forcing the women to hold the closed shop open.[57]

When Theresa Doland, the attorney for the Detroit women conductors, appeared before the NWLB in Washington on 18 January 1919, she argued John Marshall's classic broad definition of "necessity"; pleaded for equal employment opportunities; and raised an issue that she rarely heard discussed—the relative contributions of the fathers of the race.[58] All of this she considered important despite Joint Chairman Taft's admonition at the preliminary hearing five weeks earlier that "necessity" constituted the only relevant issue.[59] At the preliminary hearing, she had sat stunned while a union spokesman condemned the employment of the women as "a fester and a disgrace upon the fair name of Detroit." He had called the women conductors not only unnecessary and inefficient employees but also homewreckers who took further advantage of the collective efforts of the men because no other firm in Detroit paid men and women the same wages for the same work.[60] His crudeness had outraged Taft, who later suggested that he belonged in a cage.[61] But in Washington, Doland could capitalize on no such behavior from the carmen union's smoothest and most respected attorney, James H. Vahey of Boston.

Vahey, champion of street-railway workers in countless NWLB cases and defender of the Kansas City women conductors, apologized for what he was about to do. He was at his best. He denied a strict necessity for employing the women conductors and then argued a traditional defense for the union. Streetcar conducting, he said, was unfit work for a woman. This was a standard argument in the war years, voiced by some of the same men and women who had earlier promoted protective legislation. The job endangered women's health, Vahey explained, gave good women a bad reputation, and threatened their safety. Certainly, he would not want his daughter to conduct a streetcar but would hope for something "better and higher and . . . larger" for her and for all American working women. Besides, since a woman could fulfill "the loftiest function in the world, to be the mother of the human race," she surely should avoid jostling cars.[62]

For almost four hours Basil Manly silently watched Doland build her case toward the climax that he knew would come. The women conductors, Doland said, wanted their jobs partly because the work was the most pleasant that they had ever done. They previously had been factory workers, laundresses, janitors, or waitresses, and as conductors, they had doubled, trebled, or quadrupled their incomes.[63] For these women, the fight to stay on the cars involved both economics and principle, and they would fight, she said, just as hard as men for higher wages. Arguing that motherhood and fatherhood conveyed equal responsibilities, Doland used the women conductors to prove her point. One hundred twenty of them provided, in whole or in part, for 154 minors. None of the men who worried about the women's health and lofty functions, she added, had offered to support those children. Then came the moment that Manly had waited for, when Doland introduced Mary Van Kleeck's four-page report on a nineteen-volume study of the prewar status of working women and children. While the fathers of the race were still at home, the study of four major industries showed, the men had been able to earn only 34 to 56 percent of the family income. "The percentage of the total income of the family?" Manly questioned. "I believe that is correct," Doland answered. "I know that is correct," said Manly, "because I wrote that report."[64] Neatly, Doland and Manly had shattered the myth of an all-providing father in peacetime.

The award, which discounted the question of suitability and was said to be based solely on interpretation of contracts and "necessity," brought victory to the women conductors. They had no contracts, they were not necessary, they would probably be considered "not well adapted to the service" in peacetime, and the company was ordered to hire only men in the future. But since the women already employed had not been warned of their temporary status by either the company or the union, "equity" and "fair dealing" demanded their retention. The union "must be content with" that.⁶⁵ For Doland, Van Kleeck, Ethel M. Smith of the National Women's Trade Union League—and no doubt for their behind-the-scenes confidant, Basil Manly—the victory was marred by the women's failure to extract from the NWLB a commitment to equal employment opportunities. Instead, the award blocked their future entrance into a new field of employment.⁶⁶ For Taft, who encouraged the expansion of occupations for women that spring in *The Ladies' Home Journal*, the NWLB's narrow jurisdiction permitted no broader statement.⁶⁷ Even had he believed that it did, no award so radical could have won the board's approval.

At the Cleveland rehearing two months later, the women's supporters launched a last assault against tradition. Under sharp questioning from Taft, Vahey presented his case both quickly and half-heartedly. Rose Moriarty, meanwhile, had prepared a long brief for the women's new attorney, Frank Walsh.⁶⁸ His appearance constituted a self-described "penance" for the NWLB's ruling of 3 December.⁶⁹ Walsh had resigned as joint chairman, believing that he could do more for employees and for organized labor as a private attorney. Now, when organized labor in Cleveland denounced him, he shrugged. His conversion to the cause of the women conductors, although late, had been complete. "I just cannot see any justice in the stand taken by these men against the Cleveland women," he explained to a friend.⁷⁰

Walsh put Ethel Smith on the stand to remind the board of the women conductors' contributions to the Kansas City local and to cite new medical evidence that showed accepted woman's work such as that of waitress was more strenuous than conducting a streetcar. Anna Howard Shaw, the head of the Women's Committee of the Council of National Defense, then made the most eloquent plea on behalf of women's rights ever delivered before the NWLB. The women of America, Shaw said, believed that the war had been fought to extend liberty to people and that women were as much "people" as men. To deprive them of the right to a livelihood, in whatever work they could do, was to deprive them of liberty. As for protecting women, Shaw continued, "I have never known any body of people who sought to impose an injustice upon another group of people who did not do it for the benefit of the people upon whom they imposed it." The time had come when it was neither right nor duty nor justice for men to decide what was right for women. "If we fail, then let us fail, but do not let us fail by the direction of men."⁷¹

As expected, the Cleveland award of 17 March ordered the women conductors reinstated, but the award addressed none of the larger issues raised at the hearing. Rather, it mirrored the Detroit decision.[72] "Of course, I was pleased" at the reversal, Walsh wrote to Manly, but "what a busting decision could have been made along the right of all women and men to live their own lives. . . . Anyway, the legalistic jinx was put on that Board months ago."[73] Ironically, the award itself was but a hollow victory for the Cleveland women. The board, progressively enfeebled since the Armistice, had reached its nadir. When the Cleveland Railway Company declined to put the award into effect because the union threatened to walk out, the women remained off the cars.

The NWLB's principle on equal pay had implied a bold step in the evolution of governmental policy toward working women. Nevertheless, the board's actions demonstrated that it had not escaped the dual heritage of law and tradition. It was unable to accept women as responsible partners in the formation and administration of policy because, fundamentally, it rejected the basic equality of women in industrial matters. That attitude was most evident in Obenauer's defeat, the board's failure to support the addition of women to its ranks, and the first Cleveland ruling. In the context of 1918, however, that attitude was almost inevitable. Politically disfranchised and economically depressed, women had little power as an interest group, and the NWLB was preoccupied with balancing the needs of organized labor and business.

Despite all that, the NWLB's interpretation of its equal-pay principle and its decisions at Detroit and Cleveland in the spring of 1919 ran counter to long-standing ideas about women's role in the work force. In forty-eight cases, sixteen of which involved women streetcar conductors, the board awarded women equal pay. Among the forty-eight, even the fourteen cases that also set lower minimums for women helped to reduce the vast discrepancy between male and female pay scales.[74] At Detroit, although the board warned against the headlong rush of women into unacceptable occupations, it also called for an end to prejudice.[75] At Cleveland, it encouraged women such as Ethel Smith to believe in a better future. Even if the women conductors were not reinstated, Smith explained to Frank Walsh after the March ruling, the NWLB reversal had meant "a great deal in this fight to have established the principle of equal rights through a national agency."[76]

In reality, of course, the war provided women with limited gains. Mary Van Kleeck's wartime Women in Industry Service eased into permanence as the Women's Bureau in the Department of Labor. A few progressive state legislatures even translated the NWLB's equal-pay principle into law, thereby charting the course for the federal equal-pay law and governmental withdrawal from its protective mentality almost a half-century later.[77] But in March 1919, the New York State Department of Labor estimated that two-thirds of the women who had replaced men in jobs in the state still received less than the $15 weekly "living wage" that the NWLB often awarded. After examining this and other studies, A. B. Wolfe and Helen Olson of the University of Texas reached a grim conclusion:

> If the scattering investigations which have been made are a safe guide, it is certain that outside of government plants and the relatively few cases where the War Labor Board or other agencies forced employers to raise wages, even the pressure of war demand for labor failed to bring the wages of a vast number of women up to the level necessary to "maintain the worker in health and reasonable comfort."
>
> That other ideal of justice sponsored, in theory at least, by the National War Labor Board—equal pay for equal work—does not appear to have appealed to more than a limited percentage of employers.[78]

High-sounding principles and moral precedents alone, it seemed, had been unable to effect widespread reform, even temporarily, for an interest group that throughout the war had remained at odds with far more powerful political, economic, and historic forces.

 ## From War to Peace

> It has been my policy, insofar as I can, never to indulge in vain regrets, and I feel, at the close of this work, that I have really taken my part in a great accomplishment, as we so often agreed that the promulgation of the principles which govern this Board is a great step forward in the peaceful struggle for liberty, equality and fraternity.
>
> —Frank P. Walsh to Victor Olander,
>   4 December 1918

The story of the National War Labor Board after the November Armistice is the saga of a war agency destroyed by peace. Employers evaded its edicts, employees became skeptical about its ability to function, and the NWLB members dropped all pretense of harmony. The labor members worked to perpetuate wartime gains; the businessmen pushed to hasten the transition to the status quo ante. In that sense, the business members won an important point when, with Taft's support, they limited the board's subsequent caseload to jointly submitted disputes. Such a step seemed necessary to enable the NWLB to deal with an enormous backlog, but it also effectively kept new cases off the docket after 5 December. The new procedure, although it did not prevent the reopening of old cases, was a sure sign of declining governmental intervention in labor relations. So, too, were the resignation of Frank P. Walsh and the flagging interest of William Howard Taft in the NWLB's work. Within the federal government itself, the board lost important support when the War and Navy departments began to cancel contracts with many private employers who had been affected by previous awards. Finally, interagency jealousies flared when the Post Office Department and the Railroad Administration resented NWLB interference in their own labor relations problems. For these reasons, the NWLB had little influence in 1919. Only once, when President Wilson asked the board to ignore procedure, did it undertake a case of major importance, and even with the president's backing, it failed to make a viable settlement. By spring, the NWLB had become moribund, a war relic that rekindled passions like any other battlefield souvenir and to as little avail.

From the outset, the joint chairmen understood the implications of an armistice. At war's end, Taft believed, the NWLB would have "nothing to live for." The board's jurisdiction rests "on the exigency of war," he told his brother Horace in early November, "and when that passes the employers and employees may go to strikes and lockouts to their full bent." He was, he added, "going to get out . . . if I can."[1] Frank Walsh resigned on 3 December, fully expecting Taft to follow suit. The NWLB had become ineffective, Walsh wrote Victor Olander, and "cannot be anything but a disappointing mirage to the working people of the country."[2]

Yet, Taft and Walsh viewed their new responsibilities differently. Walsh resigned because he did not want to be associated with what he considered a sham. Before the Armistice, he believed, the NWLB had been successful despite the efforts of the employer members, but now he saw a powerful conspiracy at work. The employer members, through "some sort of agreement," were "holding things back, both at Washington and throughout the country, so that . . . the Board cannot function." The newly approved procedure, which would permit the assumption of only jointly submitted disputes, heightened his suspicions, for it denied workers access to the NWLB without the consent of their employers. Walsh withdrew, therefore, with plans to use his private practice "to help break . . . up" any further efforts to subvert the board's remaining work.[3] Taft stayed on primarily because Secretary Wilson asked the joint chairmen to guide the NWLB through unfinished business. In the limbo between war and normalcy, Wilson wrote at the end of November, there would be "many problems of production and readjustment . . . to be dealt with."[4]

By then, the turmoil that Secretary Wilson anticipated had already begun to envelope the NWLB. Three cases, in particular, illustrated the limits of industrial cooperation in peacetime. All of these post-Armistice problems were rooted in pre-Armistice conflicts and had been dealt with in pre-Armistice awards. At the Bethlehem Steel Company, President Eugene Grace had quietly evaded the NWLB's award of 31 July. After the Armistice, Grace abandoned all pretense of trying to enforce it. In Washington, Postmaster General Albert Sidney Burleson, who had assumed control of the Western Union Company, was as contemptuous of the NWLB and its policies as Western Union President Newcomb Carlton had been. Burleson, with all the zeal—if not more—of a private employer, resisted interference with his operations while telegraphers grew ever more restless. In New York, harbor workers who had come under an earlier NWLB award jockeyed for power in a struggle that pitted the board against private boat owners, the Railroad Administration, and, ultimately, the workers themselves. In all three cases, the NWLB reasserted itself in a postwar atmosphere, and in all three cases, the impact was marginal.

At Bethlehem, Eugene Grace had finally agreed in September to accept the award, but not without strings. Grace had specifically conditioned the pay increases ordered by the NWLB for machinists on the receipt of full reimbursement—in advance—from the War and Navy departments, to whom the company was under contract on a cost-plus basis. He had moved ever so slowly to implement other provisions in the award. By the Armistice, none of the 21,000 Bethlehem machinists had received increased wages; shop-committee elections were still underway; and the local board of conciliation, which the NWLB had ordered established to hear appeals, had yet to be named. What changed things dramatically in mid-November was Eugene Grace's sudden decision to evade the award openly.[5]

On 17 November, Chief Administrator of Awards E. B. Woods was alarmed at a report from the administrative examiner in Bethlehem, Richard B. Gregg. The award, Grace had told Gregg, was dead. The company, he had said, no longer considered it necessary to pay the "arsenal rates" ordered by the joint chairmen and might also sidestep the committee system mandated by the award. An angry Woods authorized the examiner to tell the steelworkers that the award remained in effect.[6]

Eugene Grace, still undaunted ten days later, restated his position formally in a letter to the NWLB. The examiner's rulings to the contrary notwithstanding, said Grace, the company could not advance wages because of the cancellation of war orders and the failure of the War and Navy departments to provide compensatory funds. In these circumstances, Grace continued, the company wanted the NWLB to abrogate the award and to withdraw its administrative personnel from Bethlehem immediately. The company would then install its own employee representation plan, which had been devised by Bethlehem Steel and was already in use at three other company plants.[7]

In December and January, negotiations with the steel company generated more heat than light. On 6 December, Taft accused Grace of "contempt," and, he continued in an executive session of the NWLB, "I am in favor of contempt proceedings . . . and I don't care whether it is an employer or an employee, and that arouses me—my old indignation as a judge."[8] Joint Chairmen Taft and Manly then answered the Bethlehem president's letter in uncompromising terms, questioned the company's "good faith," and released the correspondence to the press.[9]

By mid-December, conditions at Bethlehem had evidently worsened. Examiner Gregg reported the progressive demoralization of the steelworkers because the company ignored complaints advanced through shop committees, laid off the committeemen, and discriminated against workers who cooperated with the committee system. "A great number of the committees," Gregg observed, "are badly shot to pieces already and the men are afraid to carry out their duties actively for fear of being fired. . . . If we were to try to go in and elect new men to take the place of any who have been wrongfully discharged, we would be unable to get men to serve except people who would merely do the bidding of the company." Gregg had little hope that Bethlehem would alter its policies unless compelled to do so.[10]

At a hearing on the case in mid-January, the company yielded nothing. Joint Chairman Taft bristled and made clear his intentions to work further with the labor members to revitalize the award. Clearly out of patience, he said in a widely quoted statement, "The present attitude of Mr. Grace and his company colors the whole situation with a sense of injustice which makes one yearn for judicial power to compel compliance, but this board has not the power."[11]

Part, but certainly not all, of the board's inability to "compel" compliance resulted from its own division of opinion. Loyall Osborne was so profoundly disturbed by Taft's statement that he decided to disclose his own ideas on the Bethlehem case. Osborne had put aside his inclinations to resign after the Armistice because he believed that important precedents could be set in the transition from war to peace. He wanted them to be right. In late January, as he prepared to sail for Europe with VanDervoort on behalf of the NICB, he wrote Taft a six-page letter that supported the company on all counts.[12]

Like the other employer members, Osborne wanted the steel company to recover home rule for two reasons; he thought that the NWLB had no further business there, and he still opposed the board's collective-bargaining policies. Osborne was "distinctly opposed to . . . the legal fiction that the war is not over . . . [for] concerns who have had their work terminated by the Government." He argued that the company should be allowed to implement an employee representation scheme of its own choosing. He had never believed that the NWLB had the right to impose its own "brand" of collective bargaining on a company and thought that the NWLB brand was rigged. "We know perfectly well," he told Taft, "that the disposition of the employee members of the Board, aided and abetted by many members of the staff, is to create a situation . . . whereby the Labor Union representatives can win control of the Committees." For Osborne, Taft had implicitly concurred in a plot to destroy the open shop that Eugene Grace had a perfect right to protect.[13]

As Osborne's letter sped to Taft, *The Nation* lamented the NWLB's "enfeebled position." Bethlehem's defiance, the magazine predicted on 25 January, was "more than likely to be effective."[14] But *The Nation* was wrong in certain particulars. The board was certainly enfeebled, but through perseverance (and publicity), Taft, Manly, and the labor members ultimately forced concessions from Eugene Grace. In February, as the award of 31 July came to its automatic end, compromise was insured. (The rout came later in the year with the steel strike of 1919.) On 4 February, the company agreed not to dislodge the shop-committee members as representatives of the steelworkers. As if by magic, the NWLB withdrew its examiner from Bethlehem. In the next few weeks, the company and its employees devised a hybrid plan, which superimposed NWLB ideals and committeemen on a bargaining scheme acceptable to both sides.[15]

The Survey watched developments at Bethlehem closely during those weeks. "The negotiations," it noted in March, "are marked by an effort on the part of the company to introduce the 'representation plan' which it favors, and by a determination on the part of the employees not to accept the 'mollycoddle' form of union but to adhere to the plan of representation originally established by the War Labor Board."[16] The compromise plan, which the NWLB dutifully recorded and approved in April, was considered "the most independent" of any contemporary representation scheme in the steel industry. As for the machinists who waited in those weeks for news of pay advances, *The Nation* was correct. Their claims remained unsettled until 1926.[17]

The Bethlehem story, of course, was more than a colorful narrative of give, take, and compromise. Beneath the headlines and news releases lay the postwar power struggle in microcosm. Knowingly or not, Eugene Grace had sent a message to other employers in November. If his defiance of the NWLB's authority succeeded, they, too, would have license to ignore wartime labor policies. In Minneapolis, employers who had fought against the NWLB in October said as much. If that defiance prevailed, the NWLB would terminate having dealt with only a small percentage of cases before it and without having eased the transition to peacetime conditions. If that happened, countless thousands of employees who had stayed on their jobs during the war with expectations of relief from the NWLB would lose faith in the federal government.

Loyall Osborne, moreover, was right. The NWLB staff was not impartial. It never had been. Richard Gregg, for example, exuded partisan feelings. He had joined the staff shortly before the Armistice specifically "to help the unions,"[18] and while serving as an examiner, he had devoted his energies to advancing the labor movement. So partisan was Gregg's record at Bethlehem that E. B. Woods had to remind him in December that an examiner was supposed to be a judge and not a participant. Furthermore, union representatives did capture the NWLB shop committees and did plan to use them to organize the Bethlehem plant. They also controlled the appointment of the three representatives whom the employees named to the local board of conciliation in mid-November. It was for that reason that the company consistently refused to appoint representatives of its own.[19]

In view of that, the company's post-Armistice position becomes, if not laudable, at least understandable, as does its willingness to work out a compromise plan of collective bargaining after the NWLB personnel was withdrawn. Bethlehem Steel also showed at least a measure of good faith by agreeing in the plan that committeemen had recourse to the secretary of labor if they were discriminated against by the company. Only in the matter of the machinists' pay was it obdurate to the end.

What, then, did the resolution of the case mean for the NWLB that spring? Clearly, the events at Bethlehem demonstrated the board's flagging powers and indicated that employers would deal with their own workers, but not in strict accordance with wartime rules or through a federal agency. The bulk of American employers who had grudgingly allowed the NWLB to tamper with the balance of power in their plants during the war—when the president nationalized recalcitrant companies—was unwilling to do so in peacetime. The Bethlehem controversy partially restored employers to their prewar status. At the same time, it spared the NWLB complete humiliation. In large measure, therefore, the case worked out in accordance with the way that Loyall Osborne and the other employer members had wanted the NWLB's wartime record to read.

The board was less successful in what became a feud with Postmaster General Burleson. Burleson maintained technical justification for ignoring the NWLB because the board was presumed to have washed its hands of the Western Union case when President Wilson nationalized the company, but S. J. Konenkamp of the Commercial Telegraphers Union of America had never stopped corresponding with the NWLB and had protested against Burleson's administration almost from the first. In early November, the NWLB asked the postmaster general to respond to repeated complaints that he had failed to enforce its recommendations for Western Union. Burleson denied the charges, then declined the request on the ground that the operation of the telegraph system was his responsibility.[20] After the Armistice, things got worse.

Ideologically and temperamentally, Albert Sidney Burleson was ill-equipped to keep a labor force content. He was an autocrat with a fragile ego. He resisted change that threatened his authority, and, to his mind, any imposed change in working conditions or in labor relations within his bailiwick did so. In 1917, he had wanted not only to prevent change but also to return to an earlier day in which employees, meekly and respectfully, appeared to be grateful to have a job. During the war years, that kind of attitude conflicted with reality.[21]

Because of that attitude, Burleson's problems with the NWLB were inevitable. Since 1917, he had sponsored policies hostile not only to the wartime goals of organized labor but also to the economic well-being of federal employees under his direction. He had urged Congress to deny federal workers the right to petition for wage increases because those requests were "unpatriotic." (Federal workers, he explained, already earned more than men fighting in the trenches.) Early that year, he had lobbied Congress successfully to deny postal workers, whose pay scales had been set in the previous decade, a general increase that was granted to other federal employees. In December, he had proposed to crack the postal employees' association with labor unions that believed in the right to strike. These organizations, he announced, were selfish, and they made employees "bold." Company unions, on the other hand, satisfied Burleson's desire to maintain order. So, too, did employees' testimony before Congress, as long as the testimony was by invitation.[22] Given all that, Burleson's inclination to support Newcomb Carlton's attitudes at Western Union should have surprised no one. Perhaps it did not. But when Burleson left Carlton to manage the company so suddenly placed under his direction in the summer of 1918, he indicated his own contempt for the recommendations of the NWLB's majority. He stood with Carlton because he thought like him.

In the post-Armistice crisis, Burleson's fundamental disagreement with the majority of the NWLB was obvious. Unlike the joint chairmen and the labor members, he did not believe that the public necessarily owed its servants a living wage. Instead, he maintained that his first responsibility was to provide the public with good service at cheap rates. When he announced new wages for telegraphers, effective 1 January 1919, his terms were less generous than those set by Newcomb Carlton before the nationalization of the company. By ending overtime for Sunday work when Sunday work was almost mandatory, Burleson in effect cut wages, which he justified by anticipating postwar economic conditions.[23] Furthermore, he did not embrace the right to organize. Burleson had officially ordered that the CTUA members whom Carlton had dismissed be rehired; but some NWLB members doubted that he ever meant for the order to be obeyed. They wrote it off as "camouflage." For whatever reason, many employees had not been taken back. Among those who had, many had not been reinstated in their old positions, as the NWLB ordered, but rather had been rehired in different jobs. That meant lost seniority and, in some cases, the denial of a bonus based on length of service with Western Union. The CTUA called both those employment policies discrimination against the union and also denounced the postmaster general's wage schedule. In the latter matter, the union was joined by members of the company union that Newcomb Carlton had set up in defiance of the NWLB. Both groups wanted the NWLB to intervene on their behalf against the postmaster general in early 1919.[24]

Like the Bethlehem controversy, the renewed Western Union clash frustrated the NWLB for months. Burleson was even more arrogant than Eugene Grace, and he knew how to stay just out of reach. He had set up a "Wire Board" to handle telegraphers' complaints, but the NWLB could find no evidence that it did anything. The postmaster general also had particular incidents of alleged discrimination investigated by postal authorities, but he would neither appear before the NWLB nor send a representative to explain what the investigations showed. Instead, to protect their "confidentiality," he insisted that the NWLB send someone to his department to study the records. The records, not surprisingly, made Burleson's administration of the wires look good; but neither the examiner who studied them nor the NWLB itself believed that the records told the whole story.[25]

Antipathy to the postmaster general in early 1919 was the one sentiment that the NWLB membership shared broadly. Even the employer members were disgusted by his behavior. On the other side, William Harman Black, who served as Basil Manly's alternate, enjoyed noting that Carlton's company union had turned into "a kind of Frankenstein." When Basil Manly got so exasperated at one executive session that he moved that Jett Lauck "remove" Burleson from office, most of his colleagues applauded. William Howard Taft, on the few occasions at which he was present when the case came up for discussion, was positively acid tongued. Only Frederick Judson, who sat in Taft's place in February while Taft toured on behalf of a league of nations, treated

Burleson with reverence—and that only because of his position in the cabinet. For most members of the NWLB, Burleson was merely another balking employer.[26]

The board, nonetheless, remained uncertain about what to do. Had it the right to claim jurisdiction on the grounds that its principles and its original recommendations in the case had been ignored? If so, should it reopen the case on behalf of the CTUA alone or should it also take cognizance of the complaints filed by members of Carlton's company union? Again, precedent was at stake. Matthew Woll, Gompers's confidant and the president of the International Photo-Engravers' Union of North America who was filling in for the ailing Victor Olander, and Jett Lauck, who now acted substantially as adviser to the labor members, were especially suspicious of the company union's appeal. To both men, its action appeared to be motivated by Western Union as a tactic to discredit the postmaster general in order to recover official home rule. At length, majority sentiment produced continued support for the telegraphers' union only.[27]

Ultimately, however, the NWLB's majority sentiment did not matter. At the end of April, CTUA president S. J. Konenkamp thanked the board for its "efforts to adjust our grievances" and gave examples to show why the efforts were not enough. Telegraphers in Seattle who had been locked out by Western Union for a year remained locked out; in New Orleans, innocent workers had been unable to recover their jobs because one of their colleagues confessed to sabotage; in Memphis, Atlanta, Richmond, Little Rock, and elsewhere, discrimination against CTUA members by Western Union was still standard operating procedure. Then Konenkamp announced that a strike vote, already underway, was expected to be completed in May.[28] Organized labor accelerated its calls for Burleson's dismissal, calls that had already become commonplace. In May, *The Nation* struck out against Woodrow Wilson's management of the home front by denouncing Burleson. "Never in our recollection," began an editorial, "has there been such an outpouring of wrath upon the head of a single official as is now being showered upon Mr. Burleson." Then, after characterizing Burleson as incompetent, ignorant, intolerant, and archaic in his attitudes toward both labor and censorship of the press, the magazine announced that not even Burleson's resignation could save Wilson from "indictment" as chief administrator of the government.[29] Burleson, of course, did not resign, and the CTUA did strike. By early July, the victory went to Burleson and to Western Union. The telegraphers' strike failed, and Burleson left the matter of reemployment of the strikers to Western Union and other telegraph companies.[30]

As the NWLB fought its way toward ineffectiveness against the postmaster general, two massive strikes paralyzed New York harbor. The strikes in early 1919 were the logical outgrowth of three distinct problems, any one of which would have made compromise difficult. The obvious employer-employee conflict was complicated by intergovernmental jealousies and by the lack of consensus within the NWLB. In November 1918, the Marine Workers Affiliation asked the NWLB to establish a harbor-wide basic eight-hour day and a "living wage." The board, hard-pressed by a heavy caseload, postponed action until December. Neither the private boat owners, who employed some 60 percent of the affected workers, nor the Railroad Administration, which controlled conditions for the other 40 percent, would accept the NWLB's jurisdiction, and the board had no alternative but to decline intervention. In January, its decision to withdraw brought on the first great strike—and with it came bitter recriminations on both sides.

The bitterness flowed naturally in light of the complicated history of wartime labor adjustments in the harbor. Since the autumn of 1917, harbor workers had pressed both private boat owners and governmental operators to set harbor-wide wages and hours. The Marine Workers Affiliation, an industrial union of fifteen thousand to sixteen thousand men, had been organized specifically to advocate the standardization of these conditions of employment. At the MWA's insistence, the U.S. Shipping Board had created a local tripartite adjustment board, which most private owners at first decried. Their employees were satisfied, the owners contended; agitation for the local adjustment board, they said, had come from only a small group of labor radicals. Thus equipped with a rationale, many private boat owners then ignored the local board's November 1917 award, and governmental operatives were equally uncooperative.[31]

In the spring of 1918, with timely support from the NWLB, the harbor adjustment board achieved some measure of effectiveness. By then, however, the Railroad Administration had promulgated an entirely different set of standards for its employees. Not until summer, did the Railroad Administration—represented now, like the private owners, on the harbor board—accept a revised local award that applied to both private and public employees. Even then, both groups of employers adhered to theoretical autonomy and hundreds of violations of the new award became a matter of public record in the next few months. To complicate matters even further, neither the private owners nor the Railroad Administration filled the inevitable vacancies that occurred on the local board, and consequently, the Marine Workers Affiliation had appealed to the NWLB in November 1918. The local board had been so undermined by both public and private employers, the MWA believed, that it could no longer function.[32]

In December, the NWLB ordered the employers to revitalize the local board. When they refused to do either that or to submit any question concerning the hours of labor to the NWLB, the controversy reached its first crisis. The employers, both private and public, said in effect that neither the local nor the national board had jurisdiction over harbor conditions because the war was over. Members of the Marine Workers Affiliation, who had issued and then withdrawn previous threats to strike during the preceding year, felt used by a government that stood for their rights on paper alone.[33]

Almost sixteen thousand angry harbor workers walked out on 9 January 1919. The marine strike, the worst in the city's history, stirred strong passions, but feelings ran especially high concerning two statements from members of the NWLB that were published that morning. The first, signed by the joint chairmen, was noncontroversial. It explained objectively the reasons for the board's decision to withdraw on 8 January. The second statement, however, lent tacit support to the strike. Signed by Joint Chairman Manly and the labor members, it was frankly partisan.[34]

Manly and the labor members had written a scathing condemnation of both public and private employers in the harbor. Responsibility for whatever happened, they said, rested solely with the employers, for the workers had exercised unqualified patience and been willing to arbitrate their demands. The boat owners, on the other hand, had

> constantly violated the awards of a board constituted by their voluntary agreement, and, as indicated in . . . [the NWLB's] unanimous statement of today, they have contemptuously refused to comply with the orders of the National War Labor Board . . . and have refused to submit to any form of arbitration. All this has been done notwithstanding the urgent request of the Secretary of Labor, the Secretary of War, the Secretary of the Navy and the Shipping Board that this matter be adjusted, and in spite of the grave consequences which may result from their attitude.[35]

The boat owners returned the fire. "The National War Labor Board has now made the decision it should have made two weeks ago," said

Joseph H. Moran, chairman of the New York Towboat Exchange. "In effect, it holds that the arbitration is either binding on all parties or on none. The Railroad Administration has refused . . . to accept any new award, and consequently all parties are freed of any obligation. This is sound common sense and fully justifies the stand we have taken."[36] Joseph J. Glatzmayer, president of the New York Boat Owners Association, described the NWLB decision as "perfectly sane," then took Manly to task for his "ludicrous" statement: "For a judge, half-baked or otherwise, to forget his judicial function and indulge in private vituperation of one of the parties before him is something new in this town." One or two more such incidents, Glatzmayer predicted, would put an end to the NWLB. As for Manly's behavior, the president of the Boat Owners Association had a ready explanation: "I understand that this young man is a socialist, recently imported from Canada or some other distant point to add to the woes of an unhappy nation. The sooner he is tagged and shipped back to his point of origin the better it will be for all concerned." (Manly, the son of a Baptist preacher, was from Greenville, South Carolina, and a graduate of Washington and Lee University.) Glatzmayer ascribed the strike to bolshevism and to the actions of "just six labor leaders."[37]

Three days later the strike ended because President Wilson cabled the NWLB from Paris to put aside procedural considerations and settle the case. All the affected agencies of the federal government, he noted, would stand behind whatever decision the board made. He mentioned specifically the Railroad Administration.[38] By Sunday, 12 January, the harbor was moving again; and on Monday morning, the NWLB convened at city hall. Joint Chairman Taft wasted no time. He appointed a four-member subcommittee to take testimony over the next few weeks. He scolded the Boat Owners Association, whose attorney had explained that the private employers could not submit to a board that included Manly and the labor members. Taft told the attorney, Paul Bonynge, that whether or not they submitted was "practically unimportant." The Railroad Administration, as if on cue, agreed to accept the NWLB's arbitration, and the Marine Workers Affiliation, represented now by attorney Frank P. Walsh, was eager to proceed.[39]

All of the rancor of early January, and even more, colored the hearings. Frank Walsh probably encouraged it. True to his resignation pledge, Walsh set out to revitalize the NWLB's principles and turned the harbor hearings into a national campaign for new employment standards. He called on Professor Ogburn, who now quoted minimum-comfort and minimum-subsistence budgets at $1,800 and

$1,500 for a family of five. Walsh demanded $1,500 for common labor. As for the basic eight-hour day, Walsh implied that the NWLB would merely follow the "customs of localities" if it granted the 16,000 harbor workers what they wanted. Over 50,000 other harbor employees, including 42,000 longshoremen, already worked that schedule. Nor did Walsh spare the boat owners. He denounced a "17th Century plan" in which they had recently offered their employees welfare capitalism if the employees would renounce the Marine Workers Affiliation. The boat owners, meanwhile, devised a way to counter Walsh and his witnesses and still deny the NWLB's jurisdiction. Only one of their number, the Red Star Towing and Transportation Company, agreed to arbitrate in order to allow its attorney, Bonynge, to participate in the hearings. Through Bonynge, the owners then dismissed Ogburn's budgetary recommendations as utopian and socialistic, called the eight-hour day impractical, and insinuated that the harbor union was bankrolled from Germany. All in all, the hearings provided New Yorkers with good reading for two weeks.[40]

The rest of the story is incredible. The NWLB's award precipitated a second strike, which the Railroad Administration and the private boat owners then resolved by granting the harbor workers virtually everything they wanted. At one time or another, almost everyone, including the boat owners' attorney, described the award as unfortunate.[41] It was the work of V. Everit Macy—NWLB umpire, millionaire banker, chairman of the National Civic Federation, and chairman of the Shipbuilding Adjustment Board—who had been called into the case because the board was split evenly when Taft unexpectedly sided with the employer members. Acting hurriedly in order to make the decision by late February, Macy left most issues to local conciliation. He made no wage adjustments and granted the basic eight-hour day to only six hundred of the sixteen thousand marine workers.[42] The strike began on 4 March because the Marine Workers Affiliation no longer trusted local or national conciliation. The MWA rank and file was especially bitter because they had felt so close to victory in the January strike. In March, their reliance on action rather than talk proved right. The Railroad Administration capitulated within four days, and within three weeks, 75 percent of the harbor workers were back on the job with generous new contracts. The episode marked the first time an industrial union had united important groups of New York harbor workers toward a single end. The MWA was jubilant.[43]

The NWLB must have been embarrassed. Not only had it failed to end a dispute, it had caused a strike. Inevitably, the episode provoked speculation as to what had gone wrong. The Marine Workers Affiliation concluded that the board had made no serious effort to arbitrate. The union had information that the employer members had agreed in advance not to yield on the basic eight-hour day. Union leaders, moreover, believed that Macy had misunderstood the case.[44] The New York *Call* supported the MWA's interpretation of things, basing its information on "inside stuff in connection with the Board's methods [that] was ladled out at union headquarters."[45] For attorney Bonynge, "red-eyed and unreasoning Bolshevism," pure and simple, lay behind the strike.[46] (Bonynge's rhetoric was at least timely, for only weeks earlier Seattle Mayor Ole Hansen had used a similar tone to discredit the general strike in his city—a strike called, ironically, in protest against an award from Macy's Shipbuilding Labor Adjustment Board.) The most perceptive comments came, however, dispassionately from *The Nation*, which found the walkout difficult to condone but easy to understand. By leaving most matters to further negotiations between the employees and employers who were "unequivocally committed against any change of hours and who had not agreed to acknowledge the award," Macy had "singularly disregarded the psychology of the situation."[47]

For obvious reasons, the speculation also touched on William Howard Taft. Why had Taft stood with the employers? Why had he not used his influence, as so often in the past, to effect a compromise acceptable to labor? And what did all of this mean concerning the future of the NWLB? Thomas L. Delahunty, president of the Marine Workers Affiliation, attributed the former president's attitude to his growing lack of interest in the NWLB's affairs.[48] Certainly, Delahunty was not wrong. Taft did spend most of February crusading for a league of nations; but *The Nation* was more nearly correct when it hinted at certain institutional weaknesses within the NWLB itself, weaknesses that appealed to Taft's perception of the board's responsibility and rendered it unfit for peacetime service. The statement is worth quoting at length:

> The failure of arbitration in this case is due primarily to the narrow interpretation which Mr. Taft put upon the scope of the War Labor Board. He held that it was authorized to intervene only because of a war emergency. . . . For this reason the case had to be limited to a consideration of any change that had come subsequent to . . . the last agreement between the employers and the men. Hence the Board, instead of hearing the case on its intrinsic merits, compared the present situation with conditions of last July. Within these limits the men attempted to argue that

they had accepted the July agreement, with its twelve-hour day, because of the shortage of labor—a factor no longer existent. As to long hours, their plea that the war had practically ended was made to a Board that could listen only to a wartime demand. This is an incongruous state of affairs, and it goes to prove that immediate steps must be taken . . . if the Board is to be maintained.[49]

That was at the crux of the harbor case, and that is why it became a watershed. On the surface, the facts of the case differed little from those at Bethlehem Steel and Western Union. In all three cases, employees asked the NWLB to support them against employers who had disregarded war-labor policies. At Bethlehem and Western Union, management had evaded or ignored an NWLB award; in the harbor, management had repeatedly violated an award concluded locally with support from the NWLB. One salient factor, however, distinguished the harbor case from the other two. Both the steelworkers and the telegraphers had asked only for an enforcement of a pre-Armistice decision, while the marine workers had asked for an abrogation of one. The Marine Workers Affiliation had thus asked a war agency to establish new wages and hours suitable for peacetime, but for Taft, that was not the function of the NWLB. This is essentially why the workers lost and why the harbor case was so significant. From time to time, of course, the NWLB did revise certain awards. Even so, nothing could diminish the impact of the harbor case—where the NWLB failed its greatest post-Armistice test.

 # Whither Industrial Cooperation?

> Mr. Taft's personal influence won over enough capitalists to ensure success, and Mr. Walsh attained the cooperation of the unions. The manufacturers, it develops, did not understand the significance of what they were doing, and now that the way has been shown toward industrial democracy, many interests are anxious to have the Board wrecked and forgotten. . . . If the public understood, enough pressure could be exerted to replace the obstructionists with men of larger vision.
>
> —*The Nation*, 22 March 1919

In the autumn of 1918, the hierarchy of the National Civic Federation wanted to believe that the war had changed everything. At Chicago shortly before the Armistice, a massive reception for Samuel Gompers echoed that hope and seemed to seal the partnership of business, labor, and government. Frank P. Walsh was there to introduce Gompers to an enthusiastic crowd. Ralph Easley of the NCF came to honor Gompers and to tell reporters flatly that the war had solved the problem of labor relations. Working to revive the NCF *Review* after a hiatus of four years, Easley already planned to use the new publication to suggest that "collective bargaining is the solution to bolshevism and socialism." His sentiments were in keeping with those of Gompers, who before six thousand cheering industrialists, labor leaders, and public officials, denounced bolshevism and socialism in short order and called America the "apotheosis of all that is right and just."[1] Progress and justice, both Easley and Gompers seemed to be saying, could result from an adaptation of war machinery to serve peacetime needs. Within days, in writing to Jett Lauck, Easley said directly that the National War Labor Board should not be dissolved unless some other agency appeared to take its place.[2]

Through Easley and others, the NCF had returned to first principles. Its formula for postwar industrial harmony was essentially the formula it had devised at the turn of the century. Only the role of the federal government was different, and this was only because most observers believed that war-labor machinery had worked. V. Everit Macy, NCF chairman and war-labor official, advocated the "better" organization of labor and capital and asked the question that seemed to need no answer: "If voluntary agreements to submit all questions in dispute to labor adjustment boards have proved of value in time of war, why should not similar boards be useful to industry in times of peace?"[3]

Yet, it was William Howard Taft who used the NCF's formula to best advantage. Although willing to see the NWLB end quickly, Taft still believed in what he thought the board had stood for. After the Armistice, he scored extremists on both sides—the "bourbons" and the "bolsheviks," he called them—and dismissed welfare capitalism as an unacceptable alternative to collective dealings between organized labor and organized capital. What Taft found most valuable in the NWLB's experience was its ability to maintain the peace. He could not praise the NWLB for dispensing "exact justice," but then justice, he believed, was sometimes less important than sensible compromise. Industrial peace, therefore, was Taft's point of emphasis when he called for the continuation of adjustment machinery patterned after his board:

> A national board consisting of . . . intelligent, conservative labor leaders on the one hand, liberal-minded, broad-visioned representatives of the employers on the other hand, should be continued as a refuge to . . . both sides of an industrial controversy about to engage in wasteful strife by strike and lockout, so that their arguments can be thrashed out and some sort of compromise approximating justice may be reached. If the national war labor board has shown the wisdom of such a board it has attained a real success.[4]

Frank Walsh had never agreed to subordinate exact justice to industrial peace. For years this had irritated the NCF, as had Walsh's commitment to free the labor movement from dependence on friendly big business. Also, the war had not softened his aversion to the emergence of government as labor's new boss. That autumn, then, Walsh wanted to lay new ground rules for postwar voluntarism, rules that would finally establish labor's independence and increase the likelihood for exact justice. In his final days on the NWLB, he proposed a package of ideals, based on a liberal interpretation of the NWLB's principles, to impose in each case still pending.[5] When that failed, he recommended the passage of two federal laws intended to recognize the two principles closest to his heart. The first, under the guise of a civil rights act, would protect labor's inalienable rights to organize and to bargain collectively through representatives of their own choosing—in essence the Wagner Act of 1935; the second would empower the government to condemn a building in which workers earned less than a living wage.[6]

Walsh also favored the continuation of voluntary adjustment of labor disputes through a national mediation agency such as Taft described. He did not, however, believe that the NWLB fit that description, and for this reason Walsh launched a sustained attack on the NWLB employer members as a class when he decided to leave the board. They had, he said publicly, come from managerial ranks; they lacked the broad vision that the NCF admired; they reflected instead the antiunion "open shop" mentality of the NAM; they were, in short, too small for the job they had been asked to do.[7] Privately, Walsh was less kind. "To sum it up in a nutshell," he wrote to St. Louis publisher William M. Reedy, "the employers upon the Board were of such caliber that nothing except the threats of the President or charges of treason could induce them to act with ordinary decency."[8] For those reasons, Walsh and his confidant, Basil Manly, set out to discredit the employer members, scratch the NWLB, and devise an entirely new board.

Discrediting the employer members was easy. Early on, Walsh explained their general lack of sympathy with war-labor principles and disclosed that the NWLB's pivotal policy decisions had come only through the close cooperation of the joint chairmen with the labor members.[9] In February 1919, Manly sent President Wilson evidence of the employer members' disloyalty. Several of them, Manly reported, not only had failed to cooperate with the board's principles, but also had made "active attempts to hinder the effective functioning of the Board and destroy its usefulness." Until the Armistice, "the pressure of patriotism and fear of public exposure" had combined to keep them manageable. Since then, however, W. H. VanDervoort had attacked the NWLB before an audience of businessmen and proclaimed that the continuance of the NWLB would be "a misfortune to the United States." H. H. Rice, meanwhile, had advised American employers that the NWLB's awards were no longer binding.[10]

Manly's real purpose in writing to the president was to resign and to suggest, in fact, that the entire NWLB resign. The president, he believed, should then establish a temporary new agency, probably led by Taft and Walsh, to serve through reconstruction. Of utmost importance to Manly was that the NWLB's successor be able to act quickly, and this meant that it needed to work through subordinate tribunals. Then, too, the board's membership must work harmoniously, so its employer members should not be appointed by the National Industrial Conference Board.[11]

Like Walsh, Manly believed that the managerial and manufacturing class that the NICB represented had limited vision. The men that he urged the president to appoint to represent employers included the nation's industrial giants, men such as J. P. Morgan, Henry Ford, Julius Rosenwald, and Walsh's old bête noire, John D. Rockefeller, Jr. These men, more than the members of the NICB, felt a "genuine responsibility for the maintenance of the nation's stability."[12] In other words, they reflected the mentality of the NCF rather than of the NAM.

When no action followed his report to the president, Manly stayed on as joint chairman and worked on plans for a permanent successor to the NWLB. Within weeks, he had devised a program to infuse postwar voluntarism with a vitality such as the NWLB had never had. His proposed National Labor Board could make the legislation that Frank P. Walsh had recommended unnecessary and could bring a national industrial policy closer to fruition than ever before. It was nothing less than an industrial government.[13]

Manly's program rested on three cornerstones: democracy, efficiency, and raw power. He asked the president to convene an industrial conference of at least one hundred representatives of labor and capital to devise the National Labor Board's basic organization and principles. Following action by such a large body, Manly believed, the new board automatically would be assured of broad-based public support. For efficiency, he still maintained that much of the board's adjustment work should be carried on through subordinate boards "organized upon an industrial rather than a geographical basis" and that its members should be inherently powerful men with significant followings of their own—the "great capitalists" and the "strongest men" in the labor movement. (The selection of the "great capitalists" and the whole matter of "public" representation on the board he left for others to decide; but the "strongest men," he was sure, could be selected only by vote of the American Federation of Labor in convention.)[14]

The most striking part of Manly's plan concerned power. He intended the National Labor Board to be a supreme court of labor relations in fact as well as in theory. He intended also that it have the legislative powers that Walsh had tried to assume for the NWLB, and, finally, that it perform the investigatory functions that had distinguished the work of the Commission on Industrial Relations. The national board itself would enter disputes of national importance only; otherwise, it would serve as a court of appeal. It would then be left free for other important work, such as the establishment of national wage and hour standards, which it could then enforce. Enforcement powers were essential. Although he insisted that the national board would in no way force compulsory arbitration, Manly meant for decisions issued in jointly submitted cases to take immediate effect. The board's investigations would also focus on national problems. It would examine troubled industries upon request and publish its findings soon after in order to influence and guide public opinion.[15]

All of this Manly submitted in a manner designed to encourage moderates and conservatives to rally in defense of American capitalism. It is "submitted," he wrote, "that while there is a tendency among the extremists in the ranks of both labor and capital to decry the existence of any effective conciliatory body, the more moderate representatives of both groups seem to be in general agreement that an effective national labor tribunal is necessary if the industrial policy and practices of the nation are to progress by orderly evolution rather than by strife and revolution." In closing, Manly reiterated his call for an industrial conference to discuss the means with which to deal with problems that he predicted would soon "threaten the entire industrial stability of the nation, if not the very existence of the government itself." The "Anglo Saxon peoples" can solve their industrial problems, he concluded, but only "if they are given an adequate opportunity." That opportunity could not exist "except through the meeting, face to face, of the responsible representatives of labor and capital, preferably under the auspices of the national government."[16]

Representatives of labor, capital, and the public met under governmental auspices that fall, seven weeks after the NWLB officially shut down, but could find no basis for cooperation. The president's First Industrial Conference convened on 6 October 1919, at the height of the great steel strike, debated for less than three weeks, and dissolved in a shambles. Wilson had announced the conference in early September, before the strike began, and tried unsuccessfully to keep steelworkers on the job until the fifty-seven conference delegates could discuss broad issues of industrial policy. Instead, the steel strike became a central issue of the conference and helped to destroy it.[17]

Given the delegates, discussion of the strike was inevitable. Some of the nation's largest employers were at the Washington meeting, including John D. Rockefeller, Jr., and Elbert H. Gary, the chairman of the U.S. Steel Corporation—two men whose persistent refusal to deal with organized labor had precipitated the walkout. Ironically, they were there at the president's invitation to represent the "public." The "employer" group consisted of smaller men and was dominated by the antiunion NICB, which appointed one-third of its number. Samuel Gompers named the bulk of the "labor" delegation, including himself, several men in the leadership of the National Committee for Organizing Iron and Steel Workers, and others who had considerable experience on the NWLB. Any talk among those men about industrial policy would as a matter of course involve collective bargaining and organized labor's role in the bargaining process, and these were the issues at the heart of the strike.[18]

The coincidence of these events brought the NICB and the AFL into their sharpest conflict since the beginning of the war. In Washington, representatives of both groups understood that whatever happened at their meeting could influence not only the outcome of the strike but also the power of the labor movement. Each delegation, therefore, wanted to get from the conference a firm commitment to the same policies that it had tried to wrest from the war-labor administration. According to the NWLB's principles, employees were guaranteed the right to organize into trade unions and to bargain collectively "through chosen representatives," but that right had been qualified by another NWLB principle that permitted employers to refuse to deal with representatives outside their direct employment. At the conference of 1919, labor wanted the guarantee without the qualifier; the NICB, on the other hand, defended the qualifier as the mainstay of the open shop.[19]

Gompers's delegation struck first in what David Brody calls "a dual attack" meant to settle policy once and for all. The delegation proposed that six members of the Industrial Conference arbitrate the steel strike, and according to principles that the labor delegation offered for approval by the conference as a whole. Labor's principles contained no surprises. They recognized the "right(s) of wage-earners" which the labor movement had supported for years and which the steelworkers were then demanding: rights "to organize in trade and labor unions," "to bargain collectively through trade and labor unions with employers," and "to be represented by representatives of their own choosing in negotiations and adjustments with employers."[20] When Judge Gary announced that the steel industry would accept no arbitration, the first part of labor's plan collapsed.[21] But the principles became the focus of the conference. If labor could win there, the strike was as good as won and so, too, was labor's longtime struggle for independence.

Had it not been for the NICB, the First Industrial Conference would have compromised its way to agreement. The labor group and the public representatives reached an accord after labor gave way on both the definition of a viable labor organization and the concept of union recognition. The new language to which both groups agreed recognized the right of the workers "to organize without discrimination, to bargain collectively, [and] to be represented by representatives of their own choosing in negotiations and adjustments with employers." It was the NWLB's principle without the qualifier. It implicitly condoned both company unions and the open shop. At the same time, however, it preserved the potential for unofficial union recognition by placing no restrictions on employee representation in the bargaining process. For that reason, the NICB balked and carried the majority of employer sentiment with it.[22]

With an eye focused squarely on the steel strike, the employer group held out for a written guarantee that "no employer should be required to deal with men or groups of men who are not his employees or chosen by and from among them." That condition, described in the principles that the NICB submitted to the conference, would prevent an "opportunity for outside interference on the part of other interests to prevent close and harmonious relations between employer and employee."[23] Because the rules of the conference required approval by majorities of all three groups before a measure could be adopted, the compromise between labor and the public failed. When that happened, Samuel Gompers angrily led his delegation out on 22 October explaining that the employer group had "legislated us out of this conference."[24]

That winter the administration tried a second and final time to forge an industrial code through private citizens. This time labor and capital had no representation. The president's Second Industrial Conference, which worked from December until March 1920, was a blue-ribbon commission of public men: corporation lawyers, former cabinet members, former governors, university presidents, businessmen-philanthropists, former mobilization officers—nineteen men in all. Herbert C. Hoover, director of the American Relief Administration, and Secretary Wilson presided. The blue-ribbon commission evaded controversial issues, however, and devoted its best energies to the establishment of an elaborate system of national and regional adjustment machinery.[25]

Even then, the proposed machinery was of limited value because the adjustment boards would have no specific principles to follow and no powers of enforcement. The only potential advantage it had over the post-Armistice NWLB was administrative. Jett Lauck considered even the administrative reforms disadvantageous because they created possibilities for fragmented rather than uniform policies. A disappointed Lauck summed up the conference's work: "The Conference got the cart before the horse. Principles were of primary and machinery of secondary importance."[26] In the end, it made little difference. No one paid much attention to the work of the Second Industrial Conference, and Congress even declined to provide the funds to publish its report.[27]

What then had happened, by the winter of 1919–20, to the American dream of peace and orderly progress through voluntary cooperation? Where were the moderates whom Basil Manly and countless others had thought stood ready to build upon the innovative war-labor program in the previous spring? Two conferences had tried and failed to devise an industrial code. Why had they failed? The same interests represented at those conferences had written principles and policies that took America through most of 1918 with no strikes of national consequence. What had changed?

Some of the answers are obvious. The end of the war had ended the rationale for federal mobilization of the economy. (Much of the mobilization machinery, including the War Industries Board, had been dismantled almost immediately.) The war experience, moreover, had left a curious antistate legacy, private interests strengthened by their service in the mobilization effort, and a public ready to defend "Americanism." The war had also failed to restructure American political beliefs. Voluntarism, on which so much of the mobilization machinery had been based theoretically, resumed its literal meaning. The war had neither solved the problem of labor relations nor left organized labor in a position to deal equally with management, even though labor had greatly increased in numbers. Business and labor organizations quit the war the same way they began it, with fundamentally different objectives. The enormous economic dislocation in 1919, coupled with organized labor's determination to solidify gains made possible in part by the NWLB, caused an unprecedented number of strikes that year. The full fury of the patriotic fervor amassed to preserve the American system against the dreaded Hun was turned inward. Spurred on by the Justice Department and the NCF, among others, America turned against itself in the Red Scare and blamed predictable labor unrest on an insidious foreign threat.[28]

The stakes were high in 1919, never a good omen for moderation or compromise. Some of the clamor for the adaptation of war-labor machinery to serve peacetime needs betrayed a kind of desperation, a fear for the future unless some mechanism was preserved to grind out a measure of industrial justice. The fear was understandable, but fear cuts several ways. It encourages those with the most to lose to shore up traditional values and those with the most to gain to demand change immediately, lest hope for change be lost. It encourages moderates to take sides or to propose "disinterested" programs, like that of the Second Industrial Conference, which neither speak to the issues nor satisfy anyone else. Those circumstances, unless managed by a government willing to compel cooperation, often give advantage to the proponents of laissez-faire. That is what happened in 1919.

American employers volunteered not to cooperate with an aggressive labor movement that year, and they won. Their most powerful spokesmen consisted of the same groups that had sent obstructionists to the NWLB.[29] Those groups were no more willing to share power with organized labor than they had been before the war, and they were just as suspicious of the federal government. Stephen C. Mason, president of the NAM, surveyed "The Road Back to Normal Times" in the spring of 1919. He spoke of "the mailed hand of government," which had gripped industrial America during the war, and of a lingering "fear . . . that some . . . of the un-American schemes grafted" onto the republic "might be permanently foisted on business by those visionaries and promoters of economic experiments who have been for some time so numerous and active."[30] In the same issue of *American Industries*, the NAM reported that delegates to its annual convention in May had resolved that "we see no occasion for the further continuance of a body similar to the National War Labor Board" except under greatly restricted circumstances.[31] For the NAM by that time, the alternative to interference with home rule, from government or organized labor, had begun to crystallize in an "open-shop" drive that recalled its response to the anthracite coal strike.[32]

The new open-shop movement, later commonly known as the "American Plan," began in places such as Seattle early in 1919 as a grass-roots response to union activity. Gradually that year, the movement swept the country as management's ultimate defense against unwanted change. The steel strike and the First Industrial Conference nationalized the open-shop movement in October and identified it as what it was: a refusal to deal with organized labor. Then, while the Second Industrial Conference deliberated, the open shop triumphed in the collapse of the strike.[33] Without governmental interference to balance labor's rights within the open-shop context, the victory stood for a decade and a half.

Franklin D. Roosevelt turned to World War I to find his precedents for action in a war against domestic emergency in 1933. The immediate result was the National Recovery Administration, a cumbersome agency whose responsibilities resembled the combined functions of the WIB and the NWLB. The creation of the new agency marked the triumph of such organizations as the NAM and the Chamber of Commerce, which had taken pride in businessmen's contributions to industrial mobilization during the war and had worked thereafter for revision of the antitrust laws and business "self-regulation." In return for these concessions in 1933, the business architects of the NRA grudgingly accepted Section 7a, which restated the NWLB's recognition of labor's rights to organize and to bargain collectively through representatives of their own choosing. One assumption behind the NRA was that business could cooperate with labor organizations voluntarily to win the war against economic disaster. That assumption was wrong.[34]

Voluntarism failed to bring industrial peace in the 1930s for a number of reasons. Business and labor organizations had reached no consensus on the issues that had troubled the NWLB and disrupted the First Industrial Conference in the fall of 1919. Indeed, spokesmen such as James Emery of the NAM and William Green, the conservative miner who had succeeded Gompers as president of the AFL in the mid-1920s, openly disagreed on the import of Section 7a before, during, and after the final drafting of the provision. Emery and the NAM, which had opposed the inclusion of that section, defined labor's rights precisely as they had tried to define the NWLB's principles, their purpose being to protect the company union. Employers generally agreed, and Section 7a spawned a flurry of new company unions in 1933 and 1934. Green and the AFL, badly weakened in the previous decade by the social climate and economic realities, insisted that the language allowed for union recognition when a majority of workers so desired. The National Labor Board, created within the NRA as somewhat of an afterthought to implement Section 7a, sided with Green; but the leaders of the NRA, General Hugh Johnson who was a veteran of the WIB and Donald Richberg, supported industry's interpretation of labor's rights. By 1934, the NLB had run so badly afoul of its parent that President Roosevelt separated the two.[35]

The new National Labor Relations Board fared no better. Like the NLB, the NLRB made prolabor decisions that it had no power to enforce. (The penalty for noncompliance was removal of the Blue Eagle.) The Justice Department, which might have intervened, was disinclined to do so, and President Roosevelt contributed to the confusion.

Although he lacked Wilson's war powers to compel, he did intervene, but only intermittently and inconsistently. He sometimes supported organized labor and sometimes did not. The NRA leadership, meanwhile, continued to identify with the objectives of businessmen. Before his welcome resignation in 1934, Johnson even made a series of vituperative attacks on workers who struck in defense of labor's interpretation of Section 7a. As a result, the NLRB proved as moribund as its predecessor. Businessmen openly defied it.[36]

The continuance of industrial unrest in 1934 and 1935 so discredited voluntarism that, by the time the Supreme Court ended the NRA, the president had reluctantly abandoned the voluntary principle and endorsed Senator Robert F. Wagner's bill to outlaw company unions and establish a permanent National Labor Relations Board to prevent unfair labor practices. The leadership of the AFL also had renounced its historic position. The Wagner Act, with the support of progressive majorities in Congress and the AFL, ended voluntarism in industrial relations in the summer of 1935. Intense opposition to the bill from the NAM, the Chamber of Commerce, and other business interests had merely underscored the necessity for decisive federal governmental intervention on behalf of the institutionally disadvantaged.[37]

The events of 1919 and after by no means suggest the wartime failure of the NWLB. Backed by the power of the White House, the board served the country well. Moreover, the NWLB set valuable precedents, which the molders of public opinion understood. Both *The Nation* and *The Survey*, for example, so appreciated the board's work that they called for a similar peacetime agency. *The Nation* described the NWLB as the "most valuable economic contribution" of the Wilson administration, and in *The Survey*, John Fitch eulogized the board as the most successful agency every established to adjust industrial disputes in the United States. In its eight months of real power, he concluded, it had "made effective principles and established practices that have deeply influenced American industry."[38]

The NWLB made its reputation, and contributed to its own success, by balancing the demands of labor and capital to labor's advantage. Equally important, it did nothing revolutionary. Its policies were meant to keep workers on the job, and they were interpreted to do just that. When Frank Walsh, supported by NWLB staff experts, announced an astounding 73-cent hour, eight-hour day as the proper standard for common laborers, the NWLB instead followed its own tamer precedent—a precedent that nonetheless identified the board as the friend of the working class. The dramatic increase at Waynesboro, Pennsylvania, from 22 to 40 cents an hour, and countless others like it, helped raise the standard of living for unskilled laborers to a new level. So, too, did the board's refusal to determine wages according to the ability of employers to pay. Although the board declined to adopt a standard workday, it granted the eight-hour day, basic and actual, and generally reduced hours enough to add significant strength to the movement for shorter hours in private employment. The NWLB's decisions also provided equal pay for women, albeit under restricted circumstances, and lent belated support to women's efforts to retain jobs secured during the war. Finally, the NWLB intervened to protect the rights of workers to organize into trade unions and to bargain collectively to a degree unprecedented by a governmental agency. Although it upheld the open shop, it refused to sanction "yellow-dog" contracts, and it imposed a shop-committee system that escaped the taint of company unionism. In these matters, NWLB policies steered a mid-course between what John Fitch called "the employers' desire to smash the unions and the demand of the organized workers for . . . the closed shop." In each instance in which labor's goals clashed with management's, the NWLB allowed for steady encroachment against what organized labor correctly identified as "industrial autocracy."[39]

On reflection, liberals associated with the NWLB credited William Howard Taft for much of the board's pre-Armistice success. Frank Walsh and Basil Manly, among others, recognized Taft's careful guidance in many of the board's most important decisions. Indeed, Walsh believed that the NWLB had worked only because Taft had continually checked the employer members, who in the summer of 1918 had "sat like hawks . . . [ready] to pounce down on any person making an effort to ameliorate the conditions of the workers any place."[40] Jett Lauck, too, admired the attitude of the former president. In affectionate exaggeration ten years after Taft's death, Lauck recalled the joint chairman's enraged sense of justice on the discovery of working conditions in American industry. He became "so radical," Lauck told a friend, "that it was quite a problem of Frank Walsh and myself to control him."[41] Taft, of course, was never radical; yet, his ability to work with Walsh—whom he found quite "amenable to reasonable argument when he is not making a speech before the public"[42]—had given the NWLB its reformist reputation.

That was the first real key to the NWLB's success—the joint chairmen's working relationship. They, essentially, made the NWLB autonomous and defined the NWLB's controversial principles. Because they agreed fundamentally, *The Nation* soberly suggested that both men simply understood their jobs, that "they saw the necessity of production, and the truth that it could be maintained only by the establishment of justice."[43] Gilson Gardner observed the same phenomenon with gleeful hyperbole: "Something has happened to ex-President Taft," he wrote in celebration of Labor Day in 1918. "However it has come about, Taft now gives every appearance of possessing a social conscience. He appears to be as enlightened on political economics as Theodore Roosevelt thought he was when he picked him to be his successor. . . . He is for the Frank Walsh program and there never was a team of vaudevillians who did their act more in harmony than Taft and Walsh in conducting the affairs of the War Labor Board."[44] It was a harmonious act that the joint chairmen played so often. Typically, Walsh made demands that he knew were unacceptable to the employers, then stepped aside to let Taft patiently effect inevitable compromise. In that way, labor got some of what it wanted; the employer members, although not happy, were relieved that labor had got no more; Walsh got publicity for his views of what ought to be; and the NWLB preserved stability through a measure of social justice.

The second key was Woodrow Wilson. Faced with the need for stable labor relations during the war, Wilson placed his faith in voluntarism for both ideological and practical reasons—as long as it worked. But stability required concessions to labor that employers had been unwilling to grant. When voluntarism quite naturally broke down before the Armistice, he commandeered the works of selected uncooperative employers. Regardless of what later happened at Western Union, the psychological impact of the president's firm action cannot be discounted. Without it, the NWLB would have failed in war as miserably as it did in peace.

The NWLB's experience also provided a valuable lesson on the efficacy of voluntarism as a tool for democratic social action. Both business and labor organizations had traditionally embraced voluntarism in an effort to protect their own freedom of action from each other and from a potentially coercive state. But business and labor organizations could not cooperate equitably unless their relative power, so grossly unequal even in 1918, was equalized. The NWLB served as an equalizer. The board's majority, with timely help from the president, turned voluntarism from a conservative instrument into a weapon of semicoercion for liberal ends. Yet the sudden official equality of labor during the war, because it was temporary and artificial, encouraged postwar reaction as well as wartime reform. This reaction contributed heavily to the decline of the labor movement in subsequent years, demonstrated the bankruptcy of voluntarism without semicoercion in peacetime, and, ultimately, led to the creation of the welfare state.

Notes

PREFACE

1. U.S., Department of Labor, *Monthly Review of the Bureau of Labor Statistics*, 8:105–6, 7:359.
2. For good insight into the importance of voluntarism in economic mobilization, see Kennedy, *Over Here*, especially chapter 2, and Cuff, *The War Industries Board*. Berkowitz and McQuaid, *Creating the Welfare State*, chapters 1–3, provides a useful overview.
3. Cuff, "Bernard Baruch," pp. 115–33; Cuff, *The War Industries Board*, pp. 135–47, chapters 9–10. For a somewhat different assessment of Baruch's role in the war years, see Jordan A. Schwarz, *The Speculator*.

CHAPTER 1

1. U.S. Congress, House of Representatives, *Industrial Commission Reports*, 19:788, 790–93, 915, 947–53. The commission was composed of five senators, five representatives, and nine other persons appointed by President McKinley and approved by the Senate.
2. Ibid., pp. 774–86.
3. See Derber, "Industrial Democracy, 1898–1915," pp. 259–86; Taylor, *Labor Policies*, pp. 156–57.
4. *Industrial Commission Reports*, 19:804–5.
5. Ibid., pp. 834–35; Derber, "Industrial Democracy, 1898–1915," pp. 261–62.
6. *Industrial Commission Reports*, 19:780–81, 796–97, 840–45, 852.
7. Ibid., p. 800.
8. Ibid., pp. 764–72, 804, 825, 915–28.
9. Ibid., pp. 797, 805–7.
10. The two NAM vice-presidents were Ellison A. Smyth of South Carolina and Daniel A. Tompkins of North Carolina. *Industrial Commission Reports*, 19:953. See Steigerwalt, *National Association of Manufacturers*, p. 178.
11. *Industrial Commission Reports*, 19:953–55.
12. See Harbaugh, *Theodore Roosevelt*, chapter 10; Brooks, *Toil and Trouble*, pp. 98–101.
13. See Rogin, "Voluntarism," pp. 527–30.
14. See Harbaugh, *Theodore Roosevelt*, pp. 165–67; Green, *National Civic Federation and Labor*, pp. 37–55; Jensen, "National Civic Federation," pp. 108–14; Weinstein, *Corporate Ideal*, pp. 3–14.
15. See Brooks, *Toil and Trouble*, p. 102; Wiebe, *Businessmen and Reform*, p. 169; Steigerwalt, *National Association of Manufacturers*, pp. 111–12; Taylor, *Labor Policies*, p. 40.
16. See Taylor, *Labor Policies*, pp. 39, 48; Wiebe, *Businessmen and Reform*, p. 193.
17. See Jensen, "National Civic Federation," pp. 32, 117–41; Green, *National Civic Federation and Labor*, chapter 2; Gompers, *Seventy Years*, 2:105–19; Weinstein, *Corporate Ideal*, p. 7.

18. Green, *National Civic Federation and Labor*, pp. 90–98; Taylor, *Labor Policies*, pp. 35–40, 121–40; Steigerwalt, *National Association of Manufacturers*, pp. 108–17, 128–32; Weinstein, *Corporate Ideal*, pp. 14–15; Wiebe, *Businessmen and Reform*, pp. 167–71.

19. See Taylor, *Labor Policies*, pp. 37–45, 160–67; Steigerwalt, *National Association of Manufacturers*, Appendix C, pp. 186–87.

20. Jensen, "National Civic Federation," pp. iv–vii, 144–54, 161–65; Weinstein, *Corporate Ideal*, pp. 18–21, 38.

21. Taft, *The A. F. of L.*, pp. 227, 264–65; Jensen, "National Civic Federation," p. 299; Weinstein, *Corporate Ideal*, pp. 21–23. For detailed discussion, see Green, *National Civic Federation and Labor*, chapters 3 and 4.

22. Taft, *The A. F. of L.*, pp. 294–97; Jensen, "National Civic Federation," pp. 302–4; Grossman, *Department of Labor*, pp. 10–11.

23. Taft, *The A. F. of L.*, pp. 266–71; Jensen, "National Civic Federation," pp. 300–301.

24. Taft, *The A. F. of L.*, p. 297; Jensen, "National Civic Federation," p. 304. For a discussion of labor politics, see also Gompers, *Seventy Years*, 2: chapter 35.

25. See Weinstein, *Corporate Ideal*, chapter 2 and pp. 74–82; Jensen, "National Civic Federation," chapter 10; Green, *National Civic Federation and Labor*, pp. 202–9; Weinstein, "Big Business" pp. 156–74.

26. Green, *National Civic Federation and Labor*, pp. 146–78; Taft, *The A. F. of L.*, pp. 228–30; Weinstein, *Corporate Ideal*, pp. 23, 120–21.

27. Taylor, *Labor Policies*, pp. 97–101, 135–39; Steigerwalt, *National Association of Manufacturers*, pp. 119–38; Jensen, "National Civic Federation," pp. 287–88, 299; Weinstein, *Corporate Ideal*, pp. 78–82; Wiebe, *Businessmen and Reform*, pp. 81, 170–73, and see also pp. 193–205.

28. Brooks, *Toil and Trouble*, p. 111; Weinstein, *Corporate Ideal*, pp. 173–82; Davis, "Campaign for the Industrial Relations Commission," pp. 211–22; Davis, *Spearheads for Reform*, pp. 208–12. For a full discussion of the origins of the Commission on Industrial Relations, see Adams, *Industrial Violence*, chapters 1 and 2.

29. See Weinstein, *Corporate Ideal*, pp. 183–86.

30. Derber, "Industrial Democracy, 1898–1915," p. 276; Adams, *Industrial Violence*, pp. 205–9; Weinstein, *Corporate Ideal*, p. 186.

31. Adams, *Industrial Violence*, pp. 208–9, 213–14, and chapter 7; Weinstein, *Corporate Ideal*, pp. 199–203; Meehan, "Frank P. Walsh," pp. 52–58, 67–68.

32. Walsh, "Low Wages," p. 110.

33. Walsh, "Let There Be Light," *Christian Socialist* (Chicago), July 1915, p. 1, New York Public Library, The Papers of Frank P. Walsh (hereafter cited as Walsh Papers), Box 146.

34. Ibid; quoted, Meehan, "Frank P. Walsh," p. 70.

35. Adams, *Industrial Violence*, pp. 209–10, quoted, p. 215; Weinstein, *Corporate Ideal*, pp. 189–91, 198, 200–202; Derber, "Industrial Democracy, 1898–1915," pp. 264–65.

36. Adams, *Industrial Violence*, p. 215.

37. "A Remedy for Every Ill," *American Industries* 16 (September 1915): 9.

38. Quoted in Derber, "Industrial Democracy, 1898–1915," p. 264.

39. Quoted, ibid.; Taft, *The A. F. of L.*, pp. 299–300.

40. Derber, "Industrial Democracy, 1898–1915," p. 265; Weinstein, *Corporate Ideal*, pp. 208–9; Adams, *Industrial Violence*, p. 217.

41. Derber, "Industrial Democracy, 1898–1915," p. 265; Weinstein, *Corporate Ideal*,

pp. 189–90, 208–11; Adams, *Industrial Violence*, pp. 216–17, 225.

42. "A Remedy for Every Ill," p. 9.

43. A sampling of the Papers of Woodrow Wilson, Library of Congress, Microfilm Edition (hereafter cited as Wilson Papers), Series 4, No. 158, Reel 232, indicates the depth of feelings that Walsh inspired in June and July 1915. Independent businessmen and merchant and manufacturing associations roundly condemned Walsh's tactics and conclusions. On the other hand, union locals and labor assemblies, as well as organizations such as the National Women's Trade Union League of America, gloried in them.

44. Quoted, Derber, "Industrial Democracy, 1898–1915," p. 268.

45. Quoted, Weinstein, *Corporate Ideal*, p. 212.

46. Ibid.

47. Ibid., pp. 198–99, 213; see also Adams, *Industrial Violence*, pp. 219–20, for samples of favorable response from important socialist organs.

48. *The New Republic*, however, was critical of Walsh because, the magazine believed, his actions and report would diminish the likelihood of future national industrial commissions. "Industrial Conflict," *The New Republic*, 28 August 1915, pp. 89–91.

49. Smith, "Organized Labor," pp. 267–74.

50. Ibid., pp. 274–76; Grossman, *Department of Labor*, pp. 12–14; Bernhardt, *Division of Conciliation*, pp. 1–11.

51. As Robert Wiebe points out, the founding of the NICB was a part of the NAM-sponsored drive to organize open-shop associations. However, the new organization, which was supported by many large corporations from the outset, devoted at least as much of its energy to promoting industrial efficiency. The NICB thus helped to moderate businessmen's policies and to "thaw" the relations between the spokesmen for large and small business. See Wiebe, *Businessmen and Reform*, pp. 31–33, 178. See also, Taylor, *Labor Policies*, p. 28, in which the NICB is described as "a research organization" established to investigate and report on industrial issues with the self-described intention "to stand between the employer and employee without partisanship."

CHAPTER 2

1. Stoddard, "No Strikes in War Time," p. 357.

2. Pringle, *William Howard Taft*, 1:129–38.

3. From Frank P. Walsh, unidentified speech, 1915, Walsh Papers, Box 146.

4. Ibid.

5. Ibid.

6. "Industrial Relations 'Committee,'" editorial, *American Industries* 16 (February 1916): 7; Green, *National Civic Federation and Labor*, pp. 234–35. The NAM also condemned the Adamson Act in "The Eight-Hour Day Railroad Statute," *American Industries* 17 (October 1916): 9–11.

7. Cuff, *The War Industries Board*, p. 41; see also Cuff, "Business, The State, and World War I," pp. 1–19.

8. Cuff, "Business, The State and World War I"; Cuff, *The War Industries Board*, chapter 1; Weinstein, *Corporate Ideal*, chapter 8; Wiebe, *Businessmen and Reform*, p. 221; Koistinen, "The 'Industrial-Military Complex' in Historical Perspective," pp. 378–403.

9. Larson, "The American Federation of Labor," pp. 67–81; Green, *National Civic Federation and Labor*, pp. 364–67; Taft, *The A. F. of L.*, pp. 342–45; Gompers, *Seventy Years*, 2:332–60.

10. Green, *National Civic Federation and Labor*, pp. 364–66.

11. From *American Federationist*, March 1916, printed in Gompers, *Labor and the Common Welfare*, pp. 242–44. In the previous issue of the AFL's monthly magazine, Gompers had stated labor's case for membership on preparedness committees: "Formulation of plans and policies must necessarily be left largely to preliminary committees and commissions. The wage earners of America are vitally interested in these plans and policies. They bear the brunt of fighting in times of war and suffer most from mistakes of militarism and lack of national preparedness. Therefore, it is essential that representatives of wage earners should be appointed to all commissions and committees that deal with these matters" (quoted, ibid., p. 242). Even earlier, Gompers had begun to redefine preparedness in a speech before the National Civic Federation in January 1916. See Larson, "The American Federation of Labor," pp. 73–74; Green, *National Civic Federation and Labor*, p. 367; Gompers, *Seventy Years*, 2:332–33.

12. Taft, *The A. F. of L.*, pp. 344–45; Gompers, *Seventy Years*, 2:359–60.

13. Taft, *The A. F. of L.*, pp. 345–47; "Convention Reports," *American Industries* 17 (June 1917): 14–15.

14. Gompers's close ties with the administration are especially evident in Smith, "Organized Labor," and Larson, "The American Federation of Labor."

15. *Report of the Activities of the War Department in the Field of Industrial Relations During the War*, pp. 10–11, quoted in National Industrial Conference Board, "Digest of War Labor Principles," p. 5, University of Virginia, Alderman Library, typescript in the Papers of W. Jett Lauck (hereafter cited as Lauck Papers), Box 102.

16. See *Chairmen's Report of National Adjustment Commission*, pp. 9–10, quoted in NICB, "Digest," pp. 7–8; Watkins, *The Development of War Labor Administration*, pp. 134–35, 143–44.

17. Both Louis B. Wehle and Samuel Gompers admitted that the Baker-Gompers agreement in no way committed the government to further the union shop. See letter, Wehle to Frank Morrison, n.d. [June 1917], and letter, Gompes to Wehle, n.d. [June 1917], *Report of the Activities of the War Department in the Field of Industrial Relations During the War*, p. 73, quoted in NICB, "Digest," pp. 5–6; Raddock, *Portrait*, pp. 91–95; Wehle, *Hidden Threads*, pp. 19–23.

18. See Wehle, *Hidden Threads*, pp. 41–44.

19. Ibid., p. 49; Bing, *War-Time Strikes*, p. 23; United States Shipping Board, *Second Annual Report*, p. 176, quoted in NICB, "Digest," pp. 9–10.

20. U.S., Department of Labor, *Monthly Review of the U.S. Bureau of Labor Statistics*, 8:308.

21. Taft, *The A. F. of L.*, p. 354; Watkins, *The Development of War Labor Administration*, pp. 152, 154.

22. Watkins, *The Development of War Labor Administration*, pp. 150–51; letter, Woodrow Wilson to Governor Ernest Lister of Washington, 16 August 1917, Wilson Papers, Series 3, Vol. 43, p. 185.

23. National Industrial Conference Board, "Statement of the National Industrial Conference Board Respecting National Labor Situation and Recommendation of means for preventing interruption by labor disputes of necessary war production, made, by invitation, to the Council of National Defense," 6 September 1917, pp. 1–8, in National Archives, Records of the National War Labor Board, RG2 (hereafter cited as NWLB Records), Entry 15.

24. Ibid., pp. 3, 6.

25. Ibid., pp. 3–8.

26. John A. Fitch, "Organized Labor in War-Time: The Convention of the American

Federation of Labor," *The Survey*, 1 December 1917, pp. 232–33.

27. Quoted in Gompers, "America's Labor Convention in War Time," *American Federationist* 25 (January 1918): 31–32.

28. Ibid.

29. Ibid., p. 32; Fitch, "Organized Labor in War-Time," p. 233.

30. Gompers, "America's Labor Convention," p. 33.

31. Watkins, *The Development of War Labor Administration*, pp. 152–54.

32. See "Memorandum of the Advisory Council to Secretary of Labor, January 19, 1918," and "Letter to the Secretary of Labor Relative to the Selection of Representatives for a Conference Committee, January 28, 1918," printed in U.S., Department of Labor, Bureau of Labor Statistics, *National War Labor Board*, p. 30.

33. Roger Babson, "Frank J. Hayes," Fitchburg *Sentinel*, 26 August 1918, NWLB Records, Entry 20; Raddock, *Portrait*, pp. 100–108; "Says War Labor Board Has Made Good," Seattle *Times*, 12 July 1918, NWLB Records, Entry 20; Taft, *Organized Labor in American History*, pp. 251–54, 381; Taft, *The A. F. of L.*, pp. 362–63, 367; Larson, "The American Federation of Labor," pp. 76–78.

34. Letter, Loyall A. Osborne to William Howard Taft, 31 May 1918, NWLB Records, Entry 15; Charles Penrose, *L. F. Loree*, p. 15; NICB, "Statement of the National Industrial Conference Board," p. 8; Steigerwalt, *National Association of Manufacturers*, Appendix A, pp. 182–83. (Brief data about all members of the WLCB / NWLB available in Bureau of Labor Statistics, *National War Labor Board*, p. 12.)

35. "Report of the War Labor Conference Board to the Secretary of Labor, March 29, 1918," printed in Bureau of Labor Statistics, *National War Labor Board*, pp. 31–33.

36. Ibid., p. 32.

37. See ibid., pp. 32–33.

38. See ibid., pp. 31–32; "Method of Presenting Complaints and Procedure of Board," printed in Bureau of Labor Statistics, *National War Labor Board*, pp. 41–42; same source, pp. 16–17.

39. John A. Fitch, "A War Program for Industrial Peace: Tentative Agreement Between Capital and Labor Drawn Up in Washington Last Week," *The Survey*, 6 April 1918, p. 4.

40. James A. Emery, "War Labor Board for Increasing Production," *New York Times*, 14 April 1918, NWLB Records, Entry 15.

41. "Method of Presenting Complaints," in Bureau of Labor Statistics, *National War Labor Board*, pp. 41–42; same source, pp. 16–17.

42. Letter, Taft to Charles Phelps Taft II, 7 May 1918, Library of Congress, the Papers of William Howard Taft (hereafter cited as Taft Papers), Series 3, Box 412.

43. National War Labor Board, Minutes of Executive Sessions, typescripts in Lauck Papers (hereafter cited as NWLB, Minutes), meeting of 21 May 1918, pp. 38–39.

44. Letter, Taft and Walsh to William B. Wilson, 22 May 1918, Library of Congress, the Papers of Felix Frankfurter (hereafter cited as Frankfurter Papers), Box 190.

45. George P. West, "The Progress of American Labor," *The Nation*, 29 June 1918, pp. 753–54.

46. C. Edwin Michael, "War Labor Conference Board," *American Industries* 18 (June 1918): 35–36.

47. Letter, Taft to Horace Taft, 9 April 1918, Taft Papers, Series 3, Box 408.

48. Interview with Walsh, conducted by Charles W. Wood, "A New Deal for American Labor," reprinted in the *Irish World and Industrial Liberator*, 1 June 1918, Walsh Papers, Scrapbook No. 39.

49. "Report of the President's Mediation Commission to the President of the United

States, 1918," p. 21, quoted in Bureau of Labor Statistics, *National War Labor Board*, p. 30.

50. "Principles and Standards: Avoidance and Adjustments of Labor Disputes a War Measure," *American Federationist* 25 (May 1918): 369–72.

CHAPTER 3

1. Western Union Telegraph Company, *The Western Union and the War Labor Board: The Company's Position* (New York, 1918), p. 4, copy in Lauck Papers, Box 103.
2. U.S., Department of Labor, *Monthly Review of the Bureau of Labor Statistics*, 6:46.
3. NWLB, Minutes, afternoon meeting of 10 May 1918, pp. 65–70.
4. Michael, "Conference Board," p. 36.
5. "Principles and Standards," p. 372.
6. Commercial Telegraphers Union of America, "What Organization Day Means," 17 March 1918, Taft Papers, Series 3, Box 413.
7. Ibid.
8. Organizing Committee of Five, "Fourth Bulletin to Savannah Commercial Telegraphers," 13 April 1918, Taft Papers, Series 3, Box 413.
9. "Snubbing the War Labor Board," *The Survey*, 8 June 1918, p. 292.
10. NWLB, Minutes, afternoon meeting of 10 May 1918, pp. 57–58.
11. Ibid., pp. 62–74.
12. Letter, Osborne to Taft, 12 May 1918, Taft Papers, Series 3, Box 413.
13. Letter, Taft to Charles Phelps Taft II, 7 May 1918, Taft Papers, Series 3, Box 412.
14. NWLB, Minutes, afternoon meeting of 10 May 1918, p. 65.
15. Western Union, *The Company's Position*, pp. 20–21.
16. Telegram, Newcomb Carlton to Taft, 22 May 1918, Taft Papers, Series 3, Box 413.
17. Ibid.
18. Telegram, Taft to Carlton, 27 May 1918, Taft Papers, Series 3, Box 414.
19. CTUA, Chicago District Council, flyer of 24 May 1918, Walsh Papers, Box 20; letter, L. L. Chambers, secretary, Wisconsin CTUA, and George Towne, state organizer, to Taft and Walsh, 15 May 1918, Taft Papers, Series 3, Box 413; letter, Albert L. Day, president, Detroit Council #11 CTUA, to Taft, 24 May 1918; telegram, J. L. Dean, president, Jacksonville CTUA, to Taft, 26 May 1918; telegram, H. E. Badger and B. A. Painers, Birmingham CTUA, to Taft, 26 May 1918, final three entries in Taft Papers, Series 3, Box 414.
20. Letter, L. F. Loree to Taft, 31 May 1918, Taft Papers, Series 3, Box 414.
21. Letter, Osborne to Taft, 31 May 1918, Taft Papers, Series 3, Box 414.
22. See NWLB Minutes, afternoon meeting of 1 June 1918.
23. Ibid.; see also Western Union, *The Company's Position*, pp. 19–27.
24. NWLB, Minutes, afternoon meeting of 1 June 1918, pp. 10–22.
25. Ibid., pp. 31–38.
26. "Snubbing the War Labor Board," p. 293.
27. Ibid., pp. 292–93; letter, J. H. McGrail to Walsh, 3 June 1918, Walsh Papers, Box 20.
28. Letter, Woodrow Wilson to Carlton, 11 June 1918, NWLB Records, Entry 13.
29. Letter, Carlton to Woodrow Wilson, 17 June 1918, printed in Boston *Monitor*, 18 June 1918, NWLB Records, Entry 20.
30. Western Union, *The Company's Position*, pp. 32–40.
31. Letter, Carlton to Wilson, 17 June 1918; telegram, Osborne to Woodrow Wilson,

17 June 1918; see also letter, Osborne to Taft, 21 June 1918, final two entries in Taft Papers, Series 3, Box 416.

32. "Making it a Test Case," editorial, *Newark Evening News*, 17 June 1918, NWLB Records, Entry 20.

33. Letter, Taft to Walsh, 17 June 1918, Taft Papers, Series 8, Yale Letterbook No. 75.

34. Letter, Taft to Osborne, 4 July 1918, Taft Papers, 8 Yale 78.

35. Telegram, Walsh to Woodrow Wilson, 20 June 1918, Wilson Papers, Series 4, No. 4341, Item Nos. 233179–80.

36. Letter, William B. Wilson to Woodrow Wilson, 22 June 1918, Wilson Papers, Series 4, No. 4341, Item Nos. 233185–87.

37. Telegram, Samuel Gompers to Woodrow Wilson, 18 June 1918, Wilson Papers, Series 4, No. 4341, Item No. 233177.

38. "Western Union and the Government," *The New Republic*, 8 June 1918, pp. 163–64.

39. Letter, Taft to Mrs. Murray Crane, 3 July 1918, Taft Papers, 8 Yale 76.

40. "Jottings," *The Survey*, 13 July 1918, p. 418.

41. "Shall the Nation be Unionized?" editorial, *New York Tribune*, 11 July 1919, NWLB Records, Entry 20.

42. H. K. Moderwell, "Labor Men's First Move Toward Unionizing Nation," *New York Tribune*, 7 July 1918, Walsh Papers, Scrapbook No. 40.

43. NWLB, Minutes, afternoon meeting of 1 June 1918, p. 21.

44. "U.S. Control of Telegraph May Prevent Strike," New York *Telegram*, 3 June 1918, NWLB Records, Entry 20.

45. Telegram, Gompers to Woodrow Wilson, 14 June 1918, Wilson Papers, Series 4, No. 142.

46. "U.S. Control of Telegraph May Prevent Strike."

47. Annual Report of the Postmaster General of the United States, 1917, quoted in Western Union, *The Company's Position*, pp. 28–31.

CHAPTER 4

1. Both the Walsh report and Theodore Roosevelt are cited in W. Jett Lauck, typescript on the living wage, n.d., Lauck Papers, Box 95. Roosevelt, in a speech before the Progressive Convention at Chicago, 6 August 1912, defined the "living wage" as follows: "The monetary equivalent of a living wage varies according to local conditions, but must include enough to secure the elements of a normal standard of living—a standard high enough to make morality possible, to provide for education and recreation, to care for immature members of the family, to maintain the family during periods of sickness, and to permit of reasonable saving for old age."

2. Quoted, Lauck, *New Industrial Revolution*, p. 106.

3. Quoted, Cronon, *Political Thought of Woodrow Wilson*, p. 264.

4. Wilson v. New, 243 U.S. 347 (1917); Bunting v. Oregon, 243 U.S. 426 (1917).

5. Stettler v. O'Hara, 243 U.S. 629 (1917).

6. "Report of the War Labor Conference Board," Bureau of Labor Statistics, *National War Labor Board*, p. 33.

7. Letter, Taft to James Ernest King of the Boston *Evening Transcript*, 7 August 1918, Taft Papers, 8 Yale 78; Application of Frank P. Walsh for Admission to the Bar, Appellate Division of the Supreme Court of the State of New York, First Department, Walsh Papers, Box 28; P. J. Morrin, "Frank P. Walsh, Our General Counsel Drops Dead in

New York," *The Bridgemen's Magazine* 39 (May 1939): 257–59, Lauck Papers, Box 46; Meehan, "Frank P. Walsh," pp. 8–11.

8. Letter, Walsh to Louis Knight, 9 July 1913, Walsh Papers, Box 2.
9. NWLB, Minutes, morning meeting of 26 July 1918, p. 79.
10. William L. Chenery, "Packington Steps Forward: The Gist and the Spirit of Judge Alschuler's Decision in the Chicago Packing Cases," *The Survey*, 13 April 1918, p. 36.
11. U.S., Department of Labor, *Monthly Review of the Bureau of Labor Statistics*, 6:115–17.
12. Ibid., pp. 122–23.
13. Ibid., pp. 123–24.
14. Letter, Walsh to John Fitzpatrick, 13 June 1918, NWLB Records, Entry 13.
15. Letter, Walsh to James P. Aylward, 12 October 1918, Walsh Papers, Box 24.
16. Letter, Clifton Reeves to H. L. Kerwin, assistant to the Secretary of Labor, 14 May 1918, in Washington National Record Center, Suitland, Maryland, NWLB Records, Casefile No. 40.
17. See telegrams, Hugh Hanna to Lauck, 22 May 1918; Hanna to Lauck, 23 May 1918; F. T. Unger to Lauck, 27 May 1918, all in NWLB Records, Casefile No. 40.
18. See Transcript of Hearing, 5 June 1918, NWLB Records, Casefile No. 40.
19. Ibid., morning session, pp. 30, 33–34, 66.
20. Ibid., see especially, morning session, p. 18; afternoon session, p. 2.
21. Ibid., afternoon session, p. 52.
22. Ibid., morning session, p. 18.
23. Ibid., morning session, pp. 28, 35.
24. Ibid., afternoon session, p. 50.
25. NWLB, Minutes, morning meeting of 10 July 1918, pp. 1–29.
26. Ibid., p. 27.
27. Ibid., p. 24.
28. Ibid., p. 32.
29. Ibid., p. 31.
30. Ibid., p. 39.
31. Ibid., p. 27.
32. Ibid., pp. 32–38; NWLB, Minutes, afternoon meeting of 10 July 1918, p. 3.
33. NWLB, Minutes, afternoon meeting of 10 July 1918, pp. 5, 7, 27–28, 48–49, 52, 54, 60–61, 64, 67–70.
34. Ibid., pp. 14–23.
35. Ibid., p. 4.
36. Ibid.
37. Ibid., pp. 29, 48–50, 52, 57.
38. Ibid., p. 59.
39. Ibid., p. 61.
40. Ibid., p. 70.
41. Ibid., p. 61.
42. National War Labor Board, "Findings in re Employees v. Frick Co., Emerson-Brantingham Co., Landis Tool Co., Landis Machine Co., Bostwick-Lyons Bronze Co., Shearer Machine Co., Victor Tool Co., and Cashman Tool Co., all of Waynesboro, Pa.," Docket No. 40, 11 July 1918, printed in Bureau of Labor Statistics, *National War Labor Board*, pp. 168–69.
43. NWLB, Minutes, morning meeting of 11 July 1918, p. 20.
44. Ibid., pp. 18–19; letters of complaint from Waynesboro employers began to pour

in almost immediately, and continued into the fall. Waynesboro employees, in general, were more pleased, but on 19 July, made a "suggested modification" of the 40 cents minimum to 50 cents. In succeeding months, they repeated their suggestion periodically. See NWLB Records, Casefile No. 40.

45. NWLB, "Findings in . . . Waynesboro, Pa.," Docket No. 40.
46. NWLB, Minutes, morning meeting of 11 July 1918, p. 12.
47. Letter, Taft to King, 7 August 1918.
48. NWLB, Minutes, morning meeting of 23 July 1918, pp. 25–36.
49. NWLB, Minutes, morning meeting of 24 July 1918, pp. 3–10.
50. On the morning of 25 July Victor Olander raised important questions about the implications of the new law, which provoked a heated debate. See NWLB, Minutes, morning meeting of 25 July 1918, especially pp. 66–82.
51. NWLB, Minutes, morning meeting of 26 July 1918, pp. 16–17.
52. NWLB, Minutes, morning meeting of 24 July 1918, pp. 29–35.
53. Ibid., pp. 44–46.
54. NWLB, Minutes, morning meeting of 26 July 1918, pp. 63–64.
55. Letter, W. H. VanDervoort to Taft, 27 July 1918, Taft Papers, Series 3, Box 419.
56. NWLB, Minutes, morning meeting of 26 July 1918, pp. 63–64.
57. Ibid., pp. 75–76.
58. Ibid.
59. Ibid., pp. 62–63.
60. NWLB, Minutes, morning meeting of 24 July 1918, pp. 18–19.
61. NWLB, Minutes, morning meeting of 26 July 1918, p. 28.
62. See, for example, NWLB, Minutes, morning meeting of 24 July 1918, p. 18; Minutes, morning meeting of 25 July 1918, pp. 50–52.
63. Letter, Taft to Wendell W. Mischler, 25 July 1918, Taft Papers, Series 3, Box 419.
64. NWLB, Minutes, morning meeting of 30 July 1918, p. 12; Minutes, morning meeting of 31 July 1918, pp. 8–24.
65. NWLB, Minutes, morning meeting of 26 July 1918, pp. 28–29.
66. Letter, Taft to King, 7 August 1918.
67. The rapprochement between the two men was evident in a note that Taft scrawled to Walsh on the back of an envelope that week. One imagines the former president passing his message to Walsh in mid-speech: "Did you ever read Holmes' Poem on 'An Insect—the Katydid'—It has a refrain—'Thou sayest an undisputed thing in such a solemn way'" (Walsh Papers, Box 21).
68. Because of the press coverage, and indeed because of the decisions themselves, Taft received a steady stream of letters from conservative critics of the NWLB. They denounced not only wage awards but the whole body of NWLB decisions. See Taft Papers for specifics.
69. Douglas, *Real Wages*, pp. 178–82.

CHAPTER 5

1. Douglas, *Real Wages*, p. 326; Benson, "The NWLB and the Crisis in Urban Transportation," p. 5.
2. Robert W. Hobbs, "War Board to Probe Street Car Wages," New York *Journal*, 24 June 1918, NWLB Records, Entry 20.
3. See Benson, "Crisis in Urban Transportation," p. 3.

4. War Board of the American Electric Railway Association, "Income Account of 365 Electric Roads for the Six Months Ended June 30, 1918, Compared with the Six Months Ended June 30, 1917," NWLB Records, Entry 15.
5. Telegram, Walsh to Taft, 5 June 1918, NWLB Records, Entry 19.
6. Letter, Walsh to James H. Vahey, 4 June 1918, Taft Papers, Series 3, Box 415.
7. United States Committee on Public Information, *Official Bulletin* No. 12, 23 June 1918, NWLB Records, Entry 15.
8. Ibid.; *Official Bulletin* No. 8, 13 June 1918.
9. Thomas N. McCarter, "Electric Railway Wage Increases Must Be Accompanied by Compensating Increases of Revenue to the Companies Concerned," address before the National War Labor Board at Washington, 24 June 1918, NWLB Records, Entry 14.
10. Philip N. Gadsden, "Brief Submitted by the War Board of the American Electric Railway Association to Honorable William Howard Taft and Mr. Frank P. Walsh, National War Labor Board, in the Matter of the Power of the President to Fix Rates of Fare on Electric Railways," 25 June 1918, NWLB Records, Entry 14.
11. Ibid.
12. United States Committee on Public Information, *Official Bulletin* No. 13, 26 June 1918, NWLB Records, Entry 15.
13. See NWLB, Minutes, afternoon meeting of 28 June 1918, pp. 7–8.
14. Ibid., pp. 2–4, 7–8.
15. Ibid., pp. 4–5.
16. Ibid., p. 4.
17. Ibid., p. 6.
18. Ibid., p. 8.
19. Kerr, "Decision for Federal Control," pp. 550–60.
20. "Federal Relief for Local Utilities," editorial, *New York Times*, 13 June 1918, NWLB Records, Entry 20.
21. "The Fourth Party," editorial, *New York Tribune*, 5 August 1918, NWLB Records, Entry 20.
22. "National Authority and Local Transit," editorial, New York *Journal of Commerce*, 3 August 1918, NWLB Records, Entry 20.
23. "National Control of Street Cars," editorial, New York *World*, 28 June 1918, NWLB Records, Entry 20.
24. "Crisis in the Street Railway Situation," reprinted from *Electric Railway Journal* in New York *Journal of Commerce*, 30 June 1918, NWLB Records, Entry 20.
25. William Howard Taft, "Street Car Men and the Rate of Fare," reprinted from Philadelphia *Public Ledger* in Boston *Transcript*, 11 July 1918, NWLB Records, Entry 20.
26. Ibid.; in this article and in private correspondence Taft repeated his analogy about fixing wages in the coal industry and his doubts about the president's ability to fix fares without express congressional authorization. See, for example, letters, Taft to William C. Hunneman and Taft to Judge David F. Pugh, both 4 July 1918, both in Taft Papers, 8 Yale 78.
27. William L. Ransom, "The Agitation for Higher Fares," *The Survey*, 20 July 1918, pp. 443–46.
28. Ibid.
29. Letter, Woodrow Wilson to Taft and Walsh, 9 July 1918, Taft Papers, Series 3, Box 418.
30. Letter, Taft to Walsh, 14 July 1918, Walsh Papers, Box 21.
31. Letter, Gus Karger to Taft, 16 July 1918, Taft Papers, Series 3, Box 418.

32. Letter, Walsh to H. H. Tammen, 14 July 1918, Walsh Papers, Box 21.
33. Letter, Taft to Walsh, 14 July 1918.
34. United States Committee on Public Information, *Official Bulletin* No. 11, 11 July 1918, NWLB Records, Entry 15.
35. On 30 July W. D. Mahon, president of the street-railway union, and James H. Vahey, its principal attorney, wrote the joint chairmen as follows: "We urge you to do your utmost to dispose of as many cases as possible tomorrow; and we make this suggestion because we know you will understand the spirit which prompts it, namely, to keep men at work in this industry.... If you cannot decide at the present time all the matters submitted to you in all the cases, may we suggest that possibly you might settle the question of wages, which is of course of primary importance? ... Whatever your decision may be, we will of course communicate it to the members of the organizations, but the constant strain of the last four months is bound to tell. It is certainly much harder to keep the men at work now than it was four months ago, and the difficulty will increase with the delay of your award." (Letter, Vahey and Mahon to Taft and Walsh, 30 July 1918, Taft Papers, Series 3, Box 419.)
36. United States Committee on Public Information, *Official Bulletin* No. 16, 1 August 1918, p. 5, NWLB Records, Entry 15.
37. For a summary of wages established in street railway awards, see Bureau of Labor Statistics, *National War Labor Board*, pp. 108–16, and American Electric Railway Association, "Summary of Awards of National War Labor Board," undated typescript in NWLB Records, Entry 17. For more specific information in the case of the International Railway Company in Buffalo, see Case File No. 152.
38. Letter, William S. Rann, Corporation Counsel of Buffalo, to Taft, 8 July 1918, Taft Papers, Series 3, Box 418; Letter, Frank C. Perkins to Walsh, 8 July 1918, NWLB Records, Entry 19.
39. Letter, Frank Perkins, president, and George C. Hillman, secretary, CCBMTACA, to Walsh, 22 August 1918, NWLB Records, Entry 19; see also public letter, "In Re International Railway Company," sent to various members of Congress by George Clinton, John L. Romer, and Ross Graves, 25 September 1918, copy in Taft Papers, Series 3, Box 424.
40. Letters, George Clinton to Taft, 10 August, 16 August, and 26 August, 1918, Taft Papers, Series 3, Boxes 420–21.
41. Letter, E. G. Connette to Lauck, 12 August 1918, NWLB Records, Entry 19.
42. Letter, Perkins and Hillman to Walsh, 22 August 1918.
43. "Complaint of International Railway Service to Public Service Commission, Mayor of Buffalo, and Frank P. Walsh," 26 August 1918, NWLB Records, Entry 19.
44. Frederic Almy, "The Buffalo Street Car Strike and Mayor Buck," *The Nation*, 21 December 1918, pp. 772–73; United States Committee on Public Information, *Official Bulletin* No. 8, 26 November 1918, NWLB Records, Entry 15.
45. National War Labor Board, "Findings in re Employees v. New Orleans Railway & Light Co.," Docket No. 98, 31 July 1918, printed in Bureau of Labor Statistics, *National War Labor Board*, p. 173.
46. Letter, D. D. Curran to Taft and Walsh, 10 August 1918, and letter, Arthur Sturgis and Joseph Chiesa to Lauck, 31 August 1918, both in NWLB Records, Entry 19.
47. Letter, Sturgis and Chiesa to Lauck, 31 August 1918.
48. Ibid.
49. Letters, Taft to Walsh, 18 October and 20 October 1918, both in Taft Papers, Series 3, Box 425.

50. National War Labor Board, "Findings in re Employees v. New Orleans Railway & Light Company," Docket No. 98, Revision of Award, 24 October 1918, printed in Bureau of Labor Statistics, *National War Labor Board*, p. 174.
51. For insight into circumstances in New Orleans in October 1918, see "The Railway Situation," editorial, New Orleans *States*, 7 October 1918, NWLB Records, Entry 20; telegrams, Lauck to Walsh, Lauck to Taft and Walsh, both 10 October, both Taft Papers, Series 3, Box 424; letter, Philip N. Gadsden to Taft, 16 October 1918, Taft Papers, Series 3, Box 425; "Carmen's Back Wage To Be Paid Soon, Company Says," New Orleans *Item*, 25 October 1918, NWLB Records, Entry 20. See also Revision of Award in Docket No. 98, in which the joint chairmen thank the city of New Orleans for its cooperation in helping to relieve the additional financial burden imposed on the company by the award.
52. "Public Utility Changes," Great Falls (Montana) *Tribune*, 10 October 1918, NWLB Records, Entry 20.
53. Judson C. Welliver, "Utility Aid Local Problem," New York *Globe*, 18 October 1918, NWLB Records, Entry 20.
54. "Increased Wages Granted by War Labor Board to Street Railway Employees," New York *Financial Chronicle*, 3 August 1918, NWLB Records, Entry 20.
55. *The Nation*, 9 November 1918, p. 541.
56. Letter, Taft to King, 7 August 1918.
57. Letters, Taft to Luther Brewer, 8 August 1918; Taft to King, 7 August 1918; Taft to Lauck, 4 August 1918, all in Taft Papers, 8 Yale 78.
58. Letter, Taft to Brewer, 8 August 1918.
59. Letter, Taft to King, 7 August 1918.
60. Letter, Taft to Lauck, 4 August 1918.
61. Letter, Charles Sweeney to Lauck, 8 August 1918, NWLB Records, Entry 13.
62. Ibid.
63. Ibid.
64. U.S. Department of Labor, National War Labor Board, *Report of the Secretary*, Appendix 1, "Special Report on the Public Utility Cases," by Charlton Ogburn, pp. 46–48; Bureau of Labor Statistics, *National War Labor Board*, p. 21.
65. Ogburn, "Special Report," pp. 46–48.
66. Douglas, *Real Wages*, pp. 326–28.

CHAPTER 6

1. U.S. Department of Labor, National War Labor Board, *Memorandum on the Eight-Hour Working Day*, pp. 5–7.
2. Frankfurter and Goldmark, *The Case for the Shorter Work Day*, pp. 1–10.
3. National War Labor Board, *Memorandum on the Eight-Hour Working Day*, p. 6; Leifur Magnusson, "Hours of Labor in American Industry with Particular Reference to the Recent 8-Hour Movement," typescript, n.d., in NWLB Records, Entry 14.
4. President Wilson himself appeared before Congress to propose what became the Adamson Act shortly after having appointed Gompers to the Advisory Committee of the Council of National Defense. Smith, "Organized Labor," p. 268.
5. National War Labor Board, *Memorandum on the Eight-Hour Working Day*, pp. 6–7.
6. Ibid., p. 11.
7. Bunting v. Oregon, 243 U.S. 426 (1917).

8. See Felix Frankfurter, "Suggestions for the Administration of the Eight-Hour Law," in National War Labor Board, *Memorandum on the Eight-Hour Working Day.*
9. Ibid., pp. 15–17.
10. Ibid., pp. 18–20.
11. Ibid., p. 22.
12. Ibid., pp. 24–25.
13. Samuel J. Rosensohn, "Memorandum to the War Labor Policies Board, June 21, 1918," in National War Labor Board, *Memorandum on the Eight-Hour Working Day*, p. 27.
14. Ibid., pp. 28–29.
15. Ibid.
16. "Report of the War Labor Conference Board," Bureau of Labor Statistics, *National War Labor Board*, p. 32.
17. National Industrial Conference Board, *The Eight Hour Day Defined*, p. 5.
18. National War Labor Board, "Employees v. Manufacturers of Newsprint Paper," Docket No. 35, 27 June 1918, printed in Bureau of Labor Statistics, *National War Labor Board*, pp. 152–63.
19. NWLB, Minutes, afternoon meeting of 9 July 1918, pp. 35–36.
20. Ibid., p. 37.
21. Ibid., pp. 42–45.
22. Ibid., pp. 42–67.
23. Ibid., p. 50.
24. Ibid., p. 43. Emphasis added.
25. Ibid.
26. Ibid., pp. 64–65.
27. Ibid., p. 58.
28. Ibid., pp. 49, 57, 60–61, 66–67.
29. Ibid., p. 49.
30. Ibid., p. 66.
31. Ibid., pp. 53–54.
32. Ibid., p. 55.
33. Ibid., p. 56.
34. Osborne's attitude reflected a viewpoint current in publications such as *Iron Age* and *American Industries*. Both journals opposed the introduction of the eight-hour day. See, for example, "Short Day Will Not Win War," *Iron Age*, 21 February 1918, p. 496; "The Eight-Hour Day and Economic Loss of Man Power," editorial, *American Industries* 18 (February 1918): 7; "The Inconsistency of the Eight-Hour Law," *American Industries* 18 (April 1918): 38.
35. NWLB, Minutes, afternoon meeting of 9 July 1918, pp. 51–52.
36. Ibid., p. 46.
37. Ibid., p. 47.
38. Ibid., pp. 63–64.
39. *New York Times*, 10 July 1918, quoted in NWLB, Minutes, morning meeting of 11 July 1918, pp. 28–32; Minutes, same meeting, pp. 32–37.
40. NWLB, Minutes, morning meeting of 11 July 1918, pp. 38–44.
41. Letter, Louis M. H. Howe to Thomas J. Savage, 10 July 1918, quoted, ibid., p. 43.
42. NWLB, Minutes, afternoon meeting of 11 July 1918, p. 2.
43. Ibid., p. 8.
44. See ibid., pp. 8–11.
45. Ibid., p. 10; National War Labor Board, "Findings in re Machinists v. Worthington

Pump & Machinery Corporation, Blake & Knowles Works, East Cambridge, Mass., and Snow-Holly Works, Buffalo, N.Y.," Docket No. 14, 11 July 1918, printed in Bureau of Labor Statistics, *National War Labor Board*, pp. 135–37.

46. Gilson Gardner, "Eight Hour Day on All War Work," St. Paul *News*, 22 July 1918, NWLB Records, Entry 20.

47. NWLB, "Findings in re Machinists v. Worthington Pump & Machinery Corporation," Docket No. 14.

48. National War Labor Board, "Findings in re Employees v. St. Joseph Lead Co., Herculaneum, Mo.," Docket No. 16, 31 July 1918; "Findings in re Employees v. Sloss Sheffield Steel and Iron Co., Birmingham, Ala.," Docket No. 12, 31 July 1918, both printed in Bureau of Labor Statistics, *National War Labor Board*, pp. 137–38, 132–35.

49. Memorandum, Executive Secretary of the War Labor Policies Board to the War Labor Board, 15 July 1918, Frankfurter Papers, Box 190.

50. Memorandum, Walsh to Frankfurter, 15 August 1918, Frankfurter Papers, Box 190.

51. Letter, Frankfurter to Walsh, 30 August 1918, Frankfurter Papers, Box 190.

52. See National War Labor Board, *Memorandum on the Eight-Hour Working Day*.

53. Loyall A. Osborne, "The Basic Eight-Hour Day: Argument on Behalf of the Employer Members of the National War Labor Board," n.d., Taft Papers, Series 3, Box 421.

54. Ibid.

55. Letter, Osborne to Taft, 29 August 1918, Taft Papers, Series 3, Box 421.

56. See letter, Taft to Osborne, 2 September 1918, Taft Papers, 8 Yale 78.

57. "Labor's Triumph and the Eight-Hour Day," NWLB Records, Entry 24; National War Labor Board, "Findings in re Employees in Munitions and Related Trades, Bridgeport, Conn.," Docket No. 132, 28 August 1918, printed in Bureau of Labor Statistics, *National War Labor Board*, pp. 198–202.

58. Letter, Osborne to Taft, 29 August 1918.

59. NWLB, Minutes, morning meeting of 28 August 1918, pp. 45–72.

60. Ibid.

61. National War Labor Board, "Decision of the Umpire in re International Association of Machinists, Local No. 818, v. Wheeling Mold & Foundry Co., Wheeling W. Va.," Docket No. 37-a, 30 October 1918; "Award in re Molders v. Wheeling Mold & Foundry Co., Wheeling W. Va.," Docket No. 37-b, 16 September 1918, both printed in Bureau of Labor Statistics, *National War Labor Board*, pp. 163, 164–67.

62. NWLB, "Decision of the Umpire," Docket No. 37-a.

63. Letter, Clark to Walsh, 16 September 1918, Walsh Papers, Box 23.

64. NWLB, "Award in re Molders v. Wheeling Mold & Foundry Co.," Docket No. 37-b.

65. Ibid.

66. Letter, Walsh to Clark, 18 September 1918, Walsh Papers, Box 23.

67. Letter, Clark to Basil M. Manly, 9 October 1918, NWLB Records, Entry 14.

68. *The Nation*, 5 October 1918, p. 359.

69. See Bureau of Labor Statistics, *National War Labor Board*, pp. 71–87; National War Labor Board, Index to Dockets, Lauck Papers, Box 411.

70. See, for example, Bing, *War-Time Strikes*, p. 179; U.S., Department of Labor, *Monthly Review of the Bureau of Labor Statistics*, 9:194.

CHAPTER 7

1. Letter, Walsh to Louis J. Irwin, 27 August 1918, Walsh Papers, Box 22.
2. John A. Fitch, "A Report on Industrial Unrest: Summary of Findings of President's Commission," *The Survey*, 16 February 1918, p. 546.
3. Quoted, Lauck and Watts, *The Industrial Code*, p. 117.
4. John A. Fitch, "Making the Bargain," *The Survey*, 15 December 1917, p. 319; John A. Fitch, "Two Years of the Rockefeller Plan," *The Survey*, 6 October 1917, pp. 14–20.
5. Quoted, Stoddard, *The Shop Committee*, p. 2; Rockefeller, *Personal Relation in Industry*, p. 117.
6. Fitch, "Two Years of the Rockefeller Plan," pp. 14–20.
7. Ibid.
8. Ibid.
9. U.S. Congress, House, Committee on Claims, *Claims of Certain Employees of Bethlehem Steel Co., Hearings*, before Committee on Claims, House of Representatives, on H. R. 10727, 67th Cong., 2d sess., 1922, pp. 20–21; U.S. Congress, Senate, *Award of the National War Labor Board in Favor of Certain Employees of the Bethlehem Steel Co., Report No. 855* to accompany H. R. 5481, 68th Cong., 2d sess., 1925, pp. 1–5, both in Lauck Papers, Box 53; NWLB, Minutes, meeting of 10 May 1918, p. 16.
10. Letter, E. P. Marsh to H. L. Kerwin, printed in U.S., House, Committee on Claims, *Hearings*, p. 50; United States Committee on Public Information, *Official Bulletin* No. 8, 11 May 1918, NWLB Records, Entry 15; NWLB, Minutes, meeting of 10 May 1918, pp. 24–25.
11. NWLB, Minutes, meeting of 10 May 1918, pp. 17–21.
12. U.S., Senate, *Report* No. 855, p. 2; NWLB, Minutes, meeting of 10 May 1918, pp. 16, 24.
13. Lauck and Hugh Hanna, Report on Bethlehem case, 9 July 1918, printed in NWLB, Minutes, morning meeting of 30 July 1918, p. 22.
14. "Two Decisions of the War Labor Board," *The Survey*, 10 August 1918, p. 545.
15. NWLB, Minutes, morning meeting of 1 June 1918, pp. 15, 17, 19.
16. Ibid., pp. 12–13, 20–21.
17. Ibid., p. 14.
18. NWLB, Minutes, meeting of 10 May 1918, p. 22.
19. "Two Decisions," p. 545.
20. NWLB, Minutes, morning meeting of 1 June 1918, pp. 15, 35.
21. Ibid., p. 23.
22. Ibid., pp. 24, 31.
23. Ibid., pp. 23–24, 30–32.
24. Ibid., pp. 24–28.
25. Ibid., pp. 32–33.
26. Ibid., p. 27.
27. Ibid., pp. 28–29, 36.
28. Ibid., pp. 43–44.
29. "U.S. Asked to End Bad Bethlehem Wage Plan," *New York Call*, 20 June 1918, NWLB Records, Entry 20.
30. Telegram, Lauck to Taft, 17 June 1918, Taft Papers, Series 3, Box 416; United States Committee on Public Information, *Official Bulletin* Nos. 14, 11, and 14, for 19, 23, and 29 June 1918, all in NWLB Records, Entry 15.
31. Letter, Lauck to Taft, 19 June 1918, Taft Papers, Series 3, Box 416.

32. Ibid.; "Pittsfield: Strike Danger Averted at General Electric Plant," Springfield *Republican*, 8 June 1918; "To Try to Adjust General Electric Matter," Springfield *Republican*, 12 June 1918, both in NWLB Records, Entry 20.

33. United States Committee on Public Information, *Official Bulletin* No. 15, 29 June 1918, NWLB Records, Entry 15.

34. "Individual Labor Contracts Barred," Boston *Advertiser*, 1 July 1918; "G. E. Workers Win," Springfield *Republican*, 6 July 1918, both in NWLB Records, Entry 20.

35. Stoddard, *The Shop Committee*, p. 12.

36. "U.S. Asked to End."

37. Ibid.

38. Ibid.

39. Letter, E. F. Kinkead to Frank P. Walsh, 2 July 1918; letter, William P. Harvey to Walsh, 8 July 1918; letter, Walsh to E. F. Kincaid [sic], 9 July 1918, all in Walsh Papers, Box 21; Memo, Harvey to Walsh, 20 June 1918, NWLB Records, Entry 13.

40. Memo, Harvey to Walsh, 20 June 1918.

41. Lauck and Hanna, Report, in NWLB, Minutes, morning meeting of 30 July 1918, pp. 15–22.

42. NWLB, Minutes, morning meeting of 30 July 1918, pp. 33–34.

43. Ibid., pp. 27, 31.

44. Ibid., pp. 36–38.

45. Ibid., pp. 36–40.

46. National War Labor Board, "Findings in re Machinists and Electrical Workers and Other Employees v. Bethlehem Steel Co., Bethlehem, Pa.," Docket No. 22, 31 July 1918, printed in Bureau of Labor Statistics, *National War Labor Board*, pp. 138–40.

47. Ibid.; National War Labor Board, "Findings in re Employees v. General Electric Company, Pittsfield Works," Docket No. 19, 31 July 1918, in U.S., National War Labor Board, *National War Labor Board Docket*, 1:3–4.

48. NWLB, "Findings in re Machinists and Electrical Workers and Other Employees v. Bethlehem Steel Co., Bethlehem, Pa.," Docket No. 22.

49. NWLB, "Findings in re Employees v. General Electric Company, Pittsfield Works," Docket No. 19.

50. NWLB, Minutes, afternoon meeting of 13 August 1918, pp. 10–22.

51. Ibid., pp. 19–25.

52. Ibid., pp. 40–51.

53. Ibid., pp. 43, 51.

54. National War Labor Board, "Findings of Section in re Employees v. Smith & Wesson Arms Co., Springfield, Mass.," Docket No. 273, 21 August 1918, printed in Bureau of Labor Statistics, *National War Labor Board*, p. 260; letter, F. N. Judson to Taft, 19 August 1918, Taft Papers, Series 3, Box 421.

55. Enclosure, letter, Walsh to Major B. H. Gitchell, 19 August 1918, NWLB Records, Entry 14.

CHAPTER 8

1. Remarks of one portly gentleman to another overheard in the smoker of a Pullman car en route from Chicago to Washington, reported in letter, Stuart Chase to Walsh, 4 November 1918, Walsh Papers, Box 25.

2. Letter, R. D. Cramer to Robert Maisel, 3 October 1918, Walsh Papers, Box 24; "Taft

and Walsh Sit in Judgment on Labor Matter," Minneapolis *Daily News*, 10 October 1918, Walsh Papers, Scrapbook No. 39.

3. Newsletter, J. M. Vallmer to friends and members of Employers' Association of Louisville, Kentucky, 2 October 1918, Walsh Papers, Box 24.

4. Letter, Walter Drew to National War Labor Board, quoted in Bangor [Maine] *Commercial*, 26 August 1918, NWLB Records, Entry 20.

5. "Bridgeport's Outlaw Strike," *Iron Age*, 5 September 1918, p. 585.

6. Brody, *Labor in Crisis*, pp. 61–62, 69; newsletter, John R. Alpine to secretaries of international unions, state federations of labor, and city central bodies, 13 September 1918, NWLB Records, Entry 14.

7. Brody, *Labor in Crisis*, pp. 63–64.

8. Gompers, "Editorials," *American Federationist* 25 (September 1918): 810.

9. Walsh, "Democracy or Destruction," clipping in Walsh Papers, Scrapbook No. 39.

10. Walsh, "Labor's Day," *American Federationist* 25 (October 1918): 897.

11. "Mr. Frank P. Walsh's Outburst," Butte *Miner*, 9 September 1918, Walsh Papers, Scrapbook No. 39.

12. "What Does He Mean?" New London [Connecticut] *Day*, 3 September 1918, Walsh Papers, Scrapbook No. 39.

13. Gilson Gardner, "Laboring People Now Favor Ex-President Taft," Dallas *Dispatch*, 6 September 1918, Taft Papers, Series 3, Box 422.

14. "Bridgeport's Outlaw Strike," *Iron Age*, pp. 584–85; "Munitions Workers Petition President to Take Over Factories," Bridgeport *Herald*, 8 September 1918, Walsh Papers, Scrapbook No. 46.

15. "Frank P. Walsh, Humanity's Champion, Acclaims New Democracy in Industry with Bridgeport As a Corner Stone," Bridgeport *Labor Leader*, 29 August 1918, Walsh Papers, Scrapbook No. 39; "Machinists Vote Confidence in War Labor Board," Bridgeport *Times*, 24 August 1918, Walsh Papers, Scrapbook No. 46.

16. "A Square Deal for Workers in New Industrial Magna Carta," Bridgeport *Labor Leader*, 29 August 1918, Walsh Papers, Scrapbook No. 39.

17. "Labor Board Decides Against Machinists in Bridgeport Case," Bridgeport *Evening Post*, 28 August 1918; "Between 4,000 & 6,000 Now on Strike Here," Bridgeport *Standard-American*, 31 August 1918; "Machinists Vote to Fight Against Award to Finish," Bridgeport *Telegram*, 31 August 1918; "The Strike Without Friends," Bridgeport *Times & Evening Farmer*, 31 August 1918, all in Walsh Papers, Scrapbook No. 46.

18. "An Industrial Truce in Bridgeport," *The Survey*, 20 July 1918, pp. 454–55; A. S. O'Brien, "Tracing the Back-Ground for the Bridgeport Munitions Workers' Strike Against the Eidlitz Award," Bridgeport *Herald*, 8 September 1918, Walsh Papers, Scrapbook No. 46.

19. Ibid.; National War Labor Board, "Findings in re Employees v. Employers in Munitions and Related Trades, Bridgeport, Conn.," Docket No. 132; "Machinists Vote to Fight Against Award."

20. O'Brien, "Tracing the Back-Ground."

21. "Smith and Wesson Firm Asks that U.S. Take Plant," Bridgeport *Telegram*, 31 August 1918, Walsh Papers, Scrapbook No. 46.

22. Letter, George P. Chapin to National War Labor Board, 29 August 1918, printed in I. R. Feinberg, "Three Cases Under the National War Labor Board (1918–1919) Reflecting the Powers of That Board," n.d. [1940–45], pp. 23–26, NWLB Records, Entry 15.

23. Ibid.; letter, Eighteen Hartford, Connecticut, Manufacturers, to Newton D.

Baker, 7 September 1918, in ibid., pp. 28–29.

24. Letter, Manufacturers to Newton D. Baker, 7 September 1918.
25. Letter, Walsh to Frank P. Walsh, Jr., 9 September 1918, Walsh Papers, Box 23.
26. Ibid.
27. "In the Interests of War Production," *The Survey*, 21 September 1918, p. 697.
28. Letter, Woodrow Wilson to District Lodge No. 55, International Association of Machinists and other striking workmen of Bridgeport, Connecticut, 13 September 1918, printed in Bureau of Labor Statistics, *National War Labor Board*, p. 36.
29. Letter, Walsh to Frank P. Walsh, Jr., 15 September 1918, Walsh Papers, Box 23; "A Poor Time to Quit Work," *The Literary Digest*, 28 September 1918, pp. 17–18, NWLB Records, Entry 20.
30. Letter, Walsh to Frank P. Walsh, Jr., 15 September 1918.
31. Letter, Woodrow Wilson to Remington Arms, U. M. C. Plant, Liberty Ordnance Company and others, 17 September 1918, printed in Bureau of Labor Statistics, *National War Labor Board*, pp. 36–37.
32. "Bridgeport Case to be Reopened," *New York Times*, 20 September 1918, NWLB Records, Entry 20.
33. "Taft Announces Winter Has Full Power to Act in Administering Award," Bridgeport *Telegram*, 24 September 1918, Walsh Papers, Scrapbook No. 46.
34. Alpheus Winter, "Rulings of the National War Labor Board in the Bridgeport Award," 23 September 1918, printed with National War Labor Board, "Findings in re Employees v. Employers in Munitions and Related Trades, Bridgeport, Conn.," Docket No. 132, in Bureau of Labor Statistics, *National War Labor Board*, pp. 202–3.
35. "Taft Announces Winter Has Full Power."
36. Memorandum, Harold Callender to Walsh, 29 August 1918, Walsh Papers, Box 22; NWLB, Minutes, afternoon meeting of 30 July 1918, pp. 2–5, 13–14; NWLB, Minutes, afternoon meeting of 31 July 1918, p. 40.
37. NWLB, Minutes, afternoon meeting of 30 July 1918, p. 15; NWLB, Minutes, afternoon meeting of 31 July 1918, pp. 33–34, 40; memorandum, Callender to Walsh, 29 August 1918.
38. Letter, Taft to Walsh, 20 October 1918, Taft Papers, Series 3, Box 425; National War Labor Board, "Award in re Employees v. General Electric Co., Lynn, Mass.," Docket No. 231, 24 October 1918, printed in Bureau of Labor Statistics, *National War Labor Board*, pp. 243–44.
39. "Election of Shop Committees," 4 October 1918, typescript, NWLB Records, Entry 15.
40. National War Labor Board, "Findings in re Employees v. General Electric Company, Pittsfield Works," Docket No. 19.
41. Letter, Taft to Osborne, 5 October 1918, Taft Papers, 8 Yale 78.
42. "Election of Shop Committees"; Stoddard, *The Shop Committee*, pp. 15, 66; letter, Magnus W. Alexander to Taft, 27 September 1918, Taft Papers, Series 3, Box 423.
43. Letter, Clarence H. Kelsey to Taft, 2 October 1918; letter, Taft to Kelsey, 4 October 1918, both in Taft Papers, Series 3, Box 424.
44. Editorial, "The Voter and His Employer," Worcester, Massachusetts, 28 September 1918, printed in Feinberg, "Three Cases," p. 30.
45. Report on the Ninth Yama Conference, enclosed in letter, Magnus W. Alexander to Taft, 26 October 1918, Taft Papers, Series 3, Box 426.
46. Ibid.
47. "Labor Should Organize Now Says Nearing," New York *Call*, 10 October 1918, NWLB Records, Entry 20.

48. Telegram, R. F. Schroder to Lauck, 30 September 1918, Walsh Papers, Box 23; "War Labor Body Opens Sessions in Minneapolis," Minneapolis *Evening Tribune*, 10 October 1918, NWLB Records, Entry 20; letter, Cramer to Maisel, 3 October 1918; "National Labor Board Attacked by Mpls. Bosses," Minneapolis *Labor Review*, 4 October 1918, NWLB Records, Entry 20.
49. Quoted, "National War Labor Board Attacked."
50. Letter, Cramer to Maisel, 3 October 1918.
51. Letter, O. P. Briggs, president of the Citizens Alliance of Minneapolis, to the Board of Arbitration of the State of Minnesota, 15 April 1918; letter, George W. Lawson, secretary of the executive council of the Minnesota State Federation of Labor, to the Board of Arbitration of the State of Minnesota, 15 April 1918; Minnesota Commission of Public Safety, Order No. 30, 16 April 1918; Minnesota Commission of Public Safety, Order No. 33, 30 April 1918, all in NWLB Records, Entry 14.
52. Minnesota Commission of Public Safety, Order No. 30.
53. Ibid.
54. Letter, Cramer to Maisel, 3 October 1918.
55. Ibid.; letter, Arthur LeSueur to Walsh, 26 September 1918, Walsh Papers, Box 23.
56. "Taft and Walsh Sit in Judgment on Labor Matter"; "War Labor Body Opens Sessions in Minneapolis."
57. Ibid.
58. Ibid.
59. "War Labor Body Opens Sessions in Minneapolis."
60. Letter, Ambrose Tighe to Taft, 27 November 1918, Taft papers, Series 3, Box 429.
61. Letter, Pierce Butler to National War Labor Board, 27 November 1918, Taft Papers, Series 3, Box 429; see Dockets No. 46, 46-b, 196, 261, 264, 473, 482, 497, 566, 570, and 571, 11 April 1919, in U.S., National War Labor Board, *Docket*; letter, Elsie Henry-Latimer to Walsh, 31 July 1919, Walsh Papers, Box 30.

CHAPTER 9

1. O'Grady, *A Legal Minimum Wage*, see chapter 8.
2. Samuel Gompers, "American Labor's Position in Peace or in War," *American Federationist* 24 (April 1917): 279.
3. Gompers, "America's Labor Convention," p. 34.
4. Muller v. Oregon, 208 U.S. 412, 28 Sup. Ct. 324, 52 L. Ed. 551 (1908).
5. Lauck and Watts, *The Industrial Code*, p. 170.
6. "Report of the War Labor Conference Board," Bureau of Labor Statistics, *National War Labor Board*, p. 32.
7. United States Committee on Public Information, *Official Bulletin* No. 15, 12 July 1918, in NWLB Records, Entry 14.
8. National War Labor Board, "Industrial Justice for Women," n.d., p. 3, typescript in NWLB Records, Entry 24.
9. Ibid., p. 4.
10. Ibid., p. 5. The awards varied slightly. See "Findings in re Employees v. General Electric Company, Pittsfield Works," Docket No. 19; "Employees v. Manufacturers of Newsprint Paper," Docket No. 35; "Findings in re Employees v. Employers in Munitions and Related Trades, Bridgeport, Conn.," Docket No. 132; "Findings in re Employees v. General Electric Co., Schenectady Works," Docket No. 127, 31 July 1918, printed in Bureau of Labor Statistics, *National War Labor Board*, p. 179.

11. Letter, Walsh to George Creel, 20 August 1918, Walsh Papers, Box 22.
12. "Women's Wages," *The Nation*, 22 February 1919, p. 271.
13. Pringle, *William Howard Taft*, 2:921–22; clipping, unidentified Chicago newspaper, enclosed with letter, Wirt W. Hallam to Taft, 10 September 1918, Taft Papers, Series 3, Box 422.
14. "Among Trade Union Women," Newark *Ledger*, 15 September 1918, NWLB Records, Entry 20.
15. Letter, Francis J. Reilly to Walsh, 30 July 1918, Walsh Papers, Box 21.
16. Letter, Walsh to Creel, 20 August 1918.
17. "To Consider Problems of Women's Work," Washington *Star*, 12 August 1918; "War Board Aids Working Women," Washington *Post*, 28 August 1918, both in NWLB Records, Entry 20.
18. Memorandum, Marie L. Obenauer, Bertha M. Nienburg, Agnes V. O'Mahoney, Caroline E. Wilson, Anna Herkner, Sarah Yeats Whrlen, and Mary R. Bacon, to Lauck, 11 November 1918, NWLB Records, Entry 13; interview with Marie Obenauer, 28 October 1918, in National Archives, Records of the Women's Bureau (Women in Industry Service), RG 86, Box 5.
19. Memorandum Concerning Awards Affecting Women, Obenauer to Lauck, 9 September 1918, Taft Papers, Series 3, Box 426; "Industrial Justice," p. 4, NWLB Records, Entry 24.
20. Memorandum, Obenauer to Lauck, 9 September 1918; [Obenauer] Memorandum Concerning Awards Affecting Women, n.d. [October 1918], Taft Papers, Series 3, Box 426.
21. Alluded to in separate memorandum, Obenauer to Lauck, 9 September 1918, NWLB Records, Entry 13.
22. Ibid.
23. Memorandum, Obenauer to Lauck, 26 September 1918, Taft Papers, Series 3, Box 426.
24. Letter, Obenauer to Lauck, 5 November 1918, Taft Papers, Series 3, Box 426.
25. Memorandum, Obenauer, Nienburg, O'Mahoney, Wilson, Herkner, Whrlen, and Bacon to Lauck, 11 November 1918.
26. Letter, Lauck to Obenauer, 13 November 1918, NWLB Records, Entry 13.
27. Letter, Obenauer, Nienburg, Herkner, and Wilson to Lauck, 12 November 1918, NWLB Records, Entry 13.
28. Letter, Mary Harriman Rumsey to George Creel, n.d., [September 1918], Walsh Papers, Box 23; *The Survey*, 5 October 1918, p. 3.
29. Letter, John R. Commons to National War Labor Board, 1 October 1918, NWLB Records, Entry 14; letter, Stephen S. Wise to Walsh, 30 September 1918, Walsh Papers, Box 23; letter, Theodore Roosevelt to Taft in Kansas City *Star*, 27 September 1918, Taft Papers, Series 4A, Reel 322; telegram, Mrs. Gifford Pinchot to William B. Wilson, 17 October 1918, NWLB Records, Entry 14; letter, Amos Pinchot to William B. Colver, 15 September 1918; letter, Colver to Walsh, 17 September 1918, final two entries in Walsh Papers, Box 23.
30. Clipping, New York *Public*, 28 September 1918, NWLB Records, Entry 20.
31. Proceedings of Conference of Trade Union Women, 4–5 October 1918, pp. 9, 18, 20, 22–24, NWLB Records, Entry 24.
32. Letter, Walsh to Colver, 20 September 1918, Walsh Papers, Box 23; letter, Walsh to Agnes Nestor, 4 October 1918; letter, Walsh to Mrs. James Leeds Laidslaw, 10 October 1918; letter, Walsh to Estelle Lauder, 17 October 1918, all in NWLB Records, Entry 14; letter, Walsh to Stephen S. Wise, 15 October 1918; letter, Walsh to Mary Anderson, As-

sistant Director, Women in Industry Service, 21 October 1918, both in Walsh Papers, Box 24.

33. Letter, Taft to Theodore Roosevelt, 2 October 1918, Taft Papers, Series 3, Box 424; see also letter, Taft to Isaac M. Ullman, 30 October 1918, Taft Papers, 8 Yale 78.

34. Letter, Walsh to Woodrow Wilson, 30 October 1918, Walsh Papers, Box 24.

35. Ibid.; letter, Wilson to Walsh, 2 November 1918, Walsh Papers, Box 25.

36. "Report of the War Labor Conference Board," Bureau of Labor Statistics, *National War Labor Board*, p. 32.

37. "Findings and Award in re Amalgamated Association of Street & Electric Railway Employees of America, Division No. 764 v. The Kansas City Railways Co.," Docket No. 265, 24 October 1918, printed in Bureau of Labor Statistics, *National War Labor Board*, pp. 250–51; Report of Hearing Before Examiners, 16 September 1918, Docket No. 265, NWLB Records, Entry 10, Group I.

38. Bureau of Labor Statistics, *National War Labor Board*, pp. 70–71; United States Committee on Public Information, *Official Bulletin*, 6 November 1918, NWLB Records, Entry 15.

39. Quoted in "Women Barred," editorial, Cleveland *News*, 24 September 1918, NWLB Records, Casefile No. 491.

40. "Battles Long for Women," "Conductorets Will Appeal," "Conductorets Get Support," unidentified Cleveland news clipping, n.d. [September 1918] NWLB Records, Casefile No. 491.

41. Letter, A. L. Faulkner to W. B. Wilson, 25 September 1918, NWLB Records, Casefile No. 491.

42. United States Committee on Public Information, *Official Bulletin*, 6 November 1918.

43. NWLB, Minutes, afternoon meeting of 3 December 1918, pp. 27–30, 39, 42–45.

44. Ibid., p. 41.

45. James H. Vahey, spokesman for the carmen's union, intimated such fears at the preliminary hearing on the Cleveland case, 8 November 1918; and on 5 December 1918, Joint Chairmen Taft and Manly narrowly allayed them by granting women collectors on the Boston Elevated 40 cents an hour and the few men who worked with them 42½ cents. The men collectors, apparently, deserved higher pay when they worked at what the company considered a "women's position." Ironically, because the women were unionized, Vahey had argued unsuccessfully for equal pay (42½ cents) for equal work at Boston. At Cleveland, the city law director implied, the company had hired the women as a punitive measure after the men had agitated for higher wages. See Transcript of Proceedings, 8 November 1918, p. 90, Docket No. 491, WNRC, Suitland, NWLB Records, Entry 5; "Employees vs. The Boston Elevated Railway Company," 13 November 1918, pp. 2–5, 18, Casefile No. 181; "Decision of Arbitrators on Appeal in re Women Collectors on Lines of Boston Elevated Railway Co.," Docket No. 181, 5 December 1918, printed in Bureau of Labor Statistics, *National War Labor Board*, p. 226; NWLB, Minutes, afternoon meeting of 3 December 1918, p. 42.

46. NWLB, Minutes, afternoon meeting of 3 December 1918, pp. 13–17, 24–26, 31–33. While Hewitt's machinists union allowed female membership under reduced dues and benefits, Hutcheson's carpenters barred women from their ranks. See U.S., Department of Labor, Women's Bureau, "The New Position of Women in American Industry," p. 157.

47. NWLB, Minutes, afternoon meeting of 3 December 1918, pp. 22–27, 38–39, 44–46.

48. "Opinion in re Employees (Women Conductors) v. Cleveland Railway Co.,"

"Findings and Recommendation," Docket No. 491, 3 December 1918, printed in Bureau of Labor Statistics, *National War Labor Board*, p. 306.

49. National War Labor Board, Division of Information and Files, Press Clipping Report, 7–10 December 1918, Taft Papers, Series 3, Box 431.
50. *The Nation*, 21 December 1918, pp. 760–61.
51. "Woman's Right to Choose Her Job," *The Survey*, 21 December 1918, p. 380.
52. Letter, Taft to J. W. Marsh, 15 December 1918, Taft Papers, 8 Yale 78.
53. See letter, Margaret Dreier Robins, et al., National Women's Trade Union League of America, to National War Labor Board, 11 December 1918, NWLB Records, Casefile No. 491.
54. Letter, Mary Van Kleeck and Mary Anderson to Lauck, 10 December 1918, NWLB Records, Casefile No. 491, quoted in NWLB, Minutes, morning meeting of 19 December 1918, pp. 26–27.
55. NWLB, Minutes, morning meeting of 19 December 1918, p. 20.
56. "Report of the War Labor Conference Board," Bureau of Labor Statistics, *National War Labor Board*, p. 32.
57. Transcript of Proceedings, 13 December 1918, pp. 25–28, Docket No. 444, NWLB Records, Entry 5.
58. Transcript of Proceedings, 18 January 1919, pp. 85–87, 90, 129–36, Docket No. 444, NWLB Records, Entry 5.
59. Transcript, 13 December 1918, pp. 44–47, 174, Docket No. 444.
60. Ibid., pp. 17–22.
61. Transcript, 18 January 1919, p. 110, Docket No. 444.
62. Ibid., pp. 95–117.
63. Such testimony from and about women conductors was frequent at NWLB hearings. See, for example, Transcript, 8 November 1918, pp. 39–40, Docket No. 491; Transcript, 13 December 1918, pp. 38, 175–80, Docket No. 444; Transcript of Proceedings, 13 March 1919, pp. 13–19, 23–24, Docket No. 491, NWLB Records, Entry 5; U.S. Department of Labor, Women's Bureau, "Women Street Car Conductors and Ticket Agents."
64. Transcript, 18 January 1919, pp. 129–36, Docket No. 444.
65. "Opinion and Order in re Employees of Detroit United Railway, Members of Amalgamated Association of Street Railway Employees of America v. Detroit United Railway, and Women Conductors Association v. Amalgamated Association of Street & Electric Railway Employees of America," Docket No. 444, 18 January 1919, printed in Bureau of Labor Statistics, *National War Labor Board*, pp. 298–300.
66. Letter, Ethel M. Smith to Walsh, 6 January 1919, Walsh Papers, Box 27; Transcript, 18 January 1919, pp. 89–91, Docket No. 444; "Opinion and Order in re Employees of Detroit United Railway," Docket No. 444.
67. Transcript, 18 January 1919, p. 90, Docket No. 444. In his article, "As I See the Future of Women," *The Ladies Home Journal* 36 (March 1919): 27, 113, Taft doubted the suitability of women for conducting streetcars and voiced other protective concerns, but nonetheless endorsed the concept of economic equality between the sexes.
68. Letter, Ethel M. Smith to Walsh, 11 January 1919; letter, Rose Moriarty to Walsh, 20 January 1919, both in Walsh Papers, Box 27; letter, Walsh to Ethel M. Smith, 8 March 1919; letter, Ethel M. Smith to Walsh, 10 March 1919, both in Walsh Papers, Box 29.
69. Transcript, 13 March 1919, p. 32, Docket No. 491.
70. Ibid., pp. 37–38; letter, Walsh to A. A. Johannsen, 30 December 1918, Walsh Papers, Box 26.
71. Transcript, 13 March 1919, pp. 19–28, Docket No. 491.

72. "Opinions in re Employees (Women Conductors) v. Cleveland Railway Co.," Docket No. 491, 17 March 1919, printed in Bureau of Labor Statistics, *National War Labor Board*, pp. 304–6.
73. Letter, Walsh to Basil Manly, 21 March 1919, Walsh Papers, Box 29.
74. Figures taken from study of final caseload as reflected in pages of National War Labor Board, *Docket*.
75. "Opinion and Order in re Employees of Detroit United Railway," Docket No. 444.
76. Letter, Ethel M. Smith to Walsh, 21 March 1919, Walsh Papers, Box 29.
77. U.S., President's Commission on the Status of Women, *American Women*, p. 37.
78. Olson and Wolfe, "War-Time Industrial Employment of Women," pp. 658–59.

CHAPTER 10

1. Letter, Taft to Horace Taft, 6 November 1918, Taft Papers, Series 3, Box 427.
2. Letter, Walsh to Victor Olander, 4 December 1918, Walsh Papers, Box 26.
3. Ibid.
4. "Taft and Walsh Asked to Serve On," *New York Times*, 23 November 1918, Walsh Papers, Scrapbook No. 39.
5. Letter, Richard B. Gregg to E. B. Woods, 11 December 1918; letter, Gregg to Woods, 16 December 1918, both in NWLB Records, Entry 15; NWLB, Minutes, afternoon meeting of 13 September 1918, p. 7.
6. Memorandum, E. B. Woods to Lauck, 17 November 1918; Woods, Memorandum Regarding Bethlehem Steel Company Award, n.d. [late November 1918], both in NWLB Records, Entry 18; Brody, *Labor in Crisis*, p. 76.
7. Letter, Eugene Grace to National War Labor Board, 27 November 1918, in NWLB press release containing correspondence between Grace and joint chairmen, 8 December 1918, NWLB Records, Entry 18.
8. NWLB, Minutes, meeting of 6 December 1918, p. 56.
9. Letter, Taft and Manly to E. G. Grace, 6 December 1918, in NWLB press release of 8 December 1918.
10. Gregg wrote his superiors in Washington frequently about difficulties he encountered trying to enforce the award. See, for example, letters, Gregg to Woods, 23 November 1918, 29 November 1918, 11 December 1918; telegram, Gregg to Taft, Manly, and Woods, 6 December 1918; and for statement cited above, Gregg to Woods, 16 December 1918, all in NWLB Records, Entry 15.
11. "Bethlehem Steel Resists War Board, Draws Rebuke from Taft," *New York Times*, 16 January 1919, Lauck Papers, Box 54.
12. Letter, Loyall Osborne to Taft, 24 January 1919, Taft Papers, Series 3, Box 436.
13. Ibid.
14. *The Nation*, 25 January 1919, p. 108.
15. Brody, *Labor in Crisis*, pp. 84–85; U.S., House, Committee on Claims, *Hearings*, pp. 27–28.
16. *The Survey*, 22 March 1919, p. 909.
17. Brody, *Labor in Crisis*, p. 177; see correspondence between P. J. O'Shaughnessy, executive officer, Bethlehem War Labor Board Award, and J. L. McCarl, Comptroller General of the United States, June 1926, Lauck Papers, Box 53.
18. Letter, Gregg to Lauck, n.d. [early October 1918], NWLB Records, Entry 14.
19. See Telegram, Gregg to Woods, Taft, and Manly, 6 December 1918.

20. See correspondence between Burleson and the NWLB, read into NWLB, Minutes, morning meeting of 12 November 1918, pp. 1–5; for examples of earlier complaints, see NWLB, Minutes, morning meeting of 27 August 1918, pp. 43–44; letter, J. W. Matthews to Frank P. Walsh, 28 September 1918, NWLB Records, Entry 14.

21. "Shall the Post Office Men Have Unions?," *The Survey*, 22 December 1917, pp. 350–51.

22. Ibid.

23. Unnumbered Order, Office of Information, Post Office Department, 31 December 1918; Press release for 12 January 1919, Office of Information, Post Office Department, 11 January 1919, both in Library of Congress, The Papers of Albert Sidney Burleson (hereafter cited as Burleson Papers), Vol. 22. (For further insight on the postmaster general's view of his responsibilities, see Cablegram, Burleson to Woodrow Wilson, 19 April 1919, Burleson Papers, Vol. 23.)

24. NWLB, Minutes, afternoon meeting of 12 November 1918, pp. 1–16; press release for 12 January 1919, Burleson Papers, Vol. 22; letter, C. P. McCutcheon, secretary-treasurer, CTUA Pittsburgh local, to Taft and Manly, 11 January 1919; letter, S. S. Ulerich of Chicago district CTUA, to Manly, 13 January 1919; resolutions from CTUA locals in Oklahoma City and Los Angeles, 12 January and 13 January 1919; letter, G. F. Sickringer and H. M. Anderson, Western Union employees committee at Milwaukee, to Manly, 11 January 1919, all in NWLB Records, Entry 15; letter, W. F. Wade and W. H. Reighner, officers of Association of Western Union Employees, Spokane, to Taft, 11 January 1919, Taft Papers, Series 3, Box 434; letters, Mary J. Macauley, president, Western New York District CTUA No. 41, to Taft, 18 February 1919, Taft Papers, Series 3, Box 438; letter, Jos. P. Hayes, president, association of Western Union Employees, to Lauck, 8 February 1919, read into record, NWLB, Minutes, afternoon meeting of 18 February 1919, pp. 41–42; NWLB, Minutes, afternoon meeting of 5 March 1919, pp. 51–53.

25. Letter, Judson to Taft and Walsh, 14 November 1918, NWLB Records, Entry 14; NWLB, Minutes, meeting of 4 February 1919, pp. 31–32; letter, A. S. Burleson to Taft, 8 February 1919, Taft Papers, Series 3, Box 437; NWLB, Minutes, afternoon meeting of 18 February 1919, pp. 39–40; NWLB, Minutes, afternoon meeting of 19 February 1919, pp. 65–78; NWLB, Minutes, afternoon meeting of 5 March 1919, pp. 54–56; NWLB, Minutes, afternoon meeting of 6 March 1919, pp. 3–12.

26. NWLB, Minutes, meeting of 4 February 1919, pp. 31–32; NWLB, Minutes, afternoon meeting of 18 February 1919, pp. 40–50.

27. NWLB, Minutes, afternoon meeting of 18 February 1919, pp. 47–50; NWLB, Minutes, afternoon meeting of 19 February 1919, pp. 65–78; NWLB, Minutes, afternoon meeting of 6 March 1919, pp. 11–12. Even pro-CTUA sentiment, however, failed to bring an official reopening of the case because Burleson continued to sidestep the board's jurisdiction. See letter, Taft to Mary J. Macauley, 2 March 1919, Taft Papers, 8 Yale 78.

28. Letter, S. J. Konenkamp to Lauck, 25 April 1919, NWLB Records, Entry 14.

29. The AFL had attacked Burleson's "autocratic" ideas toward the unions of postal employees at its first wartime convention, in November 1917. See Fitch, "Organized Labor in Wartime," p. 233. See also NWLB Division of Information and Files, Press Clippings, Daily Report, 3 March 1919, NWLB Records, Entry 15; *The Nation*, 3 May 1919, p. 647.

30. *The Survey*, 12 July 1919, p. 582.

31. For a detailed report on harbor conditions in New York during the war, see three articles by Benjamin M. Squires in U.S., Department of Labor, *Monthly Review of the*

Bureau of Labor Statistics, 7, nos. 1, 2, and 3 (July, August, and September 1918), pp. 1–21, 265–81, 477–502. For a history of adjustment efforts before spring 1918, see Squires, "The New York Harbor Wage Adjustment," ibid. (September 1918), 477–87.

32. Ibid., pp. 487–502; telegram, Manly to Taft, 28 December 1918, Taft Papers, Series 3, Box 432.

33. "Harbor Strike Now Rests on War Labor Board," New York *Evening Journal,* 21 December 1918; "War Labor Board Decides for Men in Harbor Dispute," New York *Evening World,* 21 December 1918; "Port Labor Award to Be Enforced," New York *Journal of Commerce,* 8 January 1919; "Harbor Strike May Be Friday," New York *Evening Sun,* 8 January 1919, all clippings in NWLB Records, Entry 20; letter, Judson to Taft, 9 January 1919, Taft Papers, Series 3, Box 434; letter, Manly to Walter E. Edge, Governor of New Jersey, 10 January 1919, NWLB Records, Entry 19.

34. Several newspapers quoted the two NWLB statements at length. See for example, "15,000 Ordered Out for Harbor Strike," *New York Times,* 9 January 1919; "Labor Strike at 6 A.M. To-day," New York *Journal of Commerce,* 9 January 1919; "Owners of Vessels Resist War Board," New York *Herald,* 9 January 1919, all in NWLB Records, Entry 20.

35. "Labor Strike," New York *Journal of Commerce,* 9 January 1919.

36. Ibid.

37. Ibid.; "Harbor Strike Cuts Off New York Food," Washington *Post,* 10 January 1919, NWLB Records, Entry 20.

38. Cablegram, Woodrow Wilson to J. P. Tumulty for Taft and Manly, 11 January 1919, Taft Papers, Series 3, Box 434; "Leaders Call Off Harbor Strike; War Labor Board to Decide Issue; Public Suffering Less From Tieup," New York *Sun,* 12 January 1919, NWLB Records, Entry 20.

39. "Men Agree to Accept Findings of Board," New York *Evening Sun,* 13 January 1919; "War Labor Board Takes Up Strike; Employers Demur," *New York Times,* 14 January 1919; "Harbor Dispute Taken Up by War Labor Board; Owner's Protest Fails," New York *Tribune,* 14 January 1919; "Boat Owners Rebuked at Hearing on Strike," New York *Herald,* 14 January 1919; "Taft Names Four to Hear Evidence in Harbor Strike," New York *World,* 14 January 1919; "U.S. Takes Firm Grip and Stops Harbor Strike," New York *Sun,* 14 January 1919; "Boat Owners Unmoved by Wilson's Plea," New York *American,* 14 January 1919, all in NWLB Records, Entry 20.

40. "$1,500 a Year Minimum Set As Living Pay," New York *American,* 15 January 1919; "Harbor Hearing Shows Worker's Family of 5 Can Just Live on $1,800," New York *Call,* 15 January 1919; "Hints at German Money in Strike," *New York Times,* 17 January 1919; "Sidelights on Harbor Hearing at City Hall," New York *Call,* 17 January 1919; "Strikers Evidence Stirs Boat Owners," *New York Times,* 19 January 1919; "War Board Ends Harbor Hearings," New York *Sun,* 28 January 1919, all in NWLB Records, Entry 20; Closing Argument for the Employees, delivered by Frank P. Walsh, 27 January 1919, NWLB Records, Entry 13.

41. For reaction to the award, see "Walsh Seeks to Prevent Port Strike at N. Y.; Sees President"; "Harbor Award Does Not Suit Workers at New York Port," both New York *Call,* 27 February 1919; "Port Workers Will Not Strike," New York *Evening Post,* 27 February 1919; "Plans for General Boat Strike Made," *New York Times,* 28 February 1919, all in NWLB Records, Entry 20.

42. See National War Labor Board, "Award of the National War Labor Board in the Case of Marine Workers' Affiliation of the Port of New York v. The Railroad Administration, Shipping Board, Navy Department, War Department, and Red Star Towing & Transportation Co.," Docket no. 10 and 1036, 25 February 1919, printed in Bureau of

Labor Statistics, *National War Labor Board*, pp. 126–32.

43. "Plans for General Boat Strike Made," *New York Times*, 28 February 1919; "Strike to Tie Up Harbor is Called," *New York Times*, 4 March 1919; "Port Strike Ends on Railroad Craft, 5,000 To Go Back," *New York Times*, 8 March 1919; "Railroads Make Terms with Harbor Unions," New York *Evening Post*, 8 March 1919, all in NWLB Records, Entry 20; "Back on Union Terms," *The Survey*, 22 March 1919.

44. "Plans for General Boat Strike Made," *New York Times*, 28 February 1919; NWLB, Division of Information and Files, Press Clippings, Daily Report, 1 March 1919, NWLB Records, Entry 15.

45. New York *Call*, 28 February 1919, cited in Press Clippings, Daily Report, 1 March 1919.

46. Quoted, "Strike to Tie Up Harbor Is Called," *New York Times*, 4 March 1919.

47. *The Nation*, 22 March 1919, p. 414.

48. "Port Labor Award May Be Accepted," New York *Evening Post*, 26 February 1919, NWLB Records, Entry 20.

49. *The Nation*, 22 March 1919, p. 414.

CHAPTER 11

1. "U.S. Now is an Ideal, Gompers Tells Chicago," Chicago *Evening Post*, 9 November 1918; "Gompers Put Lid on Pacifists," Boston *Herald*, 9 November 1918; "End of Labor Strife Seen as Peace Echo," Chicago *News*, 9 November 1918, all in Walsh Papers, Scrapbook No. 39; letter, R. Easley to Lauck, 18 October 1918, NWLB Records, Entry 14.

2. Letter, Easley to Lauck, 13 November 1918, NWLB Records, Entry 14.

3. Quoted, Boston *Monitor*, 4 December 1918, Walsh Papers, Scrapbook No. 39.

4. Statement by William Howard Taft, reprinted as "Chamber of Commerce Policies in Industrial Matters Coincide with Views of Ex-President Taft," San Francisco *Chamber of Commerce Activities*, vol. 5, no. 50, 12 December 1918, Taft Papers, Series 3, Box 431; John A. Fitch, "Labor Reconstruction: The Conference of the Academy of Political Science," *The Survey*, 14 December 1918, p. 336.

5. On Wednesday morning, 20 November 1918, Walsh—apparently at the suggestion of Basil Manly—proposed a new procedure that failed to win approval, six to six. The procedure would have bound the NWLB to impose the following conditions on all cases yet to be resolved: a shop committee plan as already approved by the board to maintain collective bargaining; an eight-hour day; a minimum wage of $5.80 for unskilled adult male employees; equal pay for men and women "engaged upon the same work"; reinstatement with full pay for persons discharged for joining a union or for engaging in legitimate union activities. See summary, dated 20 November 1918, Walsh Papers, Box 26; NWLB Minutes, morning meeting of 20 November 1918, pp. 42–59.

6. Frank P. Walsh, "The War Labor Board and the Living Wage," *The Survey*, 7 December 1918, p. 303.

7. Ibid., p. 301.

8. Letter, Walsh to William M. Reedy, 13 December 1918, Walsh Papers, Box 26.

9. The Walsh correspondence is filled with such suggestions. See also, Walsh, "The War Labor Board and the Living Wage," p. 301.

10. Basil Manly, "The Present Status of the National War Labor Board," 15 February 1919, Walsh Papers, Box 28.

11. Ibid.; letter, Manly to Woodrow Wilson, 25 February 1919, Walsh Papers, Box 28.

Notes to Pages 176–83   213

(The report of 15 February on the status of the NWLB was enclosed with this letter to the president.)

12. Manly, "The Present Status of the National War Labor Board."

13. Basil Manly, "Memorandum: Proposals for a National Labor Board," n.d. [April 1919], Walsh Papers, Box 29.

14. Ibid.

15. Ibid.

16. Ibid.

17. See Brody, *Labor in Crisis*, pp. 115–27; Best, "President Wilson's Second Industrial Conference," p. 507.

18. Ibid.; Lauck and Watts, *The Industrial Code*, pp. 224–27; "Some Labor News of the Week," *The Survey*, 13 September 1919, p. 849.

19. See Brody, *Labor in Crisis*, pp. 115–27; see also, Appendices A, R, and S in Lauck and Watts, *The Industrial Code*, for restatement of NWLB principles, "Statement of Principles Submitted by the Employer Group to the First Industrial Conference, Washington, October, 1919," and "Proposition Presented by Labor Group, National Industrial Conference, Washington, October, 1919," pp. 271–73, 496–505.

20. Brody, *Labor in Crisis*, p. 116.

21. Ibid., p. 119.

22. Ibid., pp. 119–26.

23. Ibid., p. 123; Quoted, Lauck and Watts, *The Industrial Code*, p. 501.

24. Brody, *Labor in Crisis*, pp. 126–27.

25. Best, "President Wilson's Second Industrial Conference," pp. 508–9, 511, 519–20; see also, Lauck and Watts, *The Industrial Code*, p. 228 and Appendix F, "Report of March 6, 1920, of the Second Industrial Conference Convened by President Wilson," pp. 326–80.

26. Lauck and Watts, *The Industrial Code*, p. 232.

27. Best, "President Wilson's Second Industrial Conference," p. 519.

28. See Kennedy, *Over Here*, chapter 5, and Murray's classic study, *Red Scare*, for valuable insights into the postwar atmosphere.

29. The NCF had also changed character by 1919. Throughout the war years, many of its leaders had become preoccupied with fighting radicalism. Thereafter, the organization became increasingly conservative. See among others, Green, *National Civic Federation and Labor*, chapters 8 and 9.

30. Stephen C. Mason, "The Road Back to Normal Times," *American Industries* 19 (June 1919): 18–19.

31. "Resolutions Adopted by the Convention," *American Industries* 19 (June 1919): 16.

32. See Wakstein, "The Origins of the Open-Shop Movement," pp. 460–75.

33. Ibid.

34. See Leuchtenburg, "The New Deal and the Analogue of War," pp. 81–143. For detailed discussion of the origins and failure of early New Deal labor policies, see Bellush, *Failure of the NRA*; Bernstein, *New Deal Collective Bargaining Policy*; and Himmelberg, *National Recovery Administration*. In this and subsequent paragraphs, I am especially indebted to the analysis provided in Bellush's careful work.

35. See Himmelberg, *National Recovery Administration*, pp. 207–9; Bellush, *Failure of the NRA*, chapters 4 and 5; Bernstein, *New Deal Collective Bargaining Policy*, chapter 3. For a description of the "paralysis" of the labor movement on the eve of the New Deal, see Bernstein, *The Lean Years*, chapter 2.

36. Bellush, *Failure of the NRA*, chapters 4–8; Bernstein, *New Deal Collective Bargaining Policy*, p. 87.

37. Bellush, *Failure of the NRA*, chapter 7; Bernstein, *New Deal Collective Bargaining Policy*, chapter 9.
38. "The War Labor Board," *The Nation*, 22 March 1919, p. 419; John A. Fitch, "The War Labor Board, A Wartime Experiment with Compulsory Arbitration," *The Survey*, 3 May 1919, p. 192.
39. Fitch, "The War Labor Board," p. 193.
40. Letter, Walsh to Victor Olander, 4 December 1918.
41. Letter, Lauck to Jacob Billikopf, 29 July 1940, Lauck Papers, Box 45.
42. Letter, Taft to King, 7 August 1918.
43. "The War Labor Board," *The Nation*, p. 419.
44. Gardner, "Laboring People Now Favor Ex-President Taft."

Selected Bibliography

The following works are of particular importance to this study either for background understanding or for essential information. The most important sources, of course, are the papers of William Howard Taft and Frank P. Walsh and the records of the NWLB. The voluminous NWLB records are arranged in twenty-seven categories or entries, which include press clippings, examiners' reports, interstaff communications, correspondence of the joint chairmen, administrative files, general correspondence, case files, and transcripts of hearings. Typescripts of the minutes of executive sessions are included in both the NWLB records and the papers of W. Jett Lauck. Newspaper and journal articles, statements of the NICB, pamphlets, and other valuable original sources found in the Taft, Walsh, or Lauck papers or in the NWLB records have been cited as part of those collections and are therefore excluded from this bibliography. Among published works, the single most valuable source is the Bureau of Labor Statistics' *National War Labor Board*. It contains a summary of the board's work, reprints important documents associated with the NWLB, and also includes over one hundred representative awards. Because of its availability to the reader, I have cited it rather than the NWLB's less-accessible five-volume *Docket* whenever possible when discussing the NWLB's awards. For the same reason, I have cited it for basic documents reprinted therein.

PRIMARY SOURCES

Manuscript Collections

Library of Congress. The Papers of Albert Sidney Burleson.
Library of Congress. The Papers of Felix Frankfurter.
Library of Congress. The Papers of William Howard Taft.
Library of Congress. The Papers of Woodrow Wilson. Microfilm Edition.
National Archives. Records of the National War Labor Board. Record Group 2.
National Archives. Records of the Women's Bureau (Women in Industry Service). Record Group 86.
New York Public Library. The Papers of Frank P. Walsh.
University of Virginia. Alderman Library. The Papers of W. Jett Lauck.

Government Documents

U.S. Congress. House of Representatives. *Industrial Commission Reports*, Vol. 19. 57th Cong., 1st sess., House Document No. 380. Washington, D.C.: 1902.
U.S. Department of Labor. *Monthly Review of the Bureau of Labor Statistics*. 1915–19.
U.S. Department of Labor. Bureau of Labor Statistics. *National War Labor Board*. Bulletin No. 287. Labor As Affected by the War Series. Washington, D.C.: Government Printing Office, 1922.
U.S. Department of Labor. National War Labor Board. *Memorandum on the Eight-Hour*

Working Day. Submitted by the Secretary, July 20, 1918. Washington, D.C.: Government Printing Office, 1918.

———. *Memorandum on the Minimum Wage and Increased Cost of Living*. Submitted by the Secretary at the Request of the Board at Its Meeting on July 12, 1918. Washington, D.C.: Government Printing Office, 1918.

———. *National War Labor Board Docket*. 5 vols. Washington, D.C.: Bureau of Applied Economics, 1919.

———. *Organization and By-laws for Collective Bargaining Committees*. Instituted by the National War Labor Board for Bridgeport, Connecticut. Bridgeport, Conn.: Sherwood-Morgan Co., 1918.

———. *Organization and Practice of the Board as Adopted and Amended to December 10, 1918*. Washington, D.C.: Government Printing Office, 1919.

———. *Principles and Rules of Procedure*. Washington, D.C.: Government Printing Office, 1919.

———. *Proclamation of the President Creating the National War Labor Board: Its Functions and Powers, Principles Governing Industry, Method of Presenting Complaints and Procedure*. Washington, D.C.: Government Printing Office, 1918.

———. *Report of the Secretary of the National War Labor Board to the Secretary of Labor, for the Twelve Months Ending May 31, 1919*. Washington, D.C.: Government Printing Office, 1920.

U.S. Department of Labor. Wage and Hour Division, Economics Branch. *Wartime Policies on Wages, Hours, and Other Labor Standards in the United States*. Washington, D.C.: May 1942.

U.S. Department of Labor. Women's Bureau. "The New Position of Women in American Industry." Bulletin No. 12. Washington, D.C.: Government Printing Office, 1920.

———. "Women Street Car Conductors and Ticket Agents." Bulletin No. 11. Washington, D.C.: Government Printing Office, 1921.

U.S. National Archives. *Preliminary Inventory of the Records of the National War Labor Board*, compiled by Herbert Fine. Washington, D.C.: August 1943.

U.S. President's Commission on the Status of Women. *American Women*. Washington, D.C.: Government Printing Office, 1963.

Periodicals (1915–1919)

American Federationist.
American Industries.
Iron Age.
The Nation.
The Nation's Business.
The New Republic.
The Survey.

Other Printed Materials

Bernhardt, Joshua. *The Division of Conciliation: Its History, Activities and Organization*. Baltimore: The Johns Hopkins Press, 1923.

Bing, Alexander M. *War-Time Strikes and Their Adjustment*. New York: E. P. Dutton & Company, 1921.

Commager, Henry Steele, ed. *Lester Frank Ward and the Welfare State*. American Heritage

Series. New York: The Bobbs-Merrill Company, Inc., 1967.
Croly, Herbert. *The Promise of American Life*. New York: The Macmillan Company, 1909.
Cronon, E. David, ed. *The Political Thought of Woodrow Wilson*. American Heritage Series. New York: The Bobbs-Merrill Company, Inc., 1965.
de Tocqueville, Alexis. *Democracy in America*. Vol. II. Edited by Phillips Bradley. New York: Vintage Books, 1945.
Fitch, John A. *The Causes of Industrial Unrest*. New York: Harper & Brothers, 1924.
Frankfurter, Felix, and Goldmark, Josephine. *The Case for the Shorter Work Day, Supreme Court of the United States, October Term, 1915, Franklin O. Bunting vs. The State of Oregon, Brief for the Defendant in Error*. Vol. I. New York: National Consumers League, n.d.
Gompers, Samuel. *American Labor and the War*. New York: George H. Doran Company, 1919.
———. *Labor and the Common Welfare*. New York: E. P. Dutton & Company, 1919.
———. *Labor and the Employer*. New York: E. P. Dutton & Company, 1920.
———. *Seventy Years of Life and Labor*. 2 vols. New York: E. P. Dutton & Company, 1925.
Gregg, Richard B. "The National War Labor Board." *Harvard Law Review* 33 (November 1919): 38–69.
Hanna, Hugh S., and Lauck, W. Jett. *Wages and the War*. Cleveland: Doyle and Waltz, 1918.
Johnson, Hugh S. *The Blue Eagle from Egg to Earth*. New York: Doubleday, Doran, & Company, Inc., 1935.
Lauck, W. Jett. *The New Industrial Revolution and Wages*. New York: Funk & Wagnalls Company, 1929.
———. *Political and Industrial Democracy, 1776–1926*. New York: Funk & Wagnalls Company, 1926.
———, and Sydenstricker, Edgar. *Conditions of Labor in American Industries: A Summarization of the Results of Recent Investigations*. New York: Funk & Wagnalls Company, 1917.
———, and Watts, Claude S. *The Industrial Code*. New York: Funk & Wagnalls Company, 1922.
Lippmann, Walter. *Drift and Mastery*. Englewood Cliffs, N.J.: Prentice-Hall, Inc., 1961.
National Consumers' League. *The Supreme Court and Minimum Wage Legislation: Comment by the Legal Profession on District of Columbia Case*. New York: New Republic, Inc., 1925.
National Industrial Conference Board. *The Eight Hour Day Defined*. Research Report No. 11. Boston: National Industrial Conference Board, 1918.
———. *Works Councils in the United States*. Research Report No. 21. Boston: National Industrial Conference Board, 1919.
O'Grady, John. *A Legal Minimum Wage*. Washington, D.C.: National Capitol Press, 1915.
Olson, Helen, and Wolfe, A. B. "War-Time Industrial Employment of Women in the United States." *Journal of Political Economy* 27 (October 1919): 639–69.
Rockefeller, John D., Jr. *The Personal Relation in Industry*. New York: Boni and Liveright, 1923.
Roosevelt, Theodore. *The New Nationalism*. Edited by William E. Leuchtenburg. Englewood Cliffs, N.J.: Prentice-Hall, Inc., 1961.
Steinmetz, Charles P. *America and the New Epoch*. New York: Harper & Brothers, 1916.
Stoddard, William Leavitt. *The Shop Committee: A Handbook for Employer and Employee*. New York: The Macmillan Company, 1920.

———. "No Strikes in War Time." *The Independent*, 1 June 1918, pp. 357, 387.
Taft, William Howard. "As I See the Future of Women." *The Ladies' Home Journal* 36 (March 1919): 27, 113.
Trachenburg, Alexander, ed. *The American Labor Yearbook, 1918-1919*. Vol. III. New York: Rand School of Social Science, 1919.
Walsh, Frank P. "Low Wages and the Low Wage Environment." *The Annals*. American Academy of Political and Social Sciences, 59 (May 1915): 104-10.
———. "The Presidential Doctrine of Labor." *The Forum*, August 1918, pp. 167-74.
Weyl, Walter E. *The New Democracy*. Revised edition. New York: The Macmillan Company, 1920.
Wilson, Woodrow. *The New Freedom: A Call for the Emancipation of the Generous Energies of a People*. New York: Doubleday, Page & Company, 1913.

SECONDARY SOURCES

Books

Adams, Graham, Jr. *Age of Industrial Violence, 1910-1915: The Activities and Findings of the United States Commission on Industrial Relations*. New York: Columbia University Press, 1966.
Arieli, Yehoshua. *Individualism and Nationalism in American Ideology*. Cambridge, Mass.: Harvard University Press, 1964.
Beal, Edwin F., and Wickersham, Edward D. *The Practice of Collective Bargaining*. Homewood, Illinois: Richard D. Irwin, Inc., 1963.
Bellush, Bernard. *The Failure of the NRA*. New York: W. W. Norton & Company, Inc., 1975.
Berkowitz, Edward, and McQuaid, Kim. *Creating the Welfare State: The Political Economy of Twentieth-Century Reform*. New York: Praeger Publishers, 1980.
Bernstein, Irving. *The New Deal Collective Bargaining Policy*. Berkeley: University of California Press, 1950.
———. *The Lean Years*. Boston: Houghton Mifflin Company, 1960.
———. *Turbulent Years*. Boston: Houghton Mifflin Company, 1970.
Brody, David. *Labor in Crisis: The Steel Strike of 1919*. New York: J. P. Lippincott Company, 1965.
———. *Steelworkers in America: The Nonunion Era*. Cambridge, Mass.: Harvard University Press, 1960.
Brooks, Robert R. R. *As Steel Goes: Unionism in a Basic Industry*. New Haven: Yale University Press, 1940.
Brooks, Thomas R. *Toil and Trouble: A History of American Labor*. New York: Dell Publishing Co., Inc., 1971.
Chamberlain, Neil W., and Kuhn, James W. *Collective Bargaining*. New York: McGraw-Hill Book Company, 1965.
Chambers, Frank P. *The War Behind the War, 1914-1918: History of the Political and Civilian Fronts*. New York: Harcourt, Brace and Company, 1939.
Commager, Henry Steele. *The American Mind: An Interpretation of American Thought and Character Since the 1880's*. New Haven: Yale University Press, 1950.
Cuff, Robert D. *The War Industries Board: Business-Government Relations during World War I*. Baltimore: The Johns Hopkins University Press, 1973.
Davis, Allen F. *Spearheads for Reform: The Social Settlements and the Progressive Movement,*

1890-1914. New York: Oxford University Press, 1967.
Douglas, Paul H. *Real Wages in the United States, 1890-1926.* Cambridge, Mass.: The Riverside Press, 1930.
Faulkner, Harold U. *The Decline of Laissez-Faire, 1897-1917.* Vol. VII of *The Economic History of the United States.* Edited by Henry David, Harold U. Faulkner, Louis M. Hacker, Curtis P. Nettels, and Fred A. Shannon. 10 vols. New York: Harper & Row, 1968.
Fine, Sidney. *Laissez Faire and the General-Welfare State: A Study of Conflict in American Thought, 1865-1901.* Ann Arbor: The University of Michigan Press, 1956.
Forcey, Charles. *The Crossroads of Liberalism: Croly, Weyl, Lippmann, and the Progressive Era, 1900-1925.* New York: Oxford University Press, 1961.
Gilbert, James. *Designing the Industrial State: The Intellectual Pursuit of Collectivism in America, 1880-1940.* Chicago: Quadrangle Books, 1972.
Graham, Otis L., Jr. *The Great Campaigns: Reform and War in America, 1900-1928.* Englewood Cliffs, N.J.: Prentice-Hall, Inc., 1971.
Green, Marguerite. *The National Civic Federation and the American Labor Movement, 1900-1925.* Washington, D.C.: The Catholic University of America Press, 1956.
Grossman, Jonathan. *The Department of Labor.* New York: Praeger Publishers, 1973.
Grubbs, Frank L., Jr. *The Struggle for Labor Loyalty: Gompers, the A.F. of L., and the Pacifists, 1917-1920.* Durham, N.C.: Duke University Press, 1968.
Haber, Samuel. *Efficiency and Uplift: Scientific Management in the Progressive Era, 1890-1920.* Chicago: The University of Chicago Press, 1964.
Harbaugh, William Henry. *The Life and Times of Theodore Roosevelt.* New York: Collier Books, 1963.
Hawley, Ellis. *The Great War and the Search for a Modern Order: A History of the American People and Their Institutions, 1917-1933.* New York: St. Martin's Press, 1979.
Himmelberg, Robert F. *The Origins of the National Recovery Administration: Business, Government, and the Trade Association Issue, 1921-1933.* New York: Fordham University Press, 1976.
Hays, Samuel P. *The Response to Industrialism: 1885-1914.* Chicago: The University of Chicago Press, 1957.
Kennedy, David M. *Over Here: The First World War and American Society.* New York: Oxford University Press, 1980.
Kerr, K. Austin. *American Railroad Politics, 1914-1920.* Pittsburgh: University of Pittsburgh Press, 1968.
Kolko, Gabriel. *The Triumph of Conservatism: A Reinterpretation of American History, 1900-1916.* New York: The Free Press, 1963.
Link, Arthur S. *Wilson: Campaigns for Progressivism and Peace, 1916-1917.* Princeton, N.J.: Princeton University Press, 1965.
———. *Wilson: Confusions and Crises, 1915-1916.* Princeton, N.J.: Princeton University Press, 1964.
———. *Woodrow Wilson and the Progressive Era, 1910-1917.* New York: Harper & Brothers, 1963.
Murray, Robert K. *Red Scare: A Study of National Hysteria, 1919-1920.* New York: McGraw-Hill Book Company, 1964.
Penrose, Charles. *L. F. Loree (1858-1940): Patriarch of the Rails.* New York: Newcomen Society in North America, 1955.
Pringle, Henry F. *The Life and Times of William Howard Taft.* 2 vols. New York: Farrar and Rinehart, 1939.
Raddock, Maxwell C. *Portrait of an American Labor Leader: William L. Hutcheson.* New

York: American Institute of Social Science, Inc., 1955.
Schwarz, Jordan A. *The Speculator: Bernard M. Baruch in Washington, 1917–1965*. Chapel Hill: The University of North Carolina Press, 1981.
Soule, George. *Prosperity Decade: From War to Depression, 1917–1929*. Vol. VIII of *The Economic History of the United States*. Edited by Henry David, Harold U. Faulkner, Louis M. Hacker, Curtis P. Nettels, and Fred A. Shannon. 10 vols. New York: Harper and Row, 1968.
Steigerwalt, Albert K. *The National Association of Manufacturers, 1895–1914: A Study in Business Leadership*. Vol. XVI of Michigan Business Studies. Ann Arbor: University of Michigan Press, 1964.
Steuben, John. *Labor in Wartime*. New York: International Publishers, 1940.
Taft, Philip. *The A. F. of L. in the Time of Gompers*. New York: Harper & Brothers, 1957.
──────. *Organized Labor in American History*. New York: Harper and Row, 1964.
Taylor, Albion Guilford. *Labor Policies of the National Association of Manufacturers*. Vol. XV, No. 1, of University of Illinois Studies in the Social Sciences. Urbana: University of Illinois, March 1927.
Urofsky, Melvin I. *Big Steel and the Wilson Administration*. Columbus: Ohio State University Press, 1969.
Watkins, Gordon S. *Labor Problems and Labor Administration in the United States During the World War*: Part II *The Development of War Labor Administration*. Vol. VIII, No. 4, of University of Illinois Studies in the Social Sciences. Urbana: University of Illinois, September 1919.
Wehle, Louis B. *Hidden Threads of History: Wilson Through Roosevelt*. New York: The Macmillan Company, 1953.
Weinstein, James. *The Corporate Ideal in the Liberal State: 1900–1918*. Boston: Beacon Press, 1968.
White, Morton. *Social Thought in America: The Revolt Against Formalism*. Boston: Beacon Press, 1957.
Wiebe, Robert H. *Businessmen and Reform: A Study of the Progressive Movement*. Cambridge, Mass.: Harvard University Press, 1962.
──────. *The Search for Order: 1877–1920*. New York: Hill and Wang, 1967.

Articles

Asher, Robert. "Business and Workers' Welfare in the Progressive Era: Workmen's Compensation Reform in Massachusetts, 1880–1911." *Business History Review* 43 (Winter 1969): 452–75.
Best, Gary Dean. "President Wilson's Second Industrial Conference, 1919–20." *Labor History* 16 (Fall 1975): 505–20.
Conner, Valerie J. "The Mothers of the Race in World War I: The National War Labor Board and Women in Industry." *Labor History* 21 (Winter 1980): 31–54.
Cuff, Robert D. "A 'Dollar-a-Year' Man in Government: George N. Peek and the War Industries Board." *Business History Review* 41 (Winter 1967): 404–20.
──────. "Bernard Baruch: Symbol and Myth in Industrial Mobilization." *Business History Review* 43 (Summer 1969): 115–33.
──────. "Business, The State, and World War I: The American Experience," in *War and Society in North America*. Edited by Robert D. Cuff and J. L. Granatstein. Montreal: Thomas Nelson and Sons (Canada) Limited, 1971.
──────. "Herbert Hoover, The Ideology of Voluntarism and War Organization During

the Great War." *The Journal of American History* 44 (September 1977): 358–72.
Davis, Allen F. "The Campaign for the Industrial Relations Commission, 1911–1913." *Mid-America* 45 (October 1963): 211–28.
Derber, Milton. "The Idea of Industrial Democracy in America, 1898–1915." *Labor History* 7 (Fall 1966): 259–86.
———. "The Idea of Industrial Democracy in America, 1915–1935." *Labor History* 8 (Winter 1967): 3–29.
Ensley, Philip C. "The Interchurch World Movement and the Steel Strike of 1919." *Labor History* 13 (Spring 1972): 217–30.
Galambos, Louis. "AFL's Concept of Big Business: A Quantitative Study of Attitudes toward the Large Corporation, 1894–1931." *The Journal of American History* 57 (March 1971): 847–63.
———. "The Emerging Organizational Synthesis in Modern American History." *Business History Review* 44 (Autumn 1970): 279–90.
Gilbert, James B. "Collectivism and Charles Steinmetz." *Business History Review* 48 (Winter 1974): 520–40.
Hessen, Robert. "The Bethlehem Steel Strike of 1910." *Labor History* 15 (Winter 1974): 3–18.
Hill, Charles. "Fighting the Twelve-Hour Day in the American Steel Industry." *Labor History* 15 (Winter 1974): 19–35.
Kerr, K. Austin. "Decision for Federal Control: Wilson, McAdoo, and the Railroads, 1917." *The Journal of American History* 44 (December 1967): 550–60.
Koistinen, Paul A. C. "The 'Industrial-Military Complex' in Historical Perspective: World War I." *Business History Review* 41 (Winter 1967): 378–403.
Larson, Simeon. "The American Federation of Labor and the Preparedness Controversy." *The Historian* 37 (November 1974): 67–81.
Leuchtenburg, William E. "The New Deal and the Analogue of War," pp. 81–143, in *Change and Continuity in Twentieth Century America*. Edited by John Braeman, et al. Columbus: Ohio State University Press, 1964.
Lubove, Roy. "Workmen's Compensation and the Prerogatives of Voluntarism." *Labor History* 8 (Fall 1967): 254–79.
McQuaid, Kim. "Corporate Liberalism in the American Business Community, 1920–1940." *Business History Review* 52 (Autumn 1978): 342–68.
Nash, Gerald D. "Experiments in Industrial Mobilization: WIB and NRA." *Mid-America* 45 (July 1963): 157–74.
———. "Franklin D. Roosevelt and Labor: The World War I Origins of Early New Deal Policy." *Labor History* 1 (Winter 1960): 39–52.
Nelson, Daniel. "Scientific Management, Systematic Management, and Labor, 1880–1915." *Business History Review* 48 (Winter 1974): 479–500.
Rogin, Michael. "Voluntarism: The Political Functions of an Antipolitical Doctrine." *Industrial and Labor Relations Review* 15 (July 1962): 521–35.
Smith, John S. "Organized Labor and Government in the Wilson Era, 1913–1921: Some Conclusions." *Labor History* 3 (Fall 1962): 265–86.
Wakstein, Allen M. "The Origins of the Open-Shop Movement, 1919–1920." *The Journal of American History* 51 (December 1964): 460–75.
Weinstein, James. "Big Business and the Origins of Workmen's Compensation." *Labor History* 8 (Spring 1967): 156–74.

Unpublished Works

Benson, Ronald M. "The NWLB and the Crisis in Urban Transportation: An Examination of Bureaucratic Initiative, 1918." Unpublished paper, Duquesne History Forum, October 1978.

Jensen, Gordon Maurice. "The National Civic Federation: American Business in an Age of Social Change and Social Reform, 1900–1910." Ph.D. dissertation, Princeton University, 1956.

Meehan, Sister Maria Eucharia, C. S. J. "Frank P. Walsh and the American Labor Movement." Ph.D. dissertation, New York University, 1962.

Wilson, James W. "The National War Labor Board of 1918 and the Right to Organize." M.A. thesis, University of Virginia, 1967.

Index

Adamson Act, 17, 20, 73–74, 94; importance of, 90
Agriculture Department, 32
Alschuler, Samuel J., 60, 68, 128; and packinghouse settlement, 52–53, 56, 97, 106
Amalgamated Association of Street and Electric Railway Employees, 68, 77, 86, 152; attitude of, toward NWLB, 75, 87; and women, 150
American Alliance for Labor and Democracy, 27
American Electric Railway Association, 75, 84
American Expeditionary Forces, 100, 113
American Federation of Labor, vii, x, 6, 35, 108, 149, 176; and NCF, 8–11; and NAM, 9–12; and national politics, 10–11, 16–17; and United States Commission on Industrial Relations, 15–16; affiliates of, pledge loyalty and seek representation in war bureaucracy, 22; proposals of, for a national war labor board, 27, 29; appointees of, to War Labor Conference Board, 28; on NWLB's principles, 33, 36; convention of, in St. Paul, 45–46, 139; and Western Union crisis, 45–47; on eight-hour day, 94; and organization of steel industry, 107, 128; and women in industry, 143, 150; and First Industrial Conference, 178–79; postwar weaknesses of, 182, 186; leadership of, renounces voluntarism, 183
American Federationist, 34, 128–29
American Industries, 12, 20, 181; on United States Commission on Industrial Relations, 14–16; on individual contracts, 36
American Plan, 181
American Railway Union, 19
American Relief Administration, 179
Anderson, Mary, 152–53
Anthracite Coal Commission, 26, 30
Anthracite coal strike, 7–8

Antiunion sentiment, 110, 126–41 *passim*, 161; and open-shop movement, 9–12, 181; of NAM, 9–12, 175, 181; at Western Union, 39, 41, 43–44; of Albert Sidney Burleson, 48, 164–66; in New York harbor case, 167–71. *See also* Open shop
Armistice: effect of, on NWLB, 141–42, 150, 158

Baker, Newton D., 23, 91, 132
Baker-Gompers Agreement, 23
Baruch, Bernard, ix
Basic eight-hour day: in packinghouse settlement, 52; and United States Shipping Board, 59; NWLB statement on, 89, 93; appeal of, to federal government in wartime, 90; employers' objections to, upheld, 93; and NICB, 94, 137; NWLB debates on, 95–104; adoption of, by United States Steel Corporation, 107; and Bethlehem Steel Company, 111–15; and New York harbor case, 167, 170–71. *See also* National War Labor Board: hours policy of; Federal government: hours policy of; Eight-hour day
Bethlehem Steel Company, 108; bonus system at, 111, 113–16, 119–22; attitude of, toward collective bargaining, 112–15; and discrimination against unions, 113–15, 119
Bethlehem Steel Company case, 111–17, 119–23, 159–63, 165, 172; award in, 109, 122–23, 127–28, 134; post-Armistice complications in, 160–63
Black common laborers, 80–83
Black, William Harman, 165
Blue Eagle, 182
Bolshevism, 173–74; and New York harbor strike, 169, 171
Bonynge, Paul, 169–71
Boston *Advertiser*, 118
Boston *Evening Transcript*, 84
Brewer, David J., 143

Brewer, Luther, 84
Bridge and Structural Iron Workers, 12, 128
Bridgeport, Connecticut, case: umpire's award in, 104, 128, 130–34; strike against award in, 129–31, 133; resolution of, 134
Bridgeport *Labor Leader*, 130
Brody, David, 178
Bryan, William Jennings, 10
Buffalo Central Council of Business Men's Taxpayers' and Citizens' Associations, 79–80
Buffalo Chamber of Commerce, 80
Buffalo City Council, 80
Bureau of Housing and Transportation, 104
Bureau of Labor Statistics, 64, 90; on NWLB and eight-hour day movement, 107
Burleson, Albert Sidney, 48; and post-Armistice Western Union case, 159, 163–67; characterization, policies, and criticisms of, 164–66
Burnquist, J. A. A., 139
Business and labor organizations: reactions of, to NWLB's principles, vii; and voluntarism, 6, 7, 185; role of, in emerging mobilization machinery, 20–31; failure of, to develop common objectives, 177–83
Business community: prewar differences within, 7–12
Business member. *See* National War Labor Board, business members of
Business organizations: hostility of, to NWLB, 126–41 *passim*
Butler, Pierce, 140–41
Butte *Miner*, 129

Cantonment Adjustment Commission, 23
Carlton, Newcomb, 35–49 *passim*, 117, 120, 137, 159; labor policies of, 35, 37, 39–40, 44–45; attitude of, toward NWLB policies, 38–39, 41, 43–45; attitude of, toward CTUA, 39; company union of, at Western Union, 40, 44, 111, 165–66; defies president and NWLB majority, 43–45; as characterized in *The New Republic*, 46; and defiance of NWLB, 48; and Albert Sidney Burleson, 48, 164
Chamber of Commerce, 21, 182–83
Chapin, George P., 131–32
Chase, Stuart, 126
Chicago *Evening News*, 14
Chicago Federation of Labor, 53, 128
Chicago, Hamilton, and Dayton Railroad, 19
Chicago *Herald*, 52
Chiesa, Joseph, 81–82
Christman, Elisabeth, 145, 147–48
Citizens' Alliance of Minneapolis, 138–39
Civil Appropriations Act, 62
Civil Rights Act, 142
Clark, Walter, 89, 105–7
Clayton Antitrust Act, 17
Cleveland Chamber of Commerce, 151
Cleveland Railway Company case: and women conductors, 150–53, 155–56; NWLB actions in, 151–52, 155–56; reactions to rulings in, 152–53, 156
Clinton, George, 79
Closed nonunion shop, and war-labor policy, 29–30, 40, 43, 131–32
Closed union shop, and NWLB principles, 29, 153
Collective bargaining: and United States Industrial Commission, 5; and NCF, 8–9; and NAM, 9; and AFL, 9, 27, 178–79; and United States Commission on Industrial Relations, 14–15; and War Labor Conference Board, 30; criticism of, at Ninth Yama Conference, 137; and First Industrial Conference, 178–79. *See also* National War Labor Board: and the right to bargain collectively
Colorado Fuel and Iron Company, 109–11
Colver, William B., 149
Commercial Telegraphers Union of America: tests right to organize, 35–49 *passim*; prods NWLB, 40–41; assessed, 47; and post-Armistice defeat, 163–67
Commission on Industrial Relations. *See* United States Commission on Industrial Relations
Committee on Industrial Relations, 20
Committee on Public Information, 145
Commons, John R.: as member of United States Commission on Industrial Rela-

Index 225

tions, 12–15; urges appointment of women to NWLB, 148
Company unions: at Postal Telegraph Company, 37, 40; at Western Union Company, 40, 44, 111, 165–66; at Colorado Fuel and Iron Company, 109–11; at William Filene's Sons Company, 109–10; at General Electric Company, Pittsfield, 118–19; at Bethlehem Steel Company, 160, 162; under NRA, Section 7a, 182; outlawed, 183
Conference of Trade Union Women, 149
Connette, E. G., 80
Conrad, E. E., 54
Council of National Defense, 22; establishment and composition of, 20–21; and correlation of federal war-labor policies, 25–26, 28–29
Covington, J. Harry, 25
Cramer, R. D., 138
Creel, George, 145
Cuff, Robert D., ix, 21
Curran, D. D., 81

Daniels, Josephus, 99–100
Debs, Eugene V., 16
Delahunty, Thomas L., 171
Delaware & Hudson Railroad, 29
Denver Chamber of Commerce, 110
Denver Post, 77
Detroit United Railway Company case: and women conductors, 150, 153–56; and closed union shop, 153; family earnings revealed in, 154; award in, 154–56
Discrimination against unions: at Western Union, 35, 37–39, 41, 43, 165–66; outlawed in packinghouse settlement, 53; at Bethlehem Steel Company, 113–15, 119; in Minneapolis, 140
Doland, Theresa, 153–55
Dollar-a-year men, ix, 21
Dreier, Mary, 148
Drew, Walter, 128

Easley, Ralph, 21, 173
Eidlitz, Otto M., 104, 130–31, 132, 134
Eight-hour day: prewar legislation on, 9–10, 90; and Frank P. Walsh, 15, 61–62, 96–98, 101–4, 106; distinction between basic and actual day, 89–90, 94; progress of, by June 1918, 90; and AFL, 94; and William Howard Taft, 101, 103–4, 107; reputation of NWLB on, 101, 107; and Henry Ford, 105, 107; and Walter Clark, 105–7. *See also* National War Labor Board: hours policy of; Federal government: hours policy of; Basic eight-hour day
Electric Railway Journal, 75
Electrical workers: at Bethlehem Steel Company, 112–15, 117, 122; at General Electric plants, 117, 135; and National Committee for Organizing Iron and Steel Workers, 128
Emergency Fleet Corporation, 32, 95–96, 104
Emery, James A., 31–32, 182
Employee-representation plans. *See* Company unions
Equal employment opportunities, and NWLB, 155
Equal Pay Amendment to Fair Labor Standards Act, x, 142
Equal pay for women, 117; NWLB principle on, vii, 30, 142–44, 150; and United States Industrial Commission, 5; in Walsh report for United States Commission on Industrial Relations, 15; in packinghouse settlement, 53; legislation on, 142, 156–57; and Marie Obenauer, 146; summary position of NWLB, 156–57
Erdman Act, 10
Existing conditions: NWLB principle on, 30, 95, 98, 100
Existing standards: debate over, as war-labor policy, 22–27

Fair Labor Standards Act, x, 142
Faulkner, A. L., 151
Federal coercion, fear of, viii, x, 3–4, 18, 185; reflected in powers of NWLB, 30–31
Federal Commission on Labor Difficulties in the Coal Fields of Colorado, 110
Federal Council of Churches of Christ of America, 50
Federal government: hours policy of, 9–10, 89–95, 101, 106, 115–16, 122;

suggested wage policies of, in wartime, 25–27; war powers of, 71–73, 76, 79; relationship of, with state and local governments in wartime, 74–77, 79; interagency jealousies in, 158, 163–65, 167
Federal Trade Commission, 149
Federal war-labor adjustment machinery, pre-NWLB, 23–24
Fitch, John, 26; on NWLB, 31, 183–84; on company unions, 109–11
Fitzpatrick, John, 128
Ford, Henry, 89, 105, 107, 176
Foster, William Z., 128
Fox, Eugene, 99
Frankfurter, Felix, 25, 58, 60, 101–2; and creation of War Labor Policies Board, 32–33; report on hours policy for War Department, 91–92, 96, 104
Frick Company, 55–56

Gadsden, Philip N., 70–72
Gardner, Gilson, 101, 185
Gary, Elbert H.: rejects arbitration of steel strike, 177–78
General Electric Company, 108
General Electric Company cases: at Pittsfield, Massachusetts, 109, 117–25, 127–28, 146; at Schenectady, New York, 117–18, 145–46; at Lynn, Massachusetts, 134–36
General Motors Company, 115, 122
Germany, 21–22, 31, 170
Glatzmayer, Joseph J., 169
Gompers, Samuel, 28, 44, 166, 182; relationship of, with Woodrow Wilson, ix, 16–17, 47; loyalty of, to war, ix, 21–27, 173; and NCF, 9–11; on Walsh, 16; and voluntarism, 16–17; conservatism of, 17, 33; and redefinition of preparedness, 21–22, 27; and formulation of war-labor policy, 22–25, 26–28; and American Alliance for Labor and Democracy, 27; victory of, in creation of NWLB, 34; warns president on Western Union, 46; on NWLB shop committees, 128–29; reception for, in Chicago, 173; at First Industrial Conference, 178–79
Grace, Eugene: and Bethlehem Steel Company case, 112–17, 120–22, 159–63; use of collective bargaining, 114–16; pre-Armistice evasiveness of, 117, 159–60; post-Armistice defiance of, 159–62, 165
Green, William, 182
Gregg, Richard B., 160–63

Hanna, Marcus A., 8
Hansen, Ole, 171
Harriman, Edward H., 29
Harriman, Mrs. J. Borden, 14
Harvey, William P., 119–20
Hayes, Frank J., 59; member of War Labor Conference Board, 28
Haywood, William D., 16
Hepburn bill, 11–12
Herkner, Anna, 142
Hewitt, Fred, 151, 207 (n. 46); in Waynesboro case, 54, 56–57; in Worthington Pump Company cases, 94–101; view of NWLB's role, 97
Hitchman Coal and Coke Company v. Mitchell, 36, 42, 124–25, 132
Hoover, Herbert C., 179
Howe, Louis M., 99–100
Hutcheson, William L., 23–24, 151, 207 (n. 46); member of War Labor Conference Board, 28

Illinois State Federation of Labor, 28
Individual employment contracts: sustained by United States Supreme Court, 10, 35–36; and Western Union Company case, 35–36, 39. *See also* Supreme Court; *Hitchman Coal and Coke Company v. Mitchell*; Yellow-dog contracts
Individualism, 6–9, 14, 65, 127
Industrial Commission. *See* United States Industrial Commission
Industrial democracy, 3; equated with collective bargaining, 4–7, 15, 108, 120; and NWLB shop-committee plan, 123, 131
Inflation, viii, 23, 50, 54–55, 57–59, 68–69
International Association of Machinists, 11, 28, 113, 207 (n. 46). *See also* Machinists
International Longshoremen's Associa-

Index   227

tion, 23
International Photo-Engravers' Union of North America, 166
International Railway Company (Buffalo) case, 78–80
International Seamen's Union, 28
International Workers of the World, 16, 20, 25, 119
Interstate Commerce Act, 19
Interstate Commerce Commission, 73–74
Iron Age, 128–29

Johnson, Hugh, 182–83
Johnston, William H., 11, 28; and Bridgeport strike, 130
Joint chairmen. *See* National War Labor Board, joint chairmen of
Judson, Frederick, 60, 98, 165–66; and Smith and Wesson Arms Company award, 124–25
Justice Department, 180, 182

Kansas City *Post*, 20, 119
Kansas City Railways Company case: and women conductors, 150, 153, 155
Karger, Gus J., 77
Kennedy, John F., x
King, James Ernest, 84
Konenkamp, S. J.: and Western Union case, 36–37, 44, 46, 48, 163–67

Labor Department, 10, 27, 56, 101, 151–52; conciliation work of, 17–18; and Bethlehem Steel case, 111–12, 114
Labor members. *See* National War Labor Board, labor members of
Labor organizations: reactions of, to NWLB summer awards, 126, 128–31, 134
Labor radicals and socialists: squelched by Gompers, ix, 27; and United States Industrial Commission, 7; opposition of, to NCF mentality, 10–11; and United States Commission on Industrial Relations, 12, 16; antiwar sentiment of, 21
Lackawanna Bridge Company, 29
Latimer, T. E., 140
Lauck, W. Jett, 54, 66, 84, 102, 125, 138, 165–66, 173; selected NWLB secretary, 32; and General Electric cases, 117–18;

and Bethlehem case, 117, 119–20, 122; and NWLB shop committees, 118, 135–36; and women in industry, 143, 146–49, 152–53; criticisms of Second Industrial Conference, 179–80; on Taft, 184
League to Enforce Peace, 20
Lennon, John B., 28
Leo XIII, 50–51
LeSueur, Arthur, 140
Lewis, John L., 28
Lippmann, Walter, 51
Living wage, 50–67 *passim*; NWLB principle on, vii, 30, 50–51, 89; prewar discussions of, 50–51; differences within NWLB on, 50, 54, 58–66; defined by Frank P. Walsh, 50–51, 58, 61–62; and packinghouse settlement, 53; absence of, at Waynesboro, 55–56; summary and effect of NWLB awards on, 66–67; in street-railway cases, 69–70, 72–73; for women, 144, 157; and Burleson, 164; and New York harbor case, 167, 170; Walsh proposal for federal legislation on, 174–75
Lockouts: condemned by War Labor Conference Board, 29
Loree, Leonor F., 41; member of War Labor Conference Board, 29
Los Angeles *Times*, 12
Louisville Employers Association, 127–28

Machinists: at Waynesboro, 54; at Worthington Pump Company, 98–99; at Wheeling Mold and Foundry Company, 104–5; at Bethlehem Steel Company, 111–17, 119–20, 122, 160, 163; at General Electric plants, 117; and National Committee for Organizing Iron and Steel Workers, 128; at Bridgeport, 129–31, 133–34
Machinists' Journal, 54
Macy, V. Everit, 170–71; on postwar labor relations, 173–74
Mahon, W. D., 152
Manly, Basil M., 107, 180; with United States Commission on Industrial Relations, 19; succeeds Walsh, 151; and women streetcar conductors, 151–56; and Bethlehem case, 160, 162; and

Burleson, 165; and New York harbor case, 168–69; background and education of, 169; assessment of, and reactions to post-Armistice NWLB, 175–76; proposes permanent National Labor Board, 176–77; on Taft, 184
Marine Workers Affiliation: and New York harbor case, 167–72
Marshall, John, 153
Martyn, Marguerite, 142
Mason, Stephen C., 181
Massachusetts Board of Arbitration, 134–35
McAdoo, William G., 71, 73; on federal relief to street-railway industry, 83
McCarter, Thomas N., 70–71
McCarthy, Charles, 13–14
McKay, Clarence, 44
Meeker, Royal, 66
Michael, C. Edwin: member of War Labor Conference Board, 29; on individual employment contracts, 36; on living wage, 50, 65
Milburn contract, 79
Minneapolis cases, 127, 138–41, 162
Minneapolis *Labor Leader*, 138
Minneapolis Steel and Machinery Company case, 138, 140–41
Minnesota Commission of Public Safety, 139–41
Minnesota State Board of Arbitration: conflict of policies of, with NWLB's, 138–41; record of, 139
Minnesota State Federation of Labor, 139
Mitchell, John, 8, 10–11
Moderwell, Hiram, 47, 84–86
Moran, Joseph H., 169
Morgan, J. P., 176
Moriarty, Rose, 151, 155
Morrison, Frank, 140, 152
Muller v. Oregon, 143

Nation, The, 107, 152, 162, 166, 171–73, 183, 185
National Adjustment Commission, 23
National Association of Manufacturers, 17, 36, 176; attitudes and labor policies of, during 1902–12, 7–12; and open shop, 9–12, 22, 175, 181; supports Taft in 1908, 12; and United States Commission on Industrial Relations, 12–16; on Walsh, 14–16, 20; on NWLB, 33, 181; and NRA, 182; and Wagner Act, 183
National Civic Federation, 20–21, 28, 43, 104, 108, 170, 175–76; program of, during 1900–1904, 8–9; conciliation work of, as model, 8–9, 12, 23; embraces welfare capitalism, 10; weakness of, 11; anxiety of, about class politics, 11–14; and United States Commission on Industrial Relations, 12–15; failure of, by 1916, 17; formula of, for postwar industrial peace, 173–74; and Red Scare, 180
National Civic Federation *Review*, 173
National Committee for Organizing Iron and Steel Workers, 128, 178
National Committee on Public Utility Conditions, 70
National Defense Advisory Commission, 22; establishment and composition of, 20–21
National Erectors' Association, 12, 128
National Industrial Conference Board, vii, 27, 31, 149, 161, 176; origins and purpose of, 17, 189 (n. 51); proposal of, for a national war labor board, 25–26, 29–30; appointees of, to War Labor Conference Board, 29; and basic eight-hour day, 94; joins opposition to NWLB, 137; Ninth Yama Conference of, criticizes war-labor policies, 137; and First Industrial Conference, 178–79
National Labor Board (proposed, 1919), 176–77
National Labor Board (1930s): problems of, within NRA, 182
National Labor Relations Board, 182–83
National Recovery Administration: failure of, to achieve voluntary cooperation, 182–83
National War Labor Board: creation, purpose, composition and principles of, vii, 28–30; and the right to organize, vii, 29, 30, 34–48 *passim*, 86, 108–9, 111, 115–16, 123, 125, 128, 135–37, 139, 141, 166, 184; wage policies of, vii, 30, 50–88 *passim*, 142–45, 150, 183–84; hours policy of, vii, 30, 89–107, 170–72, 184; and the right to bargain collectively, vii, 30,

86, 108–41 *passim*, 160–63, 184; policies of, toward women in industry, vii, 30, 142–57, 184; powers of, ix–x, 30–31; as equalizer, ix, 18, 185–86; legacy of, x, 182–83, 186; early public image of, 18; formalizes "voluntarism," 18, 31; reactions to creation of, 31–34; procedures of, 32, 135–36, 158–59; relationship of, with War Labor Policies Board, 32–33, 58, 60, 93–94, 101–2; potential of, for assuming legislative powers, 57; and the abolition of individual contracts, 86, 109, 118, 123–25; reactions to summer awards of, 126–34; post-Armistice record of, 141–42, 150–56, 158–72; Division of Women Administrative Examiners, 145–48; Division of Administration of Awards, 146; Division of Examiners, 146; Committee on Awards, 148; disposition of, toward adding women members, 149; as precedent for NRA, 182; summary assessment of, 183–86

National War Labor Board, business members of, fear of Taft's alignment with opposition, 41; support Carlton's plans for Western Union, 42, 44–45; views of, on determination of living wage, 62–65; argue NWLB's limited powers, 64; support individualism, 65; antagonism of, toward basic eight-hour day, 89, 94–98, 102–3; view of NWLB's role, 100–101; inflexibility of, 105; post-Armistice attitude of, 158–59; assessed by Walsh, 159, 175, 184; and post-Armistice Bethlehem Steel Company, 161–62

National War Labor Board employee members. *See* National War Labor Board, labor members of

National War Labor Board employer members. *See* National War Labor Board, business members of

National War Labor Board, joint chairmen of, ix, x; decline membership on War Labor Policies Board, 32–33; effect of actions of, in Western Union case, 48–49; policies of, in street railway cases, 72–73, 87; reactions of, to Bethlehem Steel Company policies, 115–16, 160–61; prestige of, as NWLB section, 117–18; opinion of, on legality of individual contracts, 124–25; role of, in autumn, 127; on New York harbor case, 168; assessment of, by Walsh, 175; working relationship of, as major factor in NWLB's success, 184–85. *See also* Taft, William Howard; Walsh, Frank P.; and Manly, Basil M.

National War Labor Board, labor members of, demand further action in Western Union case, 42; views of, on living wage, 59, 62–64; support of, for basic eight-hour day, 89, 94–98, 102–3; view of NWLB's role, 96–97, 101; and women streetcar conductors, 151–52; post-Armistice attitude of, 158; and joint chairmen, 162, 175; with Manly, attack employers in New York harbor case, 168

National War Labor Board, shop committees of, 109, 127–29, 132, 184; at Pittsfield General Electric plant, 118, 122–23, 135–36, 146; at Bethlehem Steel Company, 120–23, 160–63; at Lynn General Electric plant, 135–36; at Schenectady General Electric plant, 146

National War Labor Board, umpires of, role of, 31–32, 89, 170; and eight-hour day, 104–7

National Women's Trade Union League, 145, 148, 152, 155

Naval Appropriations Act, 90

Navy Department, 32; and federal hours policy, 95–96, 104; and basic eight-hour day, 99–100; and Bethlehem Steel Company case, 113, 122, 160; and cancellation of contracts, 158, 160

Nearing, Scott, 137–38

Newark *Evening News*, 45

Newark *Ledger*, 145

Newark *Times*, 133

New Deal, x

New Freedom, x, 16–17

Newlands Act, 17

New London *Day*, 129

New Nationalism, x

New Orleans: politics in, 81–82

New Orleans Railway and Light Company case, 80–83

New Republic, The, 16, 46, 51

New York Boat Owners Association, 169
New York *Call*, 119, 138, 171
New York harbor case: background of, 159–60, 167–68; hearings in, 169–70; NWLB failure in, 170–72
New York *Journal of Commerce*, 74
New York *Public*, 149
New York Public Service Commission, 78, 80
New York State Court of Appeals, 76
New York State Department of Labor, 157
New York *Telegram*, 152
New York Times, 31, 74–75, 98, 133
New York Towboat Exchange, 169
New York Tribune, 47, 74
New York *World*, 74
Ninth Yama Conference, 137
Nonpartisan League, 140
North Carolina Supreme Court, 105

Obenauer, Marie, 149–50, 156; challenges of, to NWLB bureaucracy, 145–48; on need for women examiners, 147; resignation of, 148
O'Connell, James, 11–12
Ogburn, Charlton: on wages in street-railway awards, 87–88
Ogburn, William F.: family subsistence and comfort budgets of, for NWLB, 58–59, 61–63, 66, 169–70
Olander, Victor A., 42, 62, 97, 148, 159, 166; member of War Labor Conference Board, 28; and Waynesboro award, 60; view of NWLB's role, 96; and right to strike, 98
Olson, Helen, 157
Open shop: NWLB policy on, vii, 29–30, 111, 128, 161–63; and NAM, 9–11, 22, 175, 181; condemned by Walsh, 15; governmental protection of, 22–24; and NICB, 26, 29, 178–79; and British wartime government, 31; as proposed alternative to voluntary cooperation, 32
Open-shop movement. *See* Antiunion sentiment
Osborne, Loyall A., 101, 135–36; member of War Labor Conference Board, 29; role in Western Union case, 38–41, 45; leads NWLB business members, 41, 58, 61, 96; on yellow-dog contracts, 42; in Waynesboro case, 58–61; defers to War Labor Policies Board, 58, 60; view of NWLB's role, 58, 60, 64–65, 96, 100–101, 103, 120–21; in living-wage debates, 58–61, 64–65; on street-railway wage policy, 72–73; in Worthington Pump Company cases, 94–101; ideas of, on NWLB hours policy, 95–98, 100–103, 104; and Bethlehem Steel Company case, 120–21, 161–63; and Cleveland women conductors, 152; reasons for remaining on NWLB, 161; opposes NWLB on collective bargaining, 161–62
Otis, Harrison Gray, 12

Packinghouse settlement. *See* Alschuler, Samuel J.
Parry, David, 9
Peoples Council of America, 27, 137
Perkins, John F., 64
Phelan, Frank M., 19
Philadelphia *Public Ledger*, 75
Piecework rates, 55, 92
Pinchot, Amos, 149
Pinchot, Cornelia Byrne, 149
Pinchot, Gifford, 149
Post, Louis F., 101
Post Office Department, 158
Postal Telegraph Company, 35, 37, 40, 44
Postwar industrial conferences: proposed by Manly, 176–77; First Industrial Conference, 177–79, 182; Second Industrial Conference, 179–81
President's Mediation Commission, 25, 27–29, 34, 109
Protective legislation: rationale and effect of, 143, 154
Public Ownership League, 77
Public Service Commission of the First District of New York State, 76
Pullman strike, 19

Railroad Administration, 32, 158; and New York harbor case, 160, 167–70
Ransom, William L., 76
Red Scare, 180
Red Star Towing and Transportation Company, 170
Reedy, William M., 175
Reeves, Clifton, 53–54

Rerum Novarum, 51
Returning soldiers: and Cleveland Railway Company case, 151–52
Rice, Herbert H.: and Bethlehem Steel Company case, 112, 115–16, 122; on post-Armistice NWLB, 175
Richberg, Donald, 182
Rickert, Thomas A., 62–63, 89, 97, 99; member of War Labor Conference Board, 28; view of NWLB's role, 96
Right to organize: and United States Industrial Commission, 5; and United States Commission on Industrial Relations, 14–15; and AFL, in wartime, 27; and War Labor Conference Board, 29–30; and Albert Sidney Burleson, 165; and Walsh proposal for federal legislation, 174–75. *See also* National War Labor Board: and the right to organize
Right to strike, 26–27, 98; denied by War Labor Conference Board, 29
Robins, Margaret Dreier, 148
Rockefeller, John D., Jr., 13, 110, 176–77
Rockefeller Plan, 116, 123, 135; at Colorado Fuel and Iron Company, 109–11
Roosevelt, Franklin D., 99, 181–83
Roosevelt, Theodore, 7, 50, 148–49, 185
Rose, Vernon, 139–40
Rosensohn, Samuel J., 92–93, 97
Rosenwald, Julius, 176
Rumsey, Mary Harriman, 148
Ryan, John, 50

Savage, Thomas J., 42, 136; member of War Labor Conference Board, 28; in Waynesboro case, 57–60; and Worthington cases, 97, 99–100; and Wheeling cases, 105; and Bethlehem Steel Company case, 112–16
Scientific management, 15, 21
Seamen's Act, 17
Search, Theodore, 9
Seattle general strike, 171
Secondary boycott, 10
Shaw, Anna Howard, 155
Sherman Antitrust Act, 9–11
Shipbuilding Labor Adjustment Board, 24, 32, 58, 170–71
Shop committees. *See* National War Labor Board, shop committees of
Sloss Sheffield Steel and Iron Company, 101
Smith and Wesson Arms Company, 141; rejects NWLB award, 131–32; support for, by other employers, 132, 136–38; seized by War Department, 133
Smith and Wesson Arms Company case: award in, 109, 125, 127–28; issues in, 124
Smith, Ethel M., 155–56
Socialists. *See* Labor radicals and socialists
Spokane *Spokesman Review*, 129
Springfield *Republican*, 118
Square Deal, 8
St. Joseph Lead Company, 101
St. Louis Businessmen's League, 19
Steam railroads: nationalization of, 73–74
Steel strike of 1919, 162, 181; and First Industrial Conference, 177–79
Stoddard, W. L., 136
Street-railway cases, 68–88; peculiarities of, 68–69; hearings in, 70–72; and voluntary cooperation, 71, 73, 76–78, 83, 86–88; wage policy in, 72–73; financial recommendations in, 78; awards in, 78–88; and women streetcar conductors, 150–56
Street-railway industry: financial problems of, 69–70; seeks federal aid, 71–72, 75, 83; debate over federal management of, 73–77, 83–84
Strikes, viii, 24–25, 28, 35, 54, 80, 86, 98–99, 111–15, 124, 129–31, 133, 135, 151, 166–68, 170–71; NWLB policy on, 29, 54
Sturgis, Arthur, 81–82
Submarine Boat Corporation, 29, 59
Supreme Court, 10–11, 35–36, 48, 51, 73, 91, 108, 124, 132, 183
Survey, The, 12–13, 26, 31, 43, 76, 109, 152, 162, 183
Sweeney, Charles, 84–87

Taft, Charles Phelps, 39
Taft, Horace, 33, 159
Taft, William Howard, vii, ix–x, 60–61, 69–70, 120, 124–25, 132, 135, 175; prewar attitudes and career of, 12, 17, 19–20; relationship of, with Walsh,

18–20, 43, 45, 48–49, 66, 127, 133–34, 184–85; and NCF ideals, 20, 43, 174; and War Labor Conference Board, 29; antagonism of, toward Frankfurter, 32–33; view of NWLB's role, 33, 76, 96, 103–4, 107, 121–22, 134; and Western Union case, 35–49 passim, 165; on individual employment contracts, 36, 39–40; on closed nonunion shops, 40; ignores Hitchman ruling, 42; in living wage debates, 65–66; on proper wage levels, 68, 72–73; supports nationalization of street railways, 74–77; on federal war powers, 75–76, 79; and street-railway awards, 78–88; on blacks, 82–83; and eight-hour day, 101, 103–4, 107; and Bethlehem Steel Company case, 115–16, 121–22, 160–62; prolabor image of, 129, 185; and Bridgeport strike, 133–34; defends unions, 136, 141; and Minneapolis cases, 140–41; and women in industry, 144–45, 149, 151–53, 155, 208 (n. 67); post-Armistice attitude of, toward NWLB, 158–59; and Burleson, 165; in New York harbor case, 169–72; on postwar industrial relations, 174. See also National War Labor Board, joint chairmen of

Tammen, Harry, 77

Temporary Committee to Urge Representation of Women on the National War Labor Board, 148, 150

Tighe, Ambrose, 141

Turner, Frederick Jackson, 13

Umpires. See National War Labor Board, umpires of

Uniform labor policies and standards, need for, ix–x, 3–6, 21, 24, 34, 58, 89, 92

Union recognition, postwar debate on, 178–79, 182–83

United Brotherhood of Carpenters and Joiners, 23, 28, 207 (n. 46)

United Garment Workers, 28, 62

United Mine Workers, 7–8, 10, 28, 36, 110–11

United States Commission on Industrial Relations, vii, 28, 32, 51, 109, 152, 176; members of, 12–13; final reports of, 14–17, 19–20

United States Housing Corporation, 104

United States Industrial Commission, 3, 9, 13, 15, 17, 21; final report of, 4–7, 10, 30; and organized labor, 4–6; and NCF, 8

United States Shipping Board, 59–60, 167

United States Steel Corporation, 107, 177

United States Supreme Court. See Surpeme Court

University of Wisconsin, 13

Urgent Deficiency Act, 71

Vahey, James H., 70, 72, 153–55

Van Kleeck, Mary, 152–53, 155–56

VanDervoort, William H., 115, 162; member of War Labor Conference Board, 29; draws fire from Walsh, 63–64; and Wheeling cases, 105; post-Armistice attack of, on NWLB, 175

Virginia Bridge and Iron Company, 29

Voluntarism. See Voluntary cooperation

Voluntary cooperation: in wartime mobilization, vii–x, 21; and Woodrow Wilson, viii, xi, 16–17, 21, 26–27, 44, 48, 70–71, 76, 133–34, 185; historic tradition of, 3, 8; and United States Industrial Commission, 4–7; appeal of, 6–7; failure of, 7–8, 17–18, 177–83, 186; and United States Commission on Industrial Relations, 15; and Samuel Gompers, 16–17; formalization of, by NWLB, 18, 31; and Western Union case, 35, 37, 41, 43–46, 48; in NWLB policy debates, 62–66, 102–4; and street-railway crisis, 71, 73, 76, 77–78, 80, 83, 86–88; and NWLB umpires, 89, 105; and Rockefeller Plan, 110; deterioration of, 126–41, 158–72; and administration's actions at Smith and Wesson and Bridgeport, 133; summary of, in NWLB experience, 185–86

"Voter and His Employer," 136–37

Wagner Act, x, 175, 183

Wagner, Robert F., 183

Walsh, Frank P., vii, ix–x, 67–69, 128, 140–41, 173, 176; as chairman of United States Commission on Industrial Relations, vii, 13–17, 19–20, 36–37, 109; on "judicial poise," 14, 19–20; and NCF,

14–15, 20, 174; supports independent labor movement, 14–15, 174; denounced by conservative press, 14–16, 129; and eight-hour day, 15, 61–62, 96–98, 101–4, 106; proposals of, for labor legislation, 15, 174–75; defines presidential doctrine of labor, 18; relationship of, with Taft, 18–20, 43, 45, 48–49, 66, 127, 133–34, 184–85; career of, during 1915–17, 20; and War Labor Conference Board, 29; and War Labor Policies Board, 32–33, 58, 101–2; view of NWLB's role, 33, 57–58, 96, 104; and Western Union case, 35–49 *passim*; and abolition of individual contracts, 36, 124–25; unconcern of, with Hitchman ruling, 42; on nationalization of telegraph systems, 44, 47; on living wage, 50–52, 57–66, 70, 144; ideals of, as shaped by early life, 51–52; in packinghouse case, 52–53; defends lower classes, 52, 63–64; proposed wage and hour standards for common laborers, 61–62, 183–84, 212 (n. 5); on president's authority to fix street-railway fares, 72–73; on local government and street railways, 77; and street-railway awards, 78–86; and Worthington cases, 98–100; lauds Clark, 106; optimism of, about NWLB's work, 108–9; defines "democracy," 108, 129; and Bethlehem Steel Company case, 115–16, 119–22; and Smith and Wesson Arms Company case, 124–25, 132–33; Labor Day message of, 129; and Bridgeport strike, 130, 133–34; on administration's actions at Smith and Wesson and Bridgeport, 133–34; and women in industry, 144–45, 149, 151, 155–56; resignation of, 151, 158–59; post-Armistice attitude of, toward NWLB, 156, 158–59; in New York harbor case, 169–70; proposal of, for generalization of NWLB settlements, 174, 212 (n. 5); attack on NWLB business members, 175. *See also* National War Labor Board, joint chairmen of
Walsh, Frank P., Jr., 133–34
War Board of the American Electric Railway Association, 70

War Department, 32–33, 145; and federal hours policy, 91–92, 96, 104; and Bethlehem Steel Company case, 113, 117, 121–22, 160; and Smith and Wesson Arms Company, 124, 131–33; cancellation of contracts, 158, 160
War Finance Corporation, 83–84
War Industries Board, ix, 32, 180, 182
War Labor Conference Board, 31, 52, 102; origins, purpose, composition, and report of, 28–30; on individual employment contracts, 36; on hours of labor, 96
War Labor Policies Board, 34, 58, 60, 62, 66, 148; origins, purpose, and composition of, 32–33; and federal hours policy, 91–93, 101–2; adopts NWLB's principles, 101; and women in industry, 143
Washington and Lee University, 169
Washington *Times*, 152
Waynesboro Iron Molders, 55
Waynesboro, Pennsylvania, case, 50, 53–61, 65, 68–69, 94, 101, 184; conflicting testimony in, 54–56; importance of, for NWLB, 56–57; award in, 60–61, 146
Webb, Beatrice, 4
Webb, Sidney, 4
Wehle, Louis B., 24
Weinstein, James, 12, 16
Welfare capitalism, 10, 40, 174
Welfare state, x, 186
Wesson, Douglas, 124, 137
Western Union Company case, 35–49, 54, 64, 69, 111, 118–19, 159, 172, 185; results of, 43, 46–49, 166–67; and federal takeover, 46–48; post-Armistice developments in, 163–67. *See also* Carlton, Newcomb; Burleson, Albert Sidney
Westinghouse Electric and Manufacturing Company, 29, 95
Wheeling Mold and Foundry Company cases, 104–7
White, C. H., 55
Wilkinson, Adam, 59
William Filene's Sons Company, 109–10
Wilson, William B., 25, 101, 149, 151, 163, 179; early career of, 10, 17; and voluntarism, 17; and War Labor Conference Board, 28–29; and War Labor Policies Board, 33; in Western Union case, 45–46; retains post-Armistice NWLB, 159

234 Index

Wilson, Woodrow, 18, 34, 52–53, 59, 108; reorganizes war mobilization machinery, vii; and voluntarism, viii–ix, 16–17, 21, 26–27, 44, 48, 70–71, 76, 110, 133–34, 185; and AFL leadership, ix, 16–17, 47; war powers of, x, 71–72, 183; election of, in 1912, 11; and United States Commission on Industrial Relations, 12, 19; concern of, about production losses, 24–25; address of, to AFL, 26–27; in Western Union case, 42, 44–48, 163; on living wage, 51; in street-railway crisis, 70–72, 76; and eight-hour day, 90–91, 93–94, 106; and Bridgeport strike, 131, 133–34; and Smith and Wesson Arms Company seizure, 133; on addition of women to NWLB, 149; and post-Armistice NWLB, 158, 169, 175–76; and First Industrial Conference, 177; and Second Industrial Conference, 179; and NWLB's success, 185

Winter, Alpheus, 134
Wisconsin Idea, 13–15
Wise, Stephen S., 149
Wolfe, A. B., 157
Woll, Matthew, 166
Women in industry, viii, 142–57, 184
Women in Industry Service, 148–50, 153, 156
Women's Bureau, 156
Women's Committee of the Council of National Defense, 155
Women's Joint Legislative Conference of New York, 148
Women's wages, 142–46, 150, 156–57
Woods, E. B., 146–48, 160, 163
Worden, B. L., 63, 98; member of War Labor Conference Board, 29; in Waynesboro case, 54, 56–57, 59–60
World War I, legacy of, 180–83
Worthington Pump Company cases: and basic eight-hour day, 94–101, 104

Yale University, 20
Yellow-dog contracts, 10, 36, 42, 184; at General Electric plant, Pittsfield, 117, 123; at Smith and Wesson Arms Company, 124–25

Publication of Supplementary Volumes to *The Papers of Woodrow Wilson* is assisted from time to time by the Woodrow Wilson Foundation in order to encourage scholarly work about Woodrow Wilson and his time. All volumes have passed the review procedures of the publishers and the Editor and the Editorial Advisory Committee of *The Papers of Woodrow Wilson*. Inquiries about the Series should be addressed to The Editor, Papers of Woodrow Wilson, Firestone Library, Princeton University, Princeton, N.J. 08540.

Inga Floto, *Colonel House in Paris: A Study of American Policy at the Paris Peace Conference 1919* (Princeton University Press, 1981)

Raymond B. Fosdick, *Letters on the League of Nations. From the Files of Raymond B. Fosdick* (Princeton University Press, 1966)

Wilton B. Fowler, *British-American Relations, 1917–1918: The Role of Sir William Wiseman* (Princeton University Press, 1969)

John M. Mulder, *Woodrow Wilson: The Years of Preparation* (Princeton University Press, 1978)

George Egerton, *Great Britain and the Creation of the League of Nations* (University of North Carolina Press, 1978)

Stephen L. Vaughn, *Holding Fast the Inner Lines: Democracy, Nationalism, and the Committee on Public Information* (University of North Carolina Press, 1980)

Robert C. Hilderbrand, *Power and the People: Executive Management of Public Opinion in Foreign Affairs, 1897–1921* (University of North Carolina Press, 1980)

Edwin A. Weinstein, *Woodrow Wilson: A Medical and Psychological Biography* (Princeton University Press, 1981)

Arthur S. Link (ed.), *Woodrow Wilson and a Revolutionary World, 1913–1921* (University of North Carolina Press, 1982)

Valerie Jean Conner, *The National War Labor Board: Stability, Social Justice, and the Voluntary State in World War I* (University of North Carolina Press, 1983)

www.ingramcontent.com/pod-product-compliance
Lightning Source LLC
Chambersburg PA
CBHW021401290426
44108CB00010B/338